FIGHTING BACK

Columbia University Press
New York   Chichester, West Sussex
Copyright © 1992 Dorothy Werner
All rights reserved

LIBRARY OF CONGRESS CATALOGING-IN-PUBLICATION DATA

Werner, Harold, d. 1989.
Fighting back : a memoir of Jewish resistance in World War II / by
Harold Werner ; edited by Mark Werner, with a foreword by Martin Gilbert.
    p. cm.
ISBN 0-231-07882-X
ISBN 0-231-07883-8 (pbk.)
1. Werner, Harold, d. 1989.   2. Jews—Poland—Biography.
3. Holocaust, Jewish (1939–1945)—Poland—Personal narratives.
4. World War, 1939–1945—Underground movements, Jewish—Poland.
5. Poland—Biography.   I. Title.
DS135.P63W418   1992
940.53'18'09438092—dc20
92–16046
CIP

∞

*Casebound editions of Columbia University Press books
printed on permanent and durable acid-free paper.*

Printed in the United States of America
c 10 9 8 7 6 5 4 3 2
p 10 9 8 7 6 5 4 3 2 1

This book is dedicated to those courageous Jewish resistance fighters who fought the Germans in the Polish forests during the Second World War.

This book is also dedicated to my loving and patient wife of forty-one years, Dorothy, without whose assistance it could never have become a reality. I also wish to thank my sons, Sidney, Mark, and Robert, for the encouragement and active involvement they provided me in writing this book.

CONTENTS

EXPLANATION OF NAMES, PLACES, AND EVENTS

The setting for this story is Poland, and every effort has been made to be true to the Polish spelling of cities, towns, and villages identified in the story. The reader should keep in mind that certain letters are pronounced differently in Polish than in English. For example, the letter *w* is pronounced as a *v*, the letters *cz* are pronounced as *ch*, and the letter *j* is pronounced as a *y*. By way of illustration, the Polish city of Parczew is pronounced as if it were spelled "Parchev," and the Army Krajowa is pronounced as if it were spelled "Army Krayova."

Throughout the story, many people are identified by nicknames (e.g., "Velvale the Patzan," "Yefim") or by their first names and places of birth (e.g., "Mortche and Yurek from Zaliszcze"). During the war, they were recognized by these names rather than by their full names. A glossary of names at the end of the book lists those individuals whom the author remembers, and who survived the war, by their wartime names and their corresponding full names.

Considerable effort went into identifying the geographic locations of the events described, either by reference to the closest town or by reference to the forest in which each event occurred. Local wooded areas, known by the closest village or town, are distinguished from much larger forests. For example, the "Hola woods" means the wooded area around the village of Hola. The Hola woods, in turn, would be part of the much larger wooded area denoted as the "Skorodnica forest."

The mention of certain military actions is selective and is not meant to be complete and exhaustive. Those military actions described in the book are actual events and were selected to illustrate the different types of situations the Jewish partisans faced; many more battles and raids occurred than are covered in the text. Of course, the description of the military activities of the Jewish partisans is limited to those details the author could recall almost fifty years after the events described.

FOREWORD

Harold Werner—A Story of Jewish Resistance

In June 1981 many thousands of survivors of the Holocaust gathered in Jerusalem. It was the first time since the end of the Second World War thirty-six years earlier that such a gathering had been held. Many of those who came to Jerusalem that month had never before participated in any form of reunion. Now they wanted to meet their fellow survivors and to find, if possible, long-lost relatives or friends with whom they had shared their terrible experiences. While in Jerusalem they were encouraged to set down their recollections, even in brief, for Yad Vashem, the Holocaust memorial established after the war by the State of Israel.

About a year after the June gathering, Dr. Shmuel Krakowski, the archivist at Yad Vashem, where I was then working on my history of the Holocaust, mentioned to me that he had just been cataloging a short but remarkable testimony. It was, he said, the first account he had read—and he was familiar with many thousands of accounts—that told the story of Jewish resistance in the Wlodawa region of Poland, the story of men and women who had survived more than two years in hiding, who had faced local hostility and German manhunts, and who had even tried to make contact with the prisoners in the death camp at Sobibor.

The archivist brought the forty-nine page testimony to my desk in the Yad Vashem library. I was moved by it in two ways. Some of the details in it brought the perils of life in hiding as vividly to mind as anything that I had read hitherto. And some passages made me cry. I used one of them, the story of the death of Yankel, in my book.

The author of these recollections was Harold Werner. His address was on the document. He lived in Miami. By chance, I was due to lecture that winter in Miami at a local temple. The rabbi, who met me at the hotel on my first morning, offered to take me to the sea. I asked him if he would drive me instead to a certain address in the town. We set off toward the address I had seen at Yad Vashem on Werner's recollection. When we arrived the house was empty. I asked the next-door neighbor if the Werners lived there. She said that a Mrs. Werner did indeed live in the house. Thinking that perhaps Mr. Werner had died, I wrote a note for Mrs. Werner and pushed it under the door, inviting her to my talk that evening, when, I told her, I would say a few words about her husband's wartime struggles.

Disappointed that I would never meet Mr. Werner, I drove away with the rabbi. We had gone some six blocks back toward town when a car passed in the opposite direction. I glanced at the driver and his woman passenger and saw typical Polish Jewish faces, such as I knew so well from my own Polish-born survivor friends in London. Those, I said to the rabbi, are Mr. and Mrs. Werner. We turned the car around and followed. The other car drove into the drive we had so recently left. We pulled up alongside, and I hurried over to the Werners' car. They seemed surprised at the apparition of a person rushing up to them. I explained my purpose, and we were invited in. As we entered, I retrieved the note that I had pushed under the door; I am looking at it as I write these words.

The story that Mr. Werner began to tell me as we sat in his living room was a remarkable one. It contained many details that were not in the relatively short piece I had seen in Jerusalem. I realized that this story ought to be set down in full. I remember thinking to myself what a fine book it would make. As we left, Mr. Werner pointed to a small nick in his left ear caused by a German bullet that, miraculously, had not gone through his head.

Two years later, when I returned to Miami to lecture, Mr. Werner came to the hall to hear me speak. I was pleased to see him and even more pleased to be able to introduce him to the surprised audience as a Jewish hero living in their midst. I remember wondering if he was recording his testimony; perhaps I even asked him if he was.

The day came when I received a letter from Mr. Werner's son Mark telling me that his father was dead. I remember being overwhelmed with a sense of sadness. I had met Harold Werner only twice, but had felt a bond of sympathy and understanding. I had heard him tell his story, modestly and yet with passion. Now only the memory of him would live on.

Mark Werner told me that his father had spent a large part of his last years in a hospital bed. It was there, encouraged by his wife Dorothy, that he devoted his energies to finishing this book. In November 1989 he completed his self-imposed task. Two weeks later he died.

I knew how much it had meant to Mr. Werner that his story should be set down, that the things that he had seen with his own eyes should not be forgotten, that the ability of the Jews to stand up to their persecutors should be recorded. Now that his book is being published, I am honored at being asked to write this foreword to it.

There are many uncomfortable aspects to the story that Harold Werner recounts, not least of which are the details he gives of local Polish and Ukrainian hostility to Jews, especially when Nazi power was at its height and the Jews most in need of help. Later, as the tide of war began to turn, the hostile neighbors—themselves no longer tyrannized by the all-pervading machine of terror, and hoping also to buy time and forgetfulness—became more willing to help.

Werner chronicles not only the war years but the prewar life of Polish Jewry, when poverty and uncertainty were the daily accompaniments for so many. We see city life and village life, a world in which Jews, however much they were surrounded by antagonistic neighbors, built for themselves a vibrant and exhilarating existence, and sought to better themselves.

Hostility to Jews was never far away. Werner recounts how, just before the war, when he was twenty-one and one of his brothers, Moishe, sixteen, they were chased through the streets of Warsaw by a gang of Polish anti-Semites. "In the distance I saw a policeman stationed on a street corner. We ran toward him for protection. As we approached, he sized up who we were and calmly turned his back on us, strolling away. Seconds later, we were seized by our pursuers and severely beaten with fists and clubs."

Both the aspirations of Polish Jewry and the threats to those aspirations were swept away in a matter of hours, as Germany launched its invasion of Poland in the early hours of September 1, 1939. Werner's account of the opening days of the war, as German bombers struck at Warsaw, is a dramatic glimpse of those first, frightening moments of the sudden and violent transition from peace to war, from hope to hopelessness. Werner's story contains many poignant moments. When the Germans bombed Warsaw, where he had begun to make a small living, "The entire top floor of that building collapsed into the courtyard, together with our four knitting machines. That was the end of our business venture and our source of livelihood."

When Warsaw was occupied, Werner recounts: "The Germans set up bread lines, handing out a loaf of bread to each person in the line, but not to Jews. I was kicked out of the bread line several times when the Poles in line pointed me out to the Germans as a Jew."

Even as the noose of Nazi rule tightened, the spirit of resistance rose. In these pages it is seen among the small rural communities of Jews who lived isolated from the great cities, yet showed the same spiritual and physical courage that enabled individuals elsewhere to take their lives into their hands and to risk all by setting off into the woods, to defy the conqueror.

Here too are the myriad uncertainties of those early months of the German occupation. Whether to cross over the River Bug into Russian territory, and if so, how. Whether to return to Warsaw or to stay in the villages. Whether to remain in the villages or set off for the woods. Whether to steal and how to steal. Whether to threaten reprisals against those who harmed Jews in hiding and how to carry out those reprisals. How to keep warm. How to keep dry. How to keep alive.

The catastrophe unfolds remorselessly in these pages. It is a catastrophe seen and recorded by one who had had so much to hope for from life, from the achievements and potential of the three million Jews of interwar Poland, from his own efforts and ingenuity, and from the comradeship of his friends and colleagues. Suddenly everything was blighted. Werner decided to leave the city and seek a safer haven in Hola, a village to the east of Warsaw, not far from the River Bug. During the journey he stopped in several villages where, he recalls, some farmers "were sorry over what had happened to Poland, but they refused to give us any food because we were Jewish."

Three Jewish families lived in Hola. In the nearby villages, other Jews lived side by side with the local peasants. There was food to buy and even a livelihood to be made; the family that gave Werner shelter had a small mill for poppyseed and linseed oil. But normal times had passed. That winter one member of that family went to the nearby town of Sosnowica to try to find a replacement for a small piece of machinery for the mill. "As he walked in the town, he failed to observe that a German was walking on the same sidewalk as he, and he did not step down. A Jew was not allowed to walk on the sidewalk when a German passed on that sidewalk. The German called him over and shot him on the spot."

Then came hunger, rumors of killings elsewhere, and German raids into the Hola area in search of Soviet soldiers who had escaped capture and were in hiding. Few of these Russians managed to evade their pursuers for long. On a journey into Wlodawa to deliver grain to the Germans on a freezing cold day, Werner saw thousands of Russian prisoners of war being kept in an open field surrounded by barbed wire. They were being literally starved and frozen to death.

The time came when the Jews of Hola and the surrounding villages were ordered into the Wlodawa ghetto. Werner and two dozen other Jews decided to seek refuge in the woods instead, to live in hiding, using their own cunning to get food and to make shelter. It was a courageous decision, the start of a saga of privation, danger, death, and escape, moving from one harsh unknown to another.

Death lurked at every turn, and not just at the hands of the German search parties. Soon after Werner's life in hiding started, a local peasant warned him that each village had a few inhabitants who acted as guards and "who walked around the village perimeter at night to make sure that no Jews or Russians would try to sneak in to get food. He also told me that in a neighboring village the local guards had caught a Jew on a farm and killed both the Jew and the farmer."

On that occasion Werner and two friends had left their group to search for food in a nearby village. Returning the next day to their hiding place, they found it empty. A peasant woman told them what happened. "A large group of about fifty villagers (without any Germans) went into the woods armed with clubs and pitchforks. They surrounded our group, forced them to march to Sosnowica, and then turned them over to the Germans. There they were all shot."

Other escapees joined, new hiding places were found, and a few weapons were acquired. But further betrayals led to more killings. Werner describes one terrible manhunt in the woods by Ukrainian villagers from Zamolodycze who were determined to catch every Jew in hiding. They locked all those they caught in one of the village houses and sent a villager to Sosnowica to fetch the Germans. A friendly peasant woman told Werner, to whom she had given shelter, the sequel: "The Germans arrived on horseback. They took the Jews out of the house one by one and shot them all."

The villagers of Zamolodycze watched in a crowd as the killings took place. In recounting this savage episode, Werner comments: "They knew all these Jews. They had grown up together, and done business together. They knew the parents and grandparents of these people as well. Zelik was the village shoemaker, who made the shoes for most of the villagers and their families. His son Mendel tried to escape. He jumped out of an attic window and started to run away, but the villagers caught him and the Germans shot him also."

Werner and his friends rebuilt their group yet again, taking in new escapees. But the tyranny of local and ancient prejudice combined with the tyranny of alien conquest to deprive the Jews of any safe haven. At one point a group of forty Russian partisans moved into their area of the woods. But this did not bring the safety Werner's group sought, as he tells: "As soon as they settled near us they started to rape the young Jewish women in our group. Although we protested, they were armed and we were not, so there was little we could do to stop them."

While some Russian soldiers who were in hiding raped Jewish women, and even murdered Jews, others protected Jews and fought alongside them against the common enemy. Werner tells of a Jewish woman who fell in love with a Russian soldier, with whom she lived in a dugout in the forest as part of a small partisan group. One day the Germans surrounded the group and ordered them out of their hiding place. "Realizing the situation was hopeless, the Russian dug a shallow trench into a wall of his dugout, placed his Jewish girlfriend in the trench and covered her with a thin layer of earth. He then emerged from the dugout and was shot immediately by the Germans. His girfriend survived undetected."

As Werner's account makes clear, many Poles and Ukrainians betrayed Jews to the Germans or killed Jews themselves, inflicting bestial cruelties on those who had once been their neighbors. Other Poles and Ukrainians, albeit a small minority, saved Jews, thereby risking their own lives and the lives of their families.

The manhunts continued throughout 1942 and 1943, increasingly carried out by German soldiers rather than by local peasants. On one occasion Werner's group scattered as hunters came toward them, shooting wildly, accompanied by their savage dogs. In fact, these Germans were really animal hunters searching for wild game in the forest. They had come across the Jewish hideout by accident. Suddenly a snowstorm caused the hunt to be called off. When the storm abated, Werner writes, "We found more than a dozen people from our group, frozen stiff exactly as they had fallen during the storm."

The strain of the seemingly endless danger broke the will of some. Werner tells of one man who, having lost his wife and four of his five children in one of the German manhunts, decided to go into the Wlodawa ghetto with his surviving, youngest daughter. Others made the same decision. The fate of those in the ghetto was deportation to Sobibor.

Illness also took its toll. Werner writes: "We were nearing the Makoszka forest, but Shainche could not make it. He closed his eyes and died quietly on the sled. We could not bury him, as the ground was frozen hard as a rock. All we could do was to lay him next to a tree and cover him with snow."

Eventually reprisals had some effect in curbing the manhunts, in particular those carried out by Ukrainian villagers. Werner describes the search for the leader of the local anti-Semitic gang that had handed over a group of Jews in hiding to the Germans. "He ran for the window, but we shot him before he could escape. Faiga recognized one of the men who had dragged her father, Zelig, out of the dugout in the woods. He was wearing her father's boots. We shot him also, and Moniek took his boots. I recognized Moishe Yohel's boots on another villager and told him to take them off. We shot him too."

By such measures the Jews managed to keep their local enemies at bay. They also managed to bring out more than a hundred Jews from the Wlodawa ghetto. They even acquired enough small arms to be able to challenge the small German garrison, ten soldiers in all, in the village nearest their hideout. "It was a tremendous uplift to our morale to be able to hit back at the Germans," Werner recalls of his group's first battle with these soldiers, in which six of the Germans were killed. "It was also important to us to show the villagers that Jews, once armed, would strike back."

By the late spring of 1943 Werner's group was about 120 strong. But their armament was limited to twenty rifles, several revolvers, and a few hand grenades. To fight the Germans effectively, they needed to be part of a larger group. In the Parczew forest, they joined another Jewish partisan group with whom they participated in acts of sabotage against German installations, bridges, and even trains. They also defended the hiding places deep inside the forest where hundreds of Jewish families were guarded and fed, and where the partisans had their own headquarters.

Known as the Tabor, the Russian word for camp, these remote hiding places, a series of islands in a virtually impenetrable swamp within the forest, became a center of Werner's activities. His description of it is the fullest we have. "Each island had someone who was a good cook," he writes. "The Tabor people would apportion the meat throughout the islands in our base. The partisans kept plates attached to their belts and had their own spoons and knives."

The battles with the Germans intensified. When a German soldier, about to be killed, called out in anguish "Mother! Mother!" one of the Jewish partisans murmured, as the Jews continued firing, "They still have mothers. We don't have our mothers. They killed all of them."

Among the Jewish partisan exploits Werner describes that add to our knowledge of the fate of the Jews of this region is the rescue of Jews from a German labor camp at Adampol. In this camp, the partisans discovered "a special section for the more attractive women and girls, picked from the trains that brought Jews from all over Europe to Sobibor." Many of these Jewish deportees were from Holland. Spared the gas chamber, they were kept alive solely for the pleasure of the Ukrainian and Latvian guards and for German soldiers. With great daring Werner and his friends managed to get through the perimeter fence and smuggle out close to one hundred of the Adampol inmates in three separate trips before the camp was liquidated by the Germans. All those who were rescued were taken for safety to the Tabor.

Werner's partisan unit even approached the heavily guarded perimeter of the Sobibor death camp, near the River Bug. Unable to break in, they fired several salvoes in the air to show the inmates of that terrible place that somebody outside knew about them and cared.

The Jewish partisans took every opportunity open to them to harass the Germans and weaken their war-making powers. One of their main activities after the harvest was the destruction of barns in which grain was stored for the German army. One such barn had belonged before the war to a friend of Werner, David Terno, whose whole property, now run by the Germans, was set on fire by the Jews. "While running from the estate," Werner writes,

I noticed a bulky form crawling on all fours, like an animal, and making very strange noises. It tried to stand upright but could not, and fell back down. I pointed it out to Symcha, running next to me, and we both decided it might be a human being, perhaps a Jew. We each took hold of one arm and dragged him along with us. The fight continued around us. We ran several miles from the estate, then stopped to rest and look at this heap of a man. He was covered with hair down to his waist. His clothes were in shreds, and he could not stand on his feet. He looked like a skeleton and had no teeth. From his mumblings I discovered that this being was my friend Yankel, David Turno's nephew from Warsaw. He was half delirious and did not recognize me. I understood from his mumblings that he had dug a hiding place under the feeding troughs for the cows. No one knew he was there, and he had been able to survive on the food in the troughs and the milk from the cows. He had been in this hiding place for almost a year, but the heat from the burning buildings had driven him out of his hiding place. We continued on to the village of Mosciska, where we put him on a wagon to take him to our base. Moniek cut his long hair, and we tried to feed him, but he could not hold down any food. He was extremely weak, and a few days later he died from his malnourished state. We buried him in the woods. Afterward we grieved for what had happened to a good human being, my friend Yankel.

It was this passage that had made me cry when I first read Harold Werner's testimony.

Toward the end of 1943, when the protective swamp was dry after a long, hot summer, an unexpected German attack led to the massacre of seventy-five of the inhabitants of the Tabor while the partisans were on raids elsewhere. But the few armed Tabor Jews, mostly boys and old men, fought back, and many Germans were killed. For almost all these Jewish defenders, writes Werner, "This was their first opportunity to avenge the cruelties that had been committed against their families. Unfortunately, for many of them, this opportunity was also their last."

During the last year of the war the situation improved dramatically. By the spring of 1944 the German army was in retreat on the Eastern Front. The Jewish partisans harassed their lines of communications and had the satisfaction of participating in the wearing down of the hated enemy, the murderers of their people. The Germans no longer displayed maps in the village squares showing the advance of their armies. "The villagers were not now certain that the Germans were going to win the war," Werner recalls. "Some villagers started sympathizing more openly with those of us who were fighting the Germans."

By this time Werner's group consisted of about four hundred Jewish partisans, led by Chiel Grynszpan. The group guarded an equal number of elderly people, women, and children in the Tabor. "The Germans did not show themselves very much in the villages now," Werner writes. "They stayed mostly in the cities, and so we were able to sleep in the village homes. We stayed in the ones closest to the woods, just in case of trouble."

The Jewish partisans blew up dozens of German road and rail bridges. They also systematically sought out and killed those villagers who, two years earlier, had handed over Jews in hiding to the Germans—on one occasion fifteen villagers were killed in a single raid, "the largest act of revenge we ever took against collaborators."

The Soviet-controlled Polish partisans, the Army Ludowa, now entrusted the Jewish partisans with a growing number of sabotage missions. "They knew they could depend on us because as Jews we had no homes to return to and no families to go back to. We had no choice but to fight. Our mission was to fight, take revenge, and destroy the enemy." Other Polish partisans, however, members of the Army Krajowa, followers in the main of the London-based Polish government, were less willing to work with Jews. In their ranks were even those who killed Jewish stragglers and Jewish partisans. Werner describes one episode when fifteen Army Ludowa partisans, including five Jews from his group, were surrounded in a village far from their base by a hundred men of the Army Krajowa. Thirteen of the Army Ludowa men were murdered.

This episode embittered the Jews who had suffered so much and fought so hard against such heavy odds. Some months later Werner found himself with a group of Grynszpan's partisans who went to the rescue of an Army Krajowa force that was in danger of being destroyed by the Germans. Werner comments, "Even this, however, did not stop the Army Krajowa from their continuous attacks on unarmed Jews and small units of our partisans."

As one reads these pages, as one hides with Werner and his band of friends and partisans, as one participates through him in the attacks on German soldiers, including one group caught unawares while attending a local wedding, as one listens to the accounts brought to the forest by a survivor of the Warsaw Ghetto uprising, or by fifteen survivors of the Sobibor death camp revolt, one is assailed by the sounds and fears of danger, by the fate of so many Jewish communities wiped out in their entirety.

No one in hiding in the forests could know what the next day would bring, whether death, or another day of life. For as long as the German army and the Nazi system were the rulers of Poland, the Jews in hiding had no safety and no way out. Yet as these pages show, the will to live and the will to fight were incredibly strong impulses, leading men to carry out remarkable acts of bravery and endurance.

The end of the war brought bitter news to men like Werner who had survived it. Meeting a neighbor from his home town, he learned that two of his four brothers, seventeen-year-old Moishe and thirteen-year-old Motel, had escaped from the ghetto into which they had been sent and had gone into hiding near their village. "One night they went to the home of a former neighbor asking for food.

He told them to wait in his barn while he brought food out to them. They waited in the barn and after a while the neighbor brought a gang of anti-Semites to the barn. The gang brought clubs into the barn and clubbed Moishe and Motel to death."

Knowledge of the fate of one's nearest and dearest was the penultimate horror. The final horror was yet to come. As the survivors returned to their homes, the historic hatreds that had plagued them before the war emerged once again. One of Werner's partisan friends, Abram Bochian, was among those Jews who returned to his town in the hope of rebuilding his life. After a few days he and the handful of other survivors in the town were attacked by local anti-Semites. "In the attack, Abram Bochian was shot and killed. Abram Bochian, the heroic partisan, who had fought so bravely against the Germans, who had lost his entire family in the woods, and who had made us laugh in the tightest situations, was not killed by a German bullet but by the Polish people in his own home town."

Bochian was one of many survivors to be murdered in Poland after the defeat of the Germans, after they had returned home.

I have read Werner's account four times. Each time I have found in it new facets that impress or move me. I can see once more his eyes looking up at me as he recounted some of the episodes recorded here, as he tried to make me understand just what a struggle it had been, just how hard any form of resistance was, just how remarkable were those with whom he hid and fought, those who were killed at his side, betrayed, murdered, hunted down like animals, or broken by the severity of two harsh winters and the cruelties of an unnatural, inhuman existence, hiding in the earth, watching their friends die with no possibility of help from outside.

Yet those in hiding, who despite their weakness were determined to challenge the Germans, remained human beings: their passions and emotions emerge in these pages, as does their unquenchable love of life. The Jews whose harsh life is described here did not seek their cruel fate, yet they rose to meet it with a nobility rare in the annals of human history.

MARTIN GILBERT
Merton College, Oxford
March 16, 1992

EDITOR'S ACKNOWLEDGMENTS

I wish to express my gratitude to my friend Sandy Feckanicz for her valuable comments, suggestions, and encouragement as well as for her patience in typing and retyping this manuscript.

I also wish to thank my wife, Arlene, for her advice, support, and understanding in encouraging me to undertake this labor of love.

PREFACE

I am a survivor of Hitler's Holocaust. Born and raised under the name Hershel Zimmerman, I survived, not in a concentration camp but in the woods of eastern Poland. This book is the story of my experiences throughout the war.

I have written this book for several reasons. The first arises out of questions posed by my children. When my three sons were younger, they would often challenge me. The three million Jews living in Poland at the outbreak of World War II constituted 10 percent of the Polish population. Why, they would ask me, did so many people not rise up to resist the roundups to the concentration camps? Why did the Jews go "like sheep to the slaughter"?

This book provides two responses to this line of questioning. The first response relates to the treatment of Jews in Poland both before and during the war. My experiences mirror those of other Polish Jews. Those experiences reveal the virulent anti-Semitism present in the Polish population. This powerful hatred directed against Poland's Jews by the local populace translated into routine beatings and the like before the war. It translated into wholesale roundups and killings during the war.

This is not to attempt to shift the blame for the Holocaust away from Nazi Germany. Nothing can ever absolve Germany for the mass genocide practiced against European Jewry, resulting in the deaths of six million Jews. Rather, it is an attempt to point out that Polish Jews could not look to a friendly local populace for help in escaping from the gas chambers and crematoriums constructed by the Germans. This was unlike some other places, such as Denmark and certain parts of Holland and France, where the Jews could look for help to friendly neighbors. In Poland, the Jews faced neighbors who were so full of hatred toward them that they voluntarily rounded up local Jews for shipment to German outposts or simply killed them on the spot. As my story will illustrate, in the absence of local assistance it was extremely difficult to evade the Germans or obtain weapons with which to resist them.

All this should not obscure the valuable aid given to Polish Jews by people mentioned in this book, such as Pakula, Kornila, and Polashka, and by many other individual non-Jewish Poles who risked their lives to do so. Holocaust survivors owe an undying debt of gratitude to those righteous Poles, some of whom were motivated by Polish patriotism and others by simple humanitarianism. However, these non-Jewish Polish heroes were vastly outnumbered by those Poles who actively cooperated in the Germans' war against the Jews.

The second response to my sons' challenge is to reject its underlying premise that Jews did not resist. There are numerous books relating stories of Jews who courageously fought the Germans in the cities and ghettos of Poland. The most renowned of these accounts of Jewish resistance relates to the gallant, but hopeless, Warsaw ghetto uprising in April 1943. However, there are very few documented accounts of the ferocious resistance carried out by Jews in the vast Polish forests.

This book provides a firsthand account of a large, organized Jewish fighting force that operated in the woods of eastern Poland. Commanded by Chiel Grynszpan, our partisan unit conducted numerous military missions against the German occupation army. We overran German outposts, blew up bridges and German trains, attacked German garrisons, ambushed German military convoys, and systematically destroyed agricultural products destined for Germany. To accomplish these feats, our unit set up radio contact with Moscow through the local Russian-backed Polish resistance movement, and received air drops of military hardware and even Polish paratroopers. We joined with the Polish resistance in large-scale military efforts, even fighting pitched battles against the German army and downing German aircraft. By 1944 our Jewish partisan force had grown to approximately four hundred fighters, both men and women. By that time, we had liberated a large expanse of Polish countryside, where German troops would not dare venture except in very large units.

The military feats of Chiel's Jewish partisans should not overshadow their humanitarian success. Because we were one of only a handful of Jewish military units operating in the woods, we were virtually the only resistance fighters concerned with saving the few Jews who managed to escape from Poland's ghettos, concentration camps, and villages. To those Jews who managed to evade the Germans, the anti-Semitic London-backed Polish resistance forces, and the Jew-hating local populace, our Tabor (the Russian word for camp) in the Polish forests represented one of the few harbors of relative safety in occupied Poland. By the conclusion of hostilities, our partisan force was protecting and feeding approximately four hundred more men, women, and children in the Tabor. Undoubtedly, most of these Jews would not have survived the war without our help.

Another reason for my writing this book is to describe what life was like in the shtetl, the typical small-town Jewish community of Eastern Europe so colorfully described in *Fiddler on the Roof.* Life in the shtetl was not so colorful. In a few short pages, my recollections of life in my small village should convey how Jews in the shtetl largely eked out a subsistence living. While shtetl life was rich in tradition, religion, and learning, it was meager with regard to material things. The German genocide of the Jews wiped out the shtetl of Eastern Europe, and my effort here is to give the reader a flavor of the shtetl culture that thrived before the war.

My primary motivation in writing about my wartime experience, however, has not been to respond to my children's questions or to recreate life in the shtetl. Rather, it is to document the gallant resistance of a particular group of Jews against the German army in the forests of Poland. Many of those courageous fighters did not live to see the liberation. With very few exceptions, those who survived have not created any written record of their experiences. It is now a half century since the outbreak of World War II. Of the small number of survivors who fought with me, many are no longer alive. The list of those with direct knowledge of our Jewish resistance force has shrunk. Those with such knowledge are spread across the globe, in countries such as Brazil, Argentina, Israel, Canada, and of course the United States. Although we still occasionally get together for reunions of our partisan unit, our reunions have gotten smaller with the passage of time.

If nothing else, my hope is that this book will preserve for future generations a story of successful Jewish resistance during the Holocaust. Each of the approximately eight hundred survivors in our partisan force and in the Tabor has a unique story to tell. Mine is just one of those stories—and it consists only of those fragmented experiences I can recall after all these years. My partisan colleagues undoubtedly can recall many additional experiences. I hope my story will do justice to the many untold accounts of those who survived as well as to the many more of those who unfortunately did not.

HAROLD WERNER
November 22, 1989

Map 1: Europe on August 31, 1939

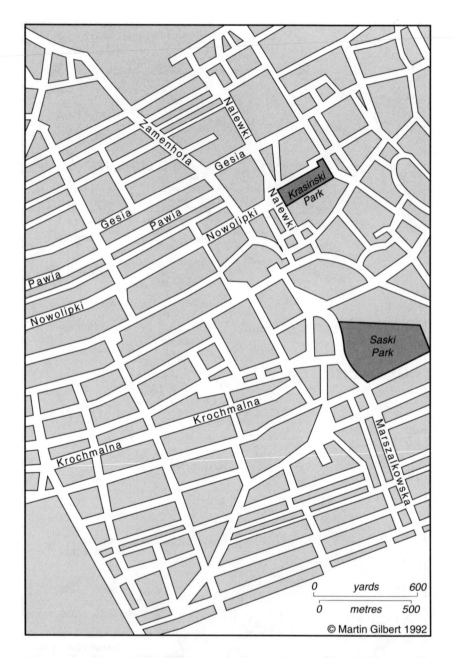

Map 2: Jewish Section of Warsaw

Map 3: Central Poland under German and Soviet occupation

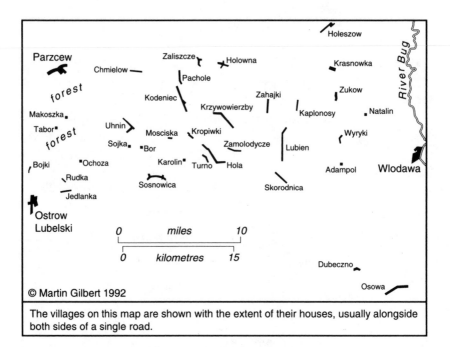

© Martin Gilbert 1992

The villages on this map are shown with the extent of their houses, usually alongside both sides of a single road.

Map 4: Polish villages between Parczew and Wlodawa—the Jewish partisans' area of operation. (The area of this map corresponds to the small rectangle on map 3.)

1

Life in Warsaw Before the Storm

It was the summer of 1938. I was Hershel Zimmerman, twenty years old and already working for myself. I had tired of working for different bosses and of being laid off periodically, so my friend Chaskel and I decided to become partners and work for ourselves. He and I were both good at operating and repairing knitting machines. We each invested 200 zlotys and together purchased two secondhand sweater-knitting machines.

Chaskel and I both lived off the courtyard at 9 Pawia Street in Warsaw. We met while working in the same knitting shop and were members of the same union. Chaskel lived with his parents on a fourth-floor walk-up, and I lived with the Freedman family in an adjacent building in a basement apartment.

Rachmiel and Chaia Freedman had two sons, twenty-three-year-old Aaron and twenty-one-year-old Shmuel, and a sixteen-year-old daughter, Manya. Rachmiel Freedman, a religious Jew with a flowing black beard, treated me like a member of the family. Both he and Chaia were especially kindly disposed toward me because I was a bachelor and hence a potential suitor for Manya. That was not an unattractive prospect for me. Manya was a tall, eye-catching high schooler, with blonde hair and blue eyes that belied her Jewish heritage. Hand in hand, Manya and I would often take long walks with her friends in Warsaw's Krasinski Park.

The Freedman apartment consisted of three rooms, which housed seven people. Manya and her parents slept in the windowless back room. The middle room had a table and chairs and two beds. The two brothers shared one bed, and I had the other one. I shared my bed with my twenty-year-old cousin Hershel, who like myself was named after our grandfather Hersh. The third room, a kitchen, also had a table and chairs. It was a small apartment and not very well ventilated. It was very sticky in the summer and on the cool side in the winter. The sole source of heat was the coal-burning cooking stove in the kitchen.

I paid a monthly rent for my living space and was glad to have it. There was a shortage of rentals in Warsaw, especially in the Jewish section. Many Jewish youngsters came to Warsaw looking for employment, which they could not find in the provinces where they lived. Major industries were located only in the larger Polish cities, such as Lublin, Warsaw, Bialystok, Lodz, and Lwów.

Unemployment and poverty were also widespread in Warsaw. Housing was scarce and many households had boarders. Some even offered meals to provide a little extra income. Rachmiel Freedman worked in a soap factory, but he was unemployed most of the year. The rent my cousin and I paid helped out a bit.

When Chaskel and I decided to open our own knitting business, we rented one room in Chaskel's parents' three-room apartment on the fourth floor facing the courtyard. We installed our two sweater-knitting machines. Then we also acquired one machine for making knitted gloves and another machine for making berets. Berets were in style then in Warsaw, as they were in France.

After we bought these machines, we did not have any capital to buy raw materials to make the sweaters. Therefore I went to a jobber who used to buy sweaters from a factory where I had worked, and who had outlets in the eastern Polish provinces near the Russian border. He provided us with the wool and cotton to make heavy knit sweaters, which were the only kind our machines could produce. Once we brought the finished sweaters to him, he paid us for the piecework. We made less than we would if we had sold directly to the stores, but we were supplied with steady orders, and it was much better than working for somebody else in a sweatshop.

The sweater industry in Warsaw was highly organized, with a strong workers' union. Wages in the factories were good when there was work, but the normal factory work season was very short. The season lasted approximately two to three months in the late summer and early fall, which was not enough to sustain a worker for a whole year.

The trouble with our jobber was that he frequently paid us with notes due one to three months later. We often could not afford to wait that long, so we had to discount the notes on the open market. It was not an organized financial market. Speculators who had money would walk in the long courtyards that ran from Nalewki Street to Zamenhofa Street, and they would buy notes at a discount. They discounted the note according to how they rated the maker of the note, and its term. Although there were some notes they would not buy, our jobber had a good enough reputation so that his were always salable. It would cost us about 10 percent of the face value of a three-month note to sell it on this market.

We were lucky to work for this jobber because he was a wealthy man and had enough money to build up his inventory of sweaters. He could keep us busy for about six months. In the slow period between seasons we picked up some work from a glove and beret jobber, which supplemented our income. This is how we managed the first year of our business venture. We saved a few hundred zlotys and were looking forward to buying a machine of a thinner knit to produce a finer sweater. Our plan was eventually to produce finer quality sweaters in small quantities and sell them to retail stores in the city, in addition to working for our jobber.

Early in the summer of 1939, a typhus epidemic broke out in Warsaw, and I came down with the disease. I remember I had bought a bunch of red cherries from a street vendor on a Saturday and had eaten them while strolling along the beach on the Vistula River. Many vendors were selling all kinds of fruits there, and I ate the cherries, unwashed, on the spot. Perhaps this was the cause of my illness.

The epidemic spread very rapidly throughout Warsaw. The city authorities tried to isolate the sick by putting them in special hospital isolation wards. Many people died. From what I could observe in my ward, it appeared that the number of fatalities was greater among the big, strong-looking people than among the weaker ones. I could not understand the reason for this phenomenon, but this was how nature seemed to work.

In the hospital isolation ward, I burned up with a high fever for about a week, and there was no medication available. The disease simply ran its course, killing some patients and sparing others. Understandably, no visitors were allowed in the isolation ward. During this time I was too sick to eat any food. At the end of the week, my temperature started to go down, and it became apparent that I was going to be one of the lucky survivors.

I was in a ward with about twenty-five or thirty beds crowded together. Like me, most of the patients had high fever, and many were delirious. Sometimes I could hear what they were saying. They boasted of how the Poles would beat the Germans. Everyone anticipated a German attack, and the outbursts of these patients made clear their belief that the Jews were at fault for the threat of war. The Poles' spirits were high. If the Germans attacked, the war would surely last less than a week, and with the aid of England and France, Poland would obliterate the Germans from the map of Europe. Such was the confidence of the Polish people.

When my temperature dropped, I was moved to a different hospital ward. There I started feeling hunger and could also receive visitors. All visitors had to be covered with a white gown from head to foot. My father came to visit me and, with his white hat and white gown, at first I could not recognize him.

After staying in the hospital for another week I was discharged. The Freedmans were glad to see me. My father and two of my brothers, Moishe and Motel, who were living in Warsaw at that time, were overjoyed that I had survived the typhus attack. My father was a very religious man and later told me that he had prayed daily for my health.

Both before and after my bout with typhus, the papers were filled with stories about the pattern of German aggression against its neighbors. The German Anschluss (takeover) of Austria had occurred in March 1938, and Germany had annexed the Sudetenland from Czechoslovakia in October 1938. In the spring of 1939, Hitler had marched into the rest of Czechoslovakia. The papers heaped criticism on Britain's prime minister, Neville Chamberlain, over his willingness to sacrifice Czech independence in order to appease Hitler and avoid war. Also in the spring, Hitler made his first demand that Poland cede the Free Port of Gdansk to Germany. Upon Poland's refusal to give up Gdansk (called "Danzig" by the Germans), Hitler denounced the 1934 nonaggression treaty between Germany and Poland. Throughout the summer, tensions heightened as Germany pressed its territorial demands against Poland. Everyone realized that German foreign minister Joachim von Ribbentrop's trip to Moscow in August, to sign a nonaggression pact between Germany and Russia, further strengthened Hitler's hand against Poland.

War preparations proceeded at a fever pitch. The Polish army was issued gas masks. People were talking about gas warfare, because they remembered the Germans using gas in World War I. Civilians were encouraged to buy their own gas masks. People in Warsaw were ordered to tape their windows and to equip their basements to make them into air raid shelters. The army ordered a partial mobilization.

The people were urged by the government, in the name of patriotism, to donate as much money as they could to help better equip
the army. The donations were given according to each individual's
financial means. Very wealthy people donated money for purchasing
bigger equipment—a piece of artillery or a tank. The less wealthy
contributed toward antiaircraft guns, which were very much needed
against the anticipated air attacks. Jews in Poland wanted to show
their patriotism and donated heavily. Despite these donations, the
main fighting force of the Polish army remained the outdated cavalry.

The Jewish Dilemma

The Jews in Poland numbered more than three million people, making up roughly 10 percent of the country's population. We had added reason to be worried about the deteriorating military and political situation. We knew the situation of the Jews would be drastically worsened if the Germans came into Poland. We were aware of the German anti-Semitic propaganda, and we had heard about Hitler's *Mein Kampf*.

Jews were desperately trying to get out of Poland, not only in 1938–39 but also much earlier, owing to the bad economic situation and rampant anti-Semitism in Poland. Anti-Semitism in Poland was fostered by the Polish Catholic clergy, which taught the blood libel fiction that Jews used the blood of a Christian to make Passover matzoh. Additionally, the clergy reminded Poles that Jews had killed Christ. Anti-Semitism took many forms, both subtle and overt. For example, the walls bordering many streets were plastered with anti-Semitic slogans like "Jews go home to Palestine."

More heavy-handed anti-Semitic activities were conducted by a right-wing political organization, the National Democratic party, popularly known as the Endek party or simply the Endecia. This was a nationalist party whose basic premise was that Poland was being exploited by its Jewish minority, which constituted a foreign people within its borders. The Endecia was a powerful force in the Polish government and was given a free hand to organize pogroms against Jewish populations in cities, towns, and villages. The most widely publicized pogrom was conducted in 1936 by the Endecia in the town of Przytyk.

After the death of the Polish dictator Marshal Joseph Pilsudski in May 1935, the anti-Semitic activities of the Endecia sharply increased. At this time, the country was in the throes of the worldwide Great Depression. To draw the population's attention away from the economic misery Poland was suffering as well as to attract more followers, the Endecia blamed the Jews for all of Poland's problems. By government decree, business establishments were required to bear the names of their owners. This was done so as to implement an Endecia-sponsored boycott of Jewish businesses. Jewish stores were picketed by young toughs to discourage non-Jews from patronizing them. Those few non-Jews who refused to honor the boycott were physically threatened by the picketers, and pictures were taken of them entering Jewish establishments. These pictures were published in the newspapers to embarrass the non-Jewish patrons. Jewish store windows were smashed and Jewish businessmen were beaten. Jewish admission to higher education was severely limited by quotas. The Polish government enacted a law forbidding the kosher slaughter of animals, to discourage Jews from following traditional dietary rules of kashruth. Pogroms increased against Jewish communities. By 1939 the Polish government had publicly adopted the Endecia position that the "Jewish problem" would only be resolved by the mass emigration of the nation's Jews.

In addition to organized anti-Semitic activities, beatings of Jewish children in public schools and of Jews in the streets were daily occurrences. In many instances I was a victim of such beatings. One such incident occurred on a beautiful spring Sunday in 1939 when I was twenty-one. My sixteen-year-old brother Moishe and I had attended a patriotic rally on Theater Place in the center of Warsaw. The government-sponsored rally was billed as a protest against the weakness of the Western European nations in giving in to German territorial demands. A crowd of many thousands turned out to listen to and cheer the government speakers criticizing Poland's Western allies.

By the end of the rally, the crowd's emotions were running high. Suddenly, the atmosphere turned violent. Instead of dispersing peacefully, parts of the crowd began to roam the streets looking for Jews to attack. Moishe and I were chased down the street by a club-wielding mob. In the distance I saw a policeman stationed on a street corner. We ran toward him for protection. As we approached, he sized up who we were and calmly turned his back on us, strolling away. Seconds later, we were seized by our pursuers and severely beaten with fists and clubs. Our bloodied heads and broken bones landed both of us in the hospital.

Because of the constant danger of street violence against Jews, many Jewish youths from different organizations—such as the Jewish Socialist Labor party (the "Bund"), the Poale Zion, and Jewish sports clubs and labor unions—organized defense groups. I joined the youth section of a defense group organized by my textile union. My group patrolled the area between Twarda and Elektoralna streets. On many occasions, we were able to intervene to save a Jew targeted by an anti-Semitic street gang and to inflict a memorable beating on the attackers. Jewish self-defense groups such as mine were declared unlawful by the authorities, and participants in these groups were subject to arrest and imprisonment.

The anti-Semitic atmosphere was compounded by the precarious economic existence faced by Polish Jews. They traditionally eked out a living as small tradesmen such as tailors, shoemakers, carpenters, blacksmiths, and shopkeepers. Jews were forbidden to hold jobs in the many nationalized industries, public transportation, and in the civil service (e.g., police force and post office). The escalating violence and boycott against Jewish businesses worsened the economic woes of Poland's Jews.

Many Jewish youths viewed emigration to British-held Palestine as an escape from the poverty and bigotry they faced in Poland. Many joined Zionist youth organizations, which advocated that Jews worldwide should move, or make *aliyah,* to a Jewish homeland in Palestine. Hachshara kibbutzim, or agricultural training camps, sprang up across Poland, where thousands of Jewish youngsters trained themselves in agricultural trades in preparation for kibbutz life in Palestine. One such hachshara kibbutz was established in my hometown of Gorzkow. It was there that my uncle Mortche met his future wife, a Warsaw native who had come to the countryside to prepare herself for kibbutz life.

Unfortunately, as the political and economic pressure on Poland's Jews to leave increased, the avenues of escape closed. Emigration to the United States was severely limited by U.S. immigration policies. In order to appease Palestinian Arabs, Great Britain issued a series of White Papers in 1931, 1937, and 1939. Each White Paper more severely restricted than previously the number of Jews permitted to immigrate to Palestine. The final White Paper was issued just a few weeks after war fever was fueled by Hitler's April 1939 renunciation of the 1934 German-Polish nonaggression treaty.

The few immigration certificates issued by the British were far too few to satisfy the desire of many Jews to leave Poland for Palestine. These immigration certificates were distributed through the Jewish Agency and were in great demand, often being sold at a dear price. But these certificates were beyond the reach of the vast majority of those seeking to leave, and very few were available to those completing their training in the hachshara kibbutzim.

Many of the Polish Jews who left for Palestine were single young men and women, who were relatively free of family responsibilities and willing to risk what was often an illegal route of escape. Very few entire families elected to face the uncertainties of emigration to Palestine. In Gorzkow, the only family head I can recall with the courage and foresight to embark on such a journey with his family was Falick Hornfeld, a first cousin of my father. One day in 1933, he announced to his family that there was no future for his children in anti-Semitic Poland and that they were going to emigrate to Palestine. Falick Hornfeld was a fervent Zionist and had helped to found the hachshara kibbutz in Gorzkow. His was a well-to-do family by Gorzkow standards. From 1933 to 1936 he planned his family's move, selling his house and worldly possessions to raise enough money for the trip. In 1936 he, his wife, and two of his five children (Dina, aged seventeen, and Shlomo, aged fifteen) left for Palestine. He did not have enough money to take his other three children, Tovah, Mordechai, and Judith (aged eighteen, fourteen, and eleven, respectively), who remained behind with their grandmother.

The four of them were smuggled out of the Polish city of Gdynia to the Free Port of Gdansk and then to Germany. They traveled through Germany and Switzerland by train to Italy, with forged papers purchased along the way. At the Italian border, they were turned back because their visas to enter Italy had expired only hours before. Forced to return to Munich, they arranged to have their visas extended but had no money to buy new train tickets to Italy. Stuck in the Munich train station, Falick and his family watched swastikaed storm troopers patrolling the streets. In desperation, Falick left his family in the train station to search for help. He entered a local jewelry store bearing a Jewish nameplate. He explained his family's plight to the Jewish jeweler, who quickly gave him the necessary train fare and wished him a safe journey. With the train fare, Falick and his family reached Genoa. Forged papers enabled them to obtain passage by ship to Palestine, where they arrived penniless. Two years later, Falick arranged to bring to Palestine his two youngest children, Mordechai and Judith. By this time, Tovah had married and so remained behind in Poland. In 1942 the family received a telegram from Poland through the Swiss Red Cross informing them that Tovah had given birth to a son, but she and her family were never heard from again.

Outbreak of War

In August 1939 I was still living with the Freedman family and working in the knitting business with my partner, Chaskel. My father lived not far from me, on Nowolipki Street, with my brother Moishe, who was seventeen years old, and my thirteen-year-old brother Motel. The rest of my family (my brothers Meyer and Irving and my sister Bella) remained in Gorzkow, with my grandfather Yisroel. I was just under twenty-one years old.

On September 1, at dawn, I was awakened by exploding bombs and an air raid siren. We all rushed into our designated air raid shelters in the basement of our building. One of the first bombs that fell that morning hit the adjacent building in which my knitting shop was located. The entire top floor of that building collapsed into the courtyard, together with our four knitting machines. That was the end of our business venture and our source of livelihood.

The entire Jewish section was heavily hit that morning. After the all-clear signal, we climbed out of the basement and gaped at the ruins of the bombardment. My block was devastated, and many buildings were on fire. People, some of them wounded and bleeding, were running in all directions carrying their belongings and trying to find members of their families. There was a little grocery store inside our courtyard operated by an old man and his daughter, where I used to buy my groceries, sometimes on credit. After this initial bombardment, the shelves in the store were emptied, and there was no food to be gotten there or elsewhere.

The bombardment of Warsaw continued for the next twenty-seven days. The Jewish section of the city, containing streets such as Na-lewki, Gesia, Zamenhofa, and Karmelicka, seemed to be bombed longer and suffered more destruction than other parts of Warsaw. The deafening noise from the antiaircraft guns was heard all over the city, but the German planes were flying so high that they seemed invisible.

Rumors were circulating that France and England had declared war on Germany. The government-controlled Polish radio broadcast encouraging news that the Polish army had repelled the Germans and was fighting on German territory. It was also reported that French divisions had attacked Germany, and the broadcasts pre-dicted that within a short time Germany would be crushed.

The bombardment was constant, and Warsaw was burning. There was no electricity, no water, no food, and no sanitary facilities. Little by little we started finding out the truth—that Warsaw was sur-rounded by the German army and that half of Poland was in German hands. The bombing continued day and night. When it got dark the German artillery surrounding Warsaw started the night shelling, which caused just as much devastation as the daytime aerial bombing. The aerial bombing hit the buildings from the top, while the people hid in the shelters. The artillery hit from the side. Sometimes an artillery shell hit a shelter and all the people in it were killed.

People were afraid to leave their shelters during a lull in the bombing to look for food. Some who ventured out were caught when the next attack started. I went out during such a lull because of a rumor that a pickle factory warehouse had been bombed on Stawki Street and that five-gallon cans of sour pickles were lying around. I rushed there and saw thousands of cans of pickles in the burned-out warehouse covered by the collapsed roof. Hundreds of people were on top of the roof trying to dig out these cans. The pickles were marked for export to America. I grabbed one can weighing about thirty pounds, and started running back just as an air raid siren sounded. Bombs began to fall in the vicinity of the pickle factory. I hid in a courtyard and waited until the raid was over, and then returned to 9 Pawia Street. I used these pickles to barter for other food.

On another occasion, I learned that a sardine warehouse on Gesia Street, near the Jewish cemetery, had been bombed and was burning. I went there with my brother Moishe and with Shmuel Freedman.

We were able to fill two and a half bags with sardine cans to take back with us. I shared my portion with my father, and we were able to sell some to buy other food.

People were starving. No food could be gotten unless you had a fortune. Some people took chances and went to the outskirts of Warsaw to find food. This was the season when vegetables were ripening, and there were plenty of vegetable fields on the outskirts of the city. It was dangerous, however, because the city was besieged by the German army, and in many cases the people searching for vege-tables were fired upon. Moishe, Shmuel, and I, along with a few other friends, ventured out of the city to look for food in the nearby fields. We came back with just a few cabbages and carrots. The fields had all been picked clean.

The city was full of Polish cavalry soldiers and their horses. They housed their horses in public buildings, theaters, and museums to protect them from the air raids. They made a shambles of these beautiful buildings. Many horses were killed in the bombing, and people cut them up right away for their meat. The streets were full of smelly horse carcasses, sewage was running in the streets, and without water supplies many houses continued to burn.

Young Polish army officers ordered the civilians to dig ditches and, in other places, to erect barricades constructed of furniture taken out of the homes. People threw furniture through their win-dows to make barricades in the streets. It was hoped this would stop the advance of the German army into the city.

Rumors were circulating that the Polish government had left Po-land on the first night of the German attack. According to these stories, the government loaded the Polish treasury onto trucks and headed in the direction of Romania.

Warsaw was being shelled into submission day and night. There was destruction and death everywhere. It took the German army eight days to conquer the Polish countryside and encircle Warsaw. The Polish army continued to resist the German advances against the capital, and in turn the Germans continued day and night bombard-ment of the starving city. The brave mayor of Warsaw, Starzynski, broadcast continual patriotic messages on the radio urging the people to resist the Germans.

The army warehouses in Warsaw were full of supplies for the military, such as uniforms, shoes, dried foods, and canned foods. As the siege of the city wore on, I heard rumors that military ordinance personnel were emptying some of these warehouses by throwing their contents out of the windows and into the street. This was being done to give the warehoused items to the Polish citizenry before the city fell to the German army and the Germans took control of the Polish army warehouses. On the basis of these rumors, I went to the Theater Place area. Boots and shoes were being thrown from the fourth- and fifth-floor windows of a military warehouse. Thousands of people were milling around in the street below, carrying away whatever they could catch. Military ordinance personnel were throwing out footwear one by one, and people in the street were practically killing each other to get at them. The Polish army boots were so heavy, especially with their heavy metal nail heads, that if they landed on someone's head they could be deadly. Many people were running around with bloody heads trying to match up a pair of boots. I was lucky to get out alive with a right and a left shoe.

Mayor Starzynski pleaded with the people to hold out and to build fortifications around the city and within it. He broadcast radio appeals to England and France asking for help. He talked on the radio to the point that he became hoarse and could hardly speak, encouraging the people to resist the invaders. Even though he kept saying that help was on its way, everyone knew the situation was hopeless. On top of all this, we heard that the Russian army had crossed the border, attacking Poland from the east. Finally, after four weeks of death and destruction, Warsaw surrendered on September 27, and the German army marched in. Poland was conquered by the Germans in eight days, but Warsaw had held out for almost a whole month.

After four weeks of bombings and hunger, and being surrounded and cut off from the world, the people of Warsaw came out of their bomb shelters into the streets. They looked and acted like wild animals, grabbing at any food they could get. The Germans set up bread lines, handing out a loaf of bread to each person in the line, but not to Jews. I was kicked out of bread lines several times when the Poles in line pointed me out to the Germans as a Jew.

As soon as the Germans occupied Warsaw, they started harassing Jews. Some Jews, mostly the Orthodox and old men, had beards and wore long black coats, called caftans. The Germans found it amusing to catch such a Jew in the street and cut his beard off, sometimes tearing it out with the skin. When the man cried out in pain they threw him to the ground and kicked him, and took pictures with their cameras, laughing at the whole spectacle. I witnessed many such horrors. Elderly Jews who did not cut their beards because of their religious beliefs wore scarfs around their faces to hide their beards.

Then came an order that all Jews had to wear white armbands bearing a blue Star of David on them. If someone disobeyed this order, the penalty was death on the spot. I complied, as did the rest of the Jews in Warsaw, but I resolved to leave the city as soon as possible.

4

The Trek Toward Russia

Chaia Freedman, in whose apartment I had boarded since coming to Warsaw in 1932, had originally come from Hola, a small farming village. Hola was located in eastern Poland, about ten miles west of the town of Wlodawa, near the Bug River. The Bug River was the dividing line between German-occupied Poland and Russian-occupied Poland, following the Polish surrender in September 1939.

Chaia Freedman's family had lived in Hola for generations, mostly occupied in farming. Rachmiel Freedman, who was from Warsaw, had decided to make his home in the big city. Before the war, the Freedman family visited their Hola relatives often during the summers. In the summer of 1937, Manya Freedman and her brother Shmuel had traveled to Hola to visit their relatives and had asked me to come along. We stayed a week and I met their uncles and aunts.

The Hola Freedmans' lives were similar to the lives of other Polish farmers. (I call the Hola family "the Freedmans," after Chaia Freedman's married name, because I do not recall the family name of her Hola relatives.) They owned land, which they inherited from their parents. They had a mill that pressed oil from poppy seeds and linseeds, they milled groats and other grains, and they kept a few cows. Because of the mill, they were considered prosperous farmers.

Chaia Freedman had a brother, Lazer, and two sisters, Shifra and

Ziesel. They all worked the family farm, operated the mill, and lived together in the family homestead. Shifra and her husband Shimon had two boys, seven and four years old. Shimon and his brother-in-law Lazar managed the families' affairs. The younger sister Ziesel, who was in her late twenties, was single and an excellent seamstress. She sewed for the local farmers and did everything the other village women did. She grew flax in the summer, dried it, and prepared it for making thread on a spinning wheel in the winter months. Then she wove the thread on a big primitive weaving machine into cloth, which she used to make clothes for the family and neighboring farmers. She also milked the cows and made butter and cream from the milk. She was a cheery, talented, energetic, and enterprising person.

The Freedman's milling business was known for miles around. Farmers from distant villages came to have their poppy seeds and linseeds pressed into oil and their groats processed. The early winter was their busiest time, and during that period they worked the mill day and night. The farmers would have to wait their turn, and sometimes they waited for days, at night often sleeping in the mill on their bags of grain.

Because of hunger and constant harassment by the occupying Germans, many Jews started leaving Warsaw in the fall of 1939. Many traveled to the Polish provinces east of Warsaw or, even further east, to Russian-occupied Poland. I went to my father and two Warsaw-based brothers, Moishe and Motel, and told them that I had decided to get out of Warsaw. I urged my father and brothers to do the same. I proposed that we travel east toward Russian-occupied territory, almost two hundred miles from Warsaw. We would have to walk the distance because there was no mechanized transportation available to the public. My father stated that he hoped the harassment of Jews by the Germans would be temporary, but he thought it was a good idea for my brothers and me to leave Warsaw. However, he felt he could not make the journey on foot at his age, and we could not persuade him to change his mind. Manya and her brother Shmuel decided to go with us. Since her older brother Aaron was married and had a baby to look after, he and his family decided to stay in Warsaw with Manya's parents.

My plan was to travel to Hola, about ten miles west of Wlodawa. We would stop at Manya's relatives' house in Hola and rest for a few days, and then proceed to Wlodawa, which was on the shores of the Bug River. From there we hoped to smuggle ourselves across the river border to Russian-occupied territory.

The five of us (Moishe, Motel, Shmuel, Manya, and myself) left Warsaw early one morning in October 1939. I wore a heavy Polish army coat and army shoes and carried a long military-issue hunting knife. The roads were crowded with many people on foot, Jews and non-Jews, leaving Warsaw. Some of the refugees leaving the city were former political leaders and high-ranking government officials. Some of them left in cars. We later saw their cars stuck on the road for lack of fuel, and they paid exorbitantly high prices to anyone who happened to have some. I heard rumors that the two main leaders of the Bund, Henryk Erlich and Viktor Alter, were also among the people leaving Warsaw at that time. I knew them from having attended their lectures on Friday nights in prewar Warsaw on Krochmalna Street.

We finished what little food we had with us during our first day on the road. We slept in barns wherever we could get in undetected, or in the woods by sleeping in an upright sitting position against a tree. When we passed through towns we usually were helped by the Jewish population there, and we slept in the towns' synagogues.

In small villages we stopped at farmers' houses and asked for food. Most of the time the farmers were helpful and expressed their remorse over the devastation of Warsaw and the loss of Polish independence. We also stopped at the homes of some farmers who were sorry over what had happened to Poland, but they refused to give us any food because we were Jewish. Many horse-drawn wagons passed us on the road, and we often got a short free ride on them. Some of them stopped but would not take us, not only because we were Jews but because they considered us "city slickers," who they felt made fun of farmers.

After about ten days on foot, we came to the city of Siedlce. It was a sizable city with a large Jewish population. We slept in one of its many synagogues and spoke with many Jews there. A stream of Jewish refugees was passing through Siedlce, migrating from German-occupied western Poland eastward toward Russian territory. The Siedlce Jews were very hospitable toward these refugees, and to us, making certain that we were invited to join local families for meals and sometimes even giving money to those refugees who needed it. The Jews there did not yet have as many restrictions imposed on them as the Jews in Warsaw. Jewish merchants kept their stores open, although there was not much to sell. One Jewish woman with a grocery store gave us some food and put us up for a night. She told us that the Polish army had put up severe resistance against the German advance before retreating from Siedlce. Her only son, who was in the Polish army, had been killed defending Poland against the

Germans. She cried as she mourned her son. I remember her saying that she was proud that the army had not given up Siedlce easily to the Germans and that many German soldiers had been killed in the battle for the city. Listening to her, I considered myself lucky. I had received my draft notice in late August, directing me to report for military induction a month later. By my induction date, Poland had already surrendered.

While we were in Siedlce, which was halfway from Warsaw to the Russian border, my two brothers Moishe and Motel had a change of heart. They decided to go home to Gorzkow in order to see what had happened to the rest of the family, and perhaps take them to Russian territory. Gorzkow was still home for my two other brothers Meyer and Irving, my little sister Bella, my grandparents, and many aunts and uncles and their respective families. In all, my Gorzkow family, including cousins, numbered over eighty people. My brothers would have to head south from Siedlce to reach Gorzkow. The journey would be about 150 miles from Siedlce, a greater distance than they would have had to cover to go east to the Russian border with us. I tried very hard to persuade Moishe and Motel to come with us, but they just wanted "to go home." They left for Gorzkow, and I never saw them again.

Shortly after Moishe and Motel left us, Manya, Shmuel Freedman and I headed southeast from Siedlce. After about another two weeks of walking, we reached the town of Parczew, about twenty miles from our destination, Hola. It happened to be market day in Parczew. Farmers from the surrounding villages came there to sell their produce and to buy supplies. Market day occurred once each week, and we were fortunate to arrive on this day. We asked the farmers if anyone was going in the direction of Hola, and we were lucky enough to encounter a neighbor of Manya's relatives. He was an elderly farmer named Kornila. He took us to Hola in his wagon, so we did not have to walk the last twenty miles.

The population east of Parczew was mostly Ukrainian. The language they used was a mixture of Ukrainian, Russian, and Polish, called Hachlacki, and the people were called Hachlakis. This Ukrainian area had belonged to Russia before World War I. The people there were very nationalistic Ukrainian, and they hated the Poles and the Polish language. This was because when the Poles occupied the area after World War I, they suppressed the local language, religion, and culture. The occupying Germans sought to win the sympathies of the Hachlacki population by exploiting their nationalistic sentiments. They allowed the Hachlackis to conduct their schools in

Ukrainian, to convert the Roman Catholic churches in the area to Russian Orthodox churches called Pravoslavny, and to use their own language for official purposes. During our ride to Hola, Kornila advised us to learn the Hachlacki language soon, or else the local people would hate us for using Polish.

In the evening we arrived in Hola. Manya gave Kornila a kerchief for his wife, to thank him for his kindness. This was a scarce item, since all manufacture of goods had stopped in Poland with the outbreak of the war. We could tell by his expression of thanks that he appreciated the gift very much.

The Freedman family in Hola was extremely happy to see us. They had heard about the siege and devastation of Warsaw and were very worried about their family there. They knew me well because they used to come to Warsaw to visit their sister Chaia and her family, and because I had previously accompanied Manya to Hola for a summer visit.

Hola was a large village with a population of close to a thousand. There were, however, only three Jewish families in the village. Some of their children lived and worked in Warsaw. They also used to come to visit the Freedmans in Warsaw, so I was familiar with them and their families. In the few weeks since the beginning of the German occupation, not much had changed for the Jews of Hola.

After staying on the Freedmans' farm for a few days, I told the family that I planned to continue on to Russian territory. Based on how I saw the Germans mistreat and kill Jews in Warsaw, I knew that I had to get as far away from the Germans as possible. Manya decided to go with me, while Shmuel decided to stay with the family on the farm. Concerned with Manya's well-being, her aunts were not happy with my plan, but they gave us money, food, and their blessings when we left.

We walked east to Wlodawa, a distance of about ten miles. It took about six or seven hours. Once there, we stopped at the home of a distant relative of Manya's. Wlodawa was a large town, with a substantial Jewish population. We found out that for five zlotys per person there were local townspeople who would take you by rowboat to Russian territory on the other side of the Bug River. Not far from the river, on the Russian side, was the small town of Tomaszewka. It also had a large Jewish population. The man we hired, originally from Tomaszewka, rowed us over to the eastern river bank at night, dropped us off, and rowed back. We walked toward Tomaszewka in the dark, but we were spotted by Russian border guards. They stopped us and asked what we were doing there. We explained that we were

Polish Jews escaping from the Germans. They walked us to a little hut where we explained again to an officer why we were there. He told us we had broken the law and explained that there was a time, several weeks earlier, when they had allowed anyone to cross the border to Russian territory. Many people had taken advantage of this opportunity, but now the border was closed and so we had to go back. He took my wristwatch and instructed the soldiers to take us back to the other side of the Bug. We were rowed back and, in accordance with the officer's instructions, left off where there were no German border guards.

The next night we tried the crossing again from another spot, using the same smuggler. But before we reached the other side of the river, we heard gunfire coming from the Russian bank. We could not tell if the shooting was directed at us or someone else. It was pitch black, and the smuggler decided to turn back. After this second unsuccessful attempt, our money and food were exhausted, so we turned back to Hola, intending to try crossing another time. However, what we learned in Hola made us question our plans.

When the Russians attacked Poland shortly after the September 1, 1939, German invasion, Russian troops advanced westward deep into Polish territory. When Poland surrendered, the Russians found themselves in control of much ground west of the Bug River. This river was predetermined to be the German-Russian border by the Ribbentrop-Molotov treaty earlier that year. By the terms of this treaty, the Russians were obligated to withdraw from the corridor of Polish territory they occupied west of the Bug. This corridor included my hometown of Gorzkow and was very heavily populated by Polish Jews.

Before pulling back to the Bug, the Russians warned the Jewish population in the region that the impending German occupation would be especially hard on the Jews, and offered the Jewish population the opportunity to pull back with them. The Russians even provided transportation for their belongings. Many young families and younger unattached single people went with the retreating Russian troops. The older family members and the very young stayed behind, hoping to ride out the war at home. Unbeknownst to me, my family experienced a similar split. My nineteen-year-old brother Meyer, as well as my stepuncle Isaac Frucht and his young family, left with the Russians. The rest of the family stayed behind in Gorzkow.

The Russian offer to move Jews to the eastern side of the Bug River had expired several weeks before our two unsuccessful attempts to cross the river. When we returned to Hola from those attempts, we were resolved to try again. However, news of those Jews who had resettled to the Russian side of the river began to trickle in to us. Often, the news was brought by Jews returning from the Russian side of the river who were passing through Hola en route back to their hometowns further west. They carried tales of hunger and overcrowding in the Jewish refugee camps set up on the Russian side of the river. They also told of mistreatment by the Russian authorities and of being forced to accept Russian passports. It was even rumored that the Russians had plans to resettle the Jews deep inside Russia itself. (This later proved to be true—and very fortunate for those resettled far from the battle theater.) There were also rumors that the Bug was not the final border and that there would be another territorial adjustment. At the same time, word spread that the English and French were fighting the Germans and that America had also entered the war against Germany (this I later learned was untrue).

All these rumors contributed to our indecision over the wisdom of attempting another crossing. In light of this situation, we remained in Hola, and I occupied myself with helping out on the farm. Before long, I learned to press the oil out of linseed at the mill. I got along well with the local farmers and quickly picked up their Hachlacki language.

Life in Hola

The first few months in Hola were peaceful. There was little visible German activity, and very seldom did we see a German patrol in the village. The three Jewish families went about their business as usual. However, it was dangerous for Jews to go to a larger neighboring town.

In these larger towns there was a significant German presence. As in Warsaw and elsewhere, Jews had to wear armbands bearing a Jewish star. In these towns, the Germans stopped any Jews they found on the street and pressed them into work gangs. The Germans established Judenrats in the towns, as well as in Polish cities. A Judenrat consisted of a committee of prominent local Jewish residents, whose job it was to implement the Germans' orders for the Jewish population.

In the nearby town of Sosnowica, the Germans established a local Judenrat. Hola and other villages in the area fell within the jurisdiction of this Judenrat. The Germans would tell the Judenrat how many Jewish men to supply for forced labor each day. The Judenrat would then tell each village under its jurisdiction how many men were to report to work from that village. The Germans also demanded certain amounts of money and gold, and the Judenrat would collect this from local Jews. If the Judenrat did not satisfy the Germans' demands, the Jewish men of Sosnowica and the surrounding

villages would be punished. Punishment consisted of additional days
of forced labor. The Germans' demands on the Judenrat progres-
sively grew heavier and heavier.

Despite the increasing burdens and hazards of the German occupation, life went on and the local Jewish population tried to make the
best of it. Jewish teenagers from the surrounding villages would come
to Hola on Saturdays to spend time at the Freedmans' big farmhouse.
This continued a practice that had existed since before the war.
Manya's Aunt Ziesel was a good hostess and served baked goods and
tea. We talked, exchanged news and rumors, and tried to have a little
fun.

In the neighboring village of Turno, there was a Jewish farmer
known as David Turno. (He, like many people, was known by his
hometown.) He was a rich landowner with hundreds of acres of
property, and with many horses, cows, and other livestock. Many
farmers worked his farm. He had a wife and one son, and his was the
sole Jewish family in the village. Well before the war, he had established a shul (synagogue) in his home, supplied it with a Torah, and
hired a chazan (cantor). The chazan read from the Torah on Saturdays and holidays, and blew the shofar on High Holidays. The chazan was a twenty-year-old Jewish orphan named Lieb, whom David
Turno had hired from a yeshiva (a Jewish high school) in Lublin.
Chazan Lieb was also the melamed, or teacher, for David Turno's
son Nuchem, a tall, good-looking twenty-year-old. Chazan Lieb had
a very pale complexion from sitting over his books all the time.

On Saturdays and holidays, Manya, her family and I, along with
all the Jews from Hola and other neighboring villages, such as Mosciska, Zamolodycze, and Kodeniec, would walk to David Turno's shul
for services. We were extended a hospitable welcome by David Turno
and his family. After every service, David Turno would host a large
kiddush meal of wine, fish, challah, and cake. Sometimes he served a
chulunt—a dish of meat, barley, and potatoes—which was stewed in
an oven overnight.

Due to starvation and German harassment in the cities, many
young Jews who had been working in Warsaw and other Polish cities
before the war began to return to their hometowns in the small
villages. One young man who came back had worked with me in a
Warsaw factory and had lived in my neighborhood. His name was
Yankel and he was David Turno's nephew. He was a few years older
than I and was lame, with one leg shorter than the other. I met him
when I came to services one day at the Turno home. We talked for a
long time, reminding each other about the good times we had had in
Warsaw.

In the fall of 1939, the Sosnowica Judenrat issued an order that each Jewish family from the neighboring villages had to supply a male member to provide three days of labor each week to the German authorities. The designated men were to assemble in the town of Sosnowica. They were to supply the labor for construction of a road from nearby Wlodawa to Sobibor (where later the infamous death camp was built). As with other German orders, the penalty for disobeying this order was death. As usual, everybody was to wear a white armband bearing the Jewish Star.

I was one of the men from the Freedman household designated for this road crew. I worked for three days and then returned to Hola. Every week I and the other Jewish men would go back and work three more days. It was backbreaking labor, and the German and Ukrainian guards would beat us with clubs and their rifle butts to work faster. Although I was beaten like the rest, I was lucky to be young and strong. Elderly Jews were beaten and, if unable to continue laboring, were shot.

The land was swampy. We had to cut trees from the nearby woods to lay a foundation. Then we added on heavy timbers from larger trees, dragged by teams of horses from farther away, to lay on top. The road was not far from the Bug River, and many times during our toil we could see Russian soldiers patrolling on the other side. I felt very bad that I was on the wrong side of the river, and I envied those Russian soldiers.

Being under the jurisdiction of the Judenrat and under the eyes of the Germans was terrible. They ordered us to do different jobs, like making roads and clearing forests, and for the smallest infraction we were beaten. Despite all this, life was still better there than in the big cities, because we still had enough food and we lived at home. The news from Warsaw was very bad. The Jews that came from there to the neighboring farms told terrible stories of hunger, degradation, and death of the Warsaw Jews. This news was echoed in the few letters I received from my father, and in Manya's letters from her father.

Assuming that the mail was read by the authorities, we were careful what we wrote back in our letters. Both our fathers asked for packages of food. I sent my father a five-pound package of chicken fat and groats. My father wrote back to tell me that he had received this package and sold it. With the money he obtained, he bought other less expensive foods to last him an entire month. After a month or two, Manya and I stopped getting responses to our letters.

Manufactured textiles, such as bolts of cloth for dresses and kerchiefs, were very scarce in the villages. Once the trains began running again, Manya and her Aunt Ziesel decided to go to Warsaw with food, like the other farmers did, to exchange for textiles. They dressed like local farm girls, with kerchiefs on their heads. Manya had blonde hair, so the two of them looked much like the other women on the train. Jews were forbidden to ride on the train. The penalty was death. Manya and Ziesel made their way to Warsaw and entered the Jewish ghetto. They found my father and Manya's father and gave them some food. They returned safely, but it was a very dangerous trip and they did not try it again.

Wintertime brought heavy snowdrifts, which blanketed the roads and houses. An order came from the Judenrat to clear the snow from the roads and highways. Groups of Jews were assigned certain sections of the roads. Often we had to walk for hours to reach the assigned workplace. You had to complete the work, regardless of when you got there. The snowdrifts were often five to ten feet high, and for not completing the assigned work a German would whip you until you fell. If this happened to an elderly Jew who could not get up after being whipped, the Germans shot him. I provided this labor three days a week, and the rest of the time I worked in the mill for Manya's relatives.

One day Shimon Freedman, Shifra's husband, went to Sosnowica to replace a broken mechanism for the mill. As he walked in the town, he failed to observe that a German was walking on the same sidewalk as he, and he did not step down. A Jew was not allowed to walk on the sidewalk when a German passed on that sidewalk. The German called him over and shot him on the spot. The family was in shock when they learned of Shimon's murder. They could not believe it. They did not immediately tell his two small boys, ages seven and four, of their father's death, but the boys eventually found out when Shimon failed to come home after several days.

The restrictions against Jews became tighter and tighter. Every week, I worked my three-day quota in Sosnowica with many other Jews. One day when we reported for work, trucks took the entire work gang to an area about forty miles to the south. This area was unfamiliar to me. We arrived at a labor camp near Osowa, named Camp Savin, halfway to the city of Chelm. There, the Germans were building a road between Chelm and Wlodawa. They put us to work on this road for twelve hours a day, with very little food. It was backbreaking. I worked there without a day's rest for about a month. We slept on straw-covered shelves in a nearby barn, and we were beaten for the slightest slowup in work. The elderly people who could not keep up the pace were shot. I realized I could not survive this regimen, as the Germans seemed intent on working us all to death, and I decided to run away. I slipped out of the barn one night and walked in the direction of Hola. I walked during the night and slept during the day. When I occasionally met a farmer, I begged for food. After four days, I made it back to Hola, where Manya's family was extremely happy to see me.

6

Work as a Farm Hand

I realized that because the Juden-rat might find out about my escape from the Osowa work gang, I was not safe in Hola. Therefore, I decided to get a job working for one of the local farmers I knew from my days of working at the mill. I thought I might be less visible to the authorities if I was on a farm rather than at the mill.

I went to the neighboring village of Lubien to a farmer named Stephan. He liked me, as I had helped him in the mill to press his linseed to oil. I offered to work for him solely in return for food and a place to sleep. Stephan agreed to take me in. I came back to Hola and told Manya and her family about my decision. I advised them to find jobs on farms also, on the basis that being out of the village of Hola would give us a better chance to survive. Also, by doing this, the Sosnowica Judenrat would not know where we were. Kornila, the neighbor across the road, found a job for Manya with a farmer in Zamolodycze, several miles from Hola, on the way to Lubien. Manya, though a city girl from Warsaw, had learned to handle all the farm chores from her Aunt Ziesel.

I went to Lubien to work for Stephan late on a Sunday afternoon in February 1940. His family was sitting down to eat dinner when I got there, and he asked me to join them. Everyone was sitting on low stools around a small table. On the table was a big bowl of mashed potatoes, containing pieces of bacon. Everyone had a spoon for the potatoes, and a cup of cabbage soup. The family consisted of Stephan, who was about thirty-five years old, his wife Marfa, their little eight-year-old girl Lanka, Stephan's mother-in-law, and a large farm dog. The dog barked at me, but Stephan told him to be quiet. After the meal, Stephan took me out and showed me his farm.

He had four horses, fifteen cows, fifty lambs, and several pigs. His little girl Lanka, who followed us as we walked, told me that they also had many chickens. He owned fifty acres of land in different plots in the same village, and about twenty acres of grassland in the woods where his cows and lambs grazed. He was considered a rich farmer. His house was nicer than average and had a tin roof. His farm equipment and even his water well were more modern than those of the other farmers. Lubien was a sizable farming village, stretching several miles along one main road. It contained a Russian Orthodox Church (which the Ukrainians had converted from a Roman Catholic Church after the Polish defeat), and there was also a farmers' cooperative grocery store. Since springtime was approaching and there was much to be done in the fields, Stephan needed me as a farm worker. And I needed his farm as a hiding place from the Judenrat and the Germans. I knew the farm work would not be easy for me, but I was young, twenty-two years old, and physically strong. My plan was to work hard and make myself indispensable to Stephan, so that he would let me stay at his farm. I explained my plan to Manya when I saw her, and encouraged her to try to do the same at her farm.

Stephan took me to the barn and showed me my sleeping place on top of the loft, where he kept the straw for the animals. He gave me a few rags from his house for bedding. Early the next morning, Stephan showed me my chores for the day. He gave me a pitchfork and told me to remove the manure from the cow barn. The manure was an accumulation from the entire winter. The cows stood all day in the cow barn. Every day fresh straw was spread out over the floor, and when it combined with the cows' excrement it made more manure. The manure was so tightly packed that it seemed impossible to penetrate it with the pitchfork. I worked very hard, and by noontime I had cleaned about half a stall. I had fourteen and a half stalls to go. Stephan came to check on me and seemed satisfied with the progress of my work. We broke for lunch on the porch of his house, after which I went back to my job. At night I was so tired I could not even finish my supper. My hands were bleeding from the pitchfork, and the powerful fumes from the stirred-up manure made me dizzy. Stephan knew that this was the hardest kind of work on the farm, but it had to be done before planting time in the spring. He gave me a hand in taking the manure into the fields, and then we both spread it.

On Sundays I did his mother-in-law's job of taking the animals out to pasture. In order to go to his grazing land in the woods, I had to take the animals through a narrow lane which was the border between his land and that of his neighbor. The neighbor's property was covered with sown crops. It was a half-mile walk from the farm to the grazing land, but the cows were trained not to get into the neighbor's fields. However, sometimes some of them strayed, and I as the shepherd had to give them a licking with a stick. Stephan's dog kept me company and helped keep the animals in line. The sheep were the biggest trouble-makers for me. Once we reached the grazing land, my job was to watch the animals. Sometimes when I had other chores to do on the farm, Stephan's mother-in-law would take the animals out to graze.

The horses were taken out to pasture on Sundays, which was a day of rest on the farm. This was strictly a man's job. You had to ride one horse and have the other three follow. I had no experience riding horses, especially bareback. The first time I took them out, we had to cross a little creek and in midstream my horse decided to take a drink of water. As he suddenly bent down, I fell over his head into the water. My only concern was that no one see my lack of experience.

Every morning, Stephan's wife Marfa would have a bag in front of the house with my food for the day. This food varied depending on her mood and what was available. Sometimes it was very sparse, but other times she gave me a piece of sausage.

I always carried a blanket with me to protect myself from the rain. Sometimes I would watch the animals while sitting under the blanket, soaked by the rain, alone in the woods, far from civilization, and twenty miles from the nearest railroad track. Yet I was happy to have this seemingly safe place to be.

Sitting there watching the animals, all kinds of memories flooded through my mind—the good old days in Warsaw, the walks in the evening in Krasinski Park with Manya, the union meetings, all the friends I had made in Warsaw in my seven years of living there. And now here I was, sitting and wondering what had happened to my father, my brothers and sister, my grandfather, uncles, aunts, and their families—wondering if I would come out of this nightmare alive. I wondered how long Stephan would keep me on his farm even though I worked for nothing and was very valuable to him. And what if the Germans found out I was here? What bothered me most was that I had not made another attempt to cross the Bug to the Russian side. I would now have been free from the German threat.

I wondered why so many Jews had come back from the Russian side to German-occupied Poland. They used to stop at Hola overnight on the way back. I could not understand why they chose to go back under German control. Didn't they know the Germans were killing Jews? The Germans made no secret of it. Maybe these refugees wanted to go back to the families they had left behind. They had told us how disappointed they were with the conditions on the Russian side. Even Polish Jews who had been communist sympathizers were disappointed with the Russian communist system, which they had glorified in Poland before the war. Maybe they thought that Germany would soon be defeated, since England and France had declared war on Germany. With all these thoughts running through my mind, I still wished I had tried again to cross the Bug.

Stephan taught me all the necessary aspects of farming. He showed me how to gather the animals back from pasture, how to prepare food for and feed the pigs, and how to spread the manure in the field. He told me he was satisfied with my work and was amazed that a city boy could learn farming in such a short time. Stephan's wife liked me too. I was a good worker who did not have to be paid. She gave me a pair of Stephan's old trousers, a straw hat, and a pair of wooden shoes. All the farmers wore wooden shoes to work. I saved my Polish army shoes that I had gotten in Warsaw. Those were my good shoes, not to be worn to tend to animals. I looked so much like any other farm hand that you could not tell I was a city boy.

Childhood Remembrances

Sitting in the field tending the animals was very boring, especially in the rain. Sometimes I got together with other local shepherds. By this time I was able to speak a perfect Hachlacki, and even they could not tell I was not from the vicinity. However, most of the time I sat alone thinking about my family and home in Gorzkow.

Gorzkow was a small farming village in eastern Poland, about forty miles southeast of the city of Lublin. To the east rose high mountains, some of which were snowcapped all year round. The village held about three hundred people, all Jewish, and was surrounded by farms for many miles. The villagers were storekeepers and tradesmen such as tailors, shoemakers, blacksmiths, and carpenters. Their clientele consisted primarily of the farmers in the surrounding area, all of whom were non-Jewish. Once a week on market day, the farmers would bring their produce to the village to sell and with the proceeds would shop in the stores in town.

All the villagers were very religious Jews. They went to religious services during portions of the morning, noon, and evening. They eked out a poor living by trading with the local farmers. Among themselves, they spoke only Yiddish; with the farmers, they conversed in Polish.

I remember a story that was told in our home in Gorzkow many times. It was set in 1920, when Poland had obtained its independence and Marshal Pilsudski had chased the Russian Bolsheviks out of Poland. Different non-Polish anti-Bolshevik military units—such as General Petlura and his Tsarist division, which had been defeated by the Bolsheviks—had not yet been disbanded. Even though the fighting was over, Petlura's troops continued roaming around our area, waiting for someone to defeat the Bolsheviks in Russia. They had been used to persecuting Jews in Russia before the war, and they undertook similar pogroms in our vicinity. The same practice was carried out by the armies of General Balackov and General Haller. General Haller's group was an expeditionary force from either France or America which had come to help defeat the Bolsheviks. They were notorious for carrying out pogroms against Jews.

I was three years old and sitting on Grandpa's large work table, which was where he did his tailoring. My mother was holding me, and we both looked out the window. We saw many of Haller's soldiers running toward us. Some came into our house and searched it from top to bottom, ripping open the feather beds and pillows. Feathers were flying all over the house. All of a sudden, in a rage an officer struck the table I was sitting on with his saber. My mother let out a scream. I can still remember her scream. She thought he had chopped off my legs. The deep cut from the saber in the table's surface was a constant reminder of this incident afterward. We later learned that this unit had been about to pull out of Gorzkow, and one of its soldiers was missing. A local farmer had falsely told the unit commander that he had seen the missing soldier enter our house. The soldiers had come in a rage, certain that the Jews had killed him. Prudently, my father and grandfather had hidden in the attic. The soldiers had made a mess of our house, and later the "missing" soldier was found lying drunk in an alley.

My mother, father, brothers, sister, and myself lived with my grandpa in his single-story house, which consisted of one very large room and a much smaller adjacent one. In the front of the house was a window overlooking the street. Just inside the window was situated grandpa's large table with his foot-pedaled sewing machine. There were many beds in the large room. Two beds were for my parents. Eventually there were five boys and one girl in our family, all of whom also slept in those two beds. Additionally, there were two beds in the large room for grandpa and my step-grandmother. When my grandfather was well into his fifties, he and my step-grandmother had two more children, who slept in their parents' two beds. In the smaller room lived my mother's younger sister Bella, her brother

Mortche, and my step-grandmother's teenage son Isaac. In total, we eventually had fifteen family members living under one roof in this two-room house.

Sanitary facilities consisted of an outhouse in the backyard. There was no electricity, and water was drawn from a hand-pumped well in the center of the village. Cooking was done on a wood-burning stove, which also kept us warm in the wintertime.

I remember my mother helping grandpa with the sewing while she rocked me in the cradle with her foot. Our neighbor, Nusen the carpenter, had made this cradle from pine wood, which smelled good. We used this cradle for my four brothers and my sister. Altogether, we were six children, in the following order: myself, Meyer, Moishe, Irving, Motel, and sister Bella. We were all born approximately two years apart.

When I was three years old, I was sent to cheder (religious school), as were all Jewish boys in the town (girls did not attend cheder). My parents made a little party for the members of the family, which at that time included my one-year-old brother Meyer. My mother baked a cake to celebrate the occasion.

There was no public school in Gorzkow at that time because the school building had burned down in the fighting during the First World War. Although Gorzkow was a small village, it contained many cheders. There were many learned men who could not find any other means to make a living, and they became the cheder teachers. The teacher for the beginning students, however, did not have to have a strong background, as he only taught the children the Hebrew alphabet and just a few Hebrew prayers.

My teacher's name was Yosel Melamed ("melamed" means "teacher" in Hebrew). My parents paid Yosel Melamed a weekly tuition for my cheder training. The townspeople donated to a local charity, which made "loans" to people who were too poor to pay for necessities and emergencies. Often, these loans were made to enable poor people to pay for cheder. The monies were called loans (although not repaid), so that the recipients could retain their pride while accepting charity.

When I started cheder, I was very scared to be left alone in a strange house with twelve boys, most of them older than myself. The melamed usually had a young helper, who brought the youngest children to and from school. In the wintertime, the helper had to carry us on his back because of the snow and sleet. Sometimes he carried two of us at a time. The young teenagers who took this job were from poor homes, or were poor homeless orphans.

On my first day, my parents walked with me to cheder at the

melamed's home. Yosel Melamed lived in a large one-room house containing a long table on one side of the room. On either side of the table were low wooden benches where the boys sat. At the other end of the room were two beds, a stove, and a large wide oven to bake bread. There was space on top of the oven to sleep. The floor was a dirt floor. The melamed had several children of his own living in the house, who also attended cheder.

My father told the melamed to treat me gently, and my mother went over to his wife to tell her to see that her husband did not hit me. He was known to have a bad temper.

The boys referred to the melamed as "Rabbi Yosel" or simply "Rabbi." He took me on his lap and with a pointer showed me the Hebrew alphabet in large print on a big square board which lay on the table. I repeated the letters after him. Two groschen (pennies) fell on the board as if from nowhere. He told me to take them. He said they had been sent from heaven by the Angel Gabriel so that I would be a good boy who would learn and make my parents proud.

Cheder started at eight o'clock in the morning. For lunch, we either walked home or my mother brought me an onion roll. At four o'clock, we were sent home for supper. At six o'clock, we returned for several more hours of cheder. Our time was spent studying Hebrew and memorizing prayers.

On the table near the rabbi was a leather whip, called a *kanchik*. I soon found out what this was for. For not knowing the name of the letter he was pointing to, he would twist your ear until it hurt. If he called on you and you were sleeping with your head on the table or you were talking, he would slap your face. For severe sins such as going to the outhouse and failing to come back quickly, he gave you a taste of the *kanchik*. The rabbi's wife would always intervene for the unfortunate boy, but not always successfully. I was lucky not to suffer such misfortunes.

The thing I liked best about the early years in cheder was when a boy was born to a family in the village. Then, Rabbi Yosel took all his students during the dinner break to the house of the newborn to say a prayer for the baby following the minchah (afternoon) prayers. We each received a bag with cookies and candies from the celebrating family. The cookies were a standard style. Each was round and had three holes in it. Afterward, in unison, we wished a "Good Night" to the mother and little baby. This went on every night for seven days until the baby's circumcision. We were happy when a boy was born. For a baby girl there was no such celebration.

After three years with Rabbi Yosel, I knew the prayers expected of me. When I was six years old, my father took me to a more advanced rabbi, Srulke Lederman, who was a distant relative of my father. There I was taught advanced Hebrew studies.

When I was seven, public school came to Gorzkow, and it was compulsory for all children. Public school was from eight o'clock in the morning through four o'clock in the afternoon. During the Catholic religious hour, taught by a local priest, Jewish children were excused. They could sit in school and not participate or go home for this hour. No one wanted to sit in school, so we all went home for the hour. After four o'clock, we went home for a bite to eat and then proceeded to cheder, which ran for about three hours. At cheder, I studied the haftorah passage for each week.

At first, I did not like public school. The change from cheder was great. Public school was roomy and sunny, and boys and girls were in the same class. Jewish and non-Jewish (or gentile) children sat together. A wooden crucifix hung on the wall, and a priest taught Catholicism in one period. Initially, I was hostile toward the gentile children and argued with them that ours was the real God. The gentile children looked at us strangely. We dressed differently. The Jewish boys, wearing curly earlocks called *payas,* were dressed in long black caftans and round hats with small visors.

The gentile children called us names, like "Christ-killers," and we often got into fights, but in the classroom everyone had to behave. The punishment for talking during the lesson was to go to the front of the classroom where the teacher would strike the child's extended palms with a ruler. Sometimes the punishment would be to stand in front of the class with arms raised for lengthy periods. Despite the fear of punishment, I began to like public school because the teacher covered many different subjects not taught in cheder, such as writing (in Polish), arithmetic, science, geography, and music. This opened a new world for me.

The Jewish children did very well in public school because they were used to sitting for long periods of study in cheder. However, I had a problem in school with getting supplies. We had to buy our own books, pencils, and crayons, and I, like many other children, did not have the money. There were other Jewish children who were not so poor, but who had trouble with their homework. I would help them with their homework and they would pay me with a pencil or crayon, and that satisfied my requirements for school supplies. I took school very seriously due to the great value placed on education by my parents.

My father, Shulim Zimmerman, was a tall, thin, wiry man with a long, full black beard. He wore the traditional Jewish garb—a black hat and black caftan. He exhibited a good sense of humor with his children and loved to take us swimming to a nearby river in the summertime. He was a great defender of his children, whenever any of us got into fights or were blamed by a neighbor for some infraction. I remember one day when my brother Moishe came home from public school with a very prominent red welt across one side of his face. My father demanded an explanation. Moishe sheepishly explained that the boy sitting next to him in school had incurred the wrath of the teacher with his disrespectful behavior. The teacher meant to give the boy a swat on the back with her punishment stick. She missed and hit Moishe's face by mistake. My father was so enraged that he accompanied Moishe to school the next day. He accosted the principal and, in an angry shouting voice which everyone in the school could hear, demanded that the teacher personally apologize to Moishe. He refused to leave the principal alone until the teacher was finally summoned to make her apology to Moishe in front of him.

My father came from a family of five girls and two boys, so he was tolerant of the fights and tensions inherent in living in crowded quarters. Three of his sisters raised families in Gorzkow, and on holidays he gave a high priority to family get-togethers with his sisters' large families. Between our family and my father's sisters' families, and with all the cousins, we could count about eighty of the village residents as relatives.

My father was a deeply religious man, but not a fanatic. He had enough training to become a rabbi, but did not want to be one. He was also self-educated in Russian and Polish. He wrote interpretations on different writings of major Hebrew scholars, which were published. He was very respected in Gorzkow as a scholar. He was also the chazan in the shul and read from the Torah.

My father was an authority on religious interpretations of the Talmud and served as an advocate in disputes among local Jews. Jews did not take their disputes to the Polish civil courts. Instead, they went before the local Jewish court, known as the Bet Din. In the Bet Din the rabbi of the village acted as the judge, and each party to a dispute would choose an advocate to argue their side of the case. My father was frequently asked to serve as the advocate for a party before the Bet Din and hardly ever lost one of these cases. He also wrote petitions in Polish to government agencies for people who had certain requests.

When I was young, my father made a decent living for the family.

He would buy grain from farmers, mill it in the local mill, and sell the flour to the townspeople out of our house. Thursday was his busiest day, because on that day the local women would buy his flour to bake challah for the Sabbath and bread for the entire week. However, as our family grew in number, it became more and more difficult for my father to conduct his flour business from our crowded house.

My mother Basha was a sweet, loving mother to the six of us, and managed to make each of us feel we were special to her. She wore the traditional wig evidencing married status. I was told that in her youth she was very attractive, with pretty brown eyes and high cheek bones, and was the center of attention of the single young men in town. As the mother of six in a poor family, she worked long hours, either on household work or by helping my father with his flour business. She was also a talented seamstress, having learned her trade at my grandfather's side. Any spare time was taken up with sewing outfits for her children. She did not seem to age from her life of toil and remained a remarkably attractive woman even after all six of us were born.

Father and mother always saw to it that the family had enough to eat. One winter, father stored a large bucket of honey in the house, and we children would eat bread smeared with honey for snacks when we were hungry. This was a very memorable treat. Another time, I remember mother cooking plums for jam for several days in big earthen pots, and we had bread and jam for an entire winter.

I remember another year when Uncle Mortche, my mother's brother who lived with us, brought us several geese. We fattened them up, had them killed by the shocket (kosher butcher), and rendered the fat, which was kept in large pots in a solid form. We children used this fat to spread on bread and thus kept from being hungry the entire winter. It even lasted beyond Passover that spring.

Other Jewish families were less fortunate. There were homes where children were kept in bed because the houses were so cold, and they did not have warm clothes. The houses were warmed with wood-burning stoves and the wood had to be purchased from local farmers, who cut it and brought it in by wagon from the woods. I remember that in one house the parents found their baby frozen to death after a very cold night.

Before the Jewish High Holidays, father would buy a cowhide from the butcher and give it to a local tannery to process into usable leather. Then he brought the leather to a cutter to cut the proper sizes, and then to a shoemaker to make the boots. The soles had to be purchased separately. From this one hide we obtained five or six pairs of boots, and we were sure to have good footwear for the entire year. We were also sure to be clothed properly. My mother the seamstress and grandpa the tailor made certain of that.

There was not much for the teenagers to do in Gorzkow. There was no industry and there were too many shoemakers, tailors, and carpenters. They worked for practically nothing. Some of the teenagers left home and went to the cities to find jobs. They were not all lucky at that either. The more religious families sent their boys to yeshivas in large cities where they were supported by the city's Jewish community. In the cities, the yeshivas organized a system where local Jewish families would take one yeshiva boy to feed one day out of each week. The boys were rotated every day to a different family. Teenage girls from poor families had even fewer options. They typically were hired out as domestics for very little pay by more affluent families in the bigger cities.

The youth that remained in Gorzkow gathered in different clubs and organizations. They would read books, newspapers, and magazines, and have debates about what they read. Most of them were Zionists who wanted to go to Palestine. There were Leftist Zionists, Rightist Zionists, and Religious Zionists.

There were also socialist organizations, and these groups were always fighting among themselves. My grandfather's stepson, Isaac Frucht, was the leader of one of the socialist groups. Grandfather called him the "Kaiser" because he was the head of his group. Isaac used to question the existence of God. Grandfather, who was deeply religious, would get very angry with him for such questioning and would refuse to talk to him for weeks, even though Isaac worked for him. Isaac, who was ten years older than I, was already a tailor. Grandfather used to tell me not to listen to Isaac, but we all lived in one house and it was difficult not to hear what Isaac said.

My grandfather Yisroel was the patriarch of the family. A tall, barrel-chested man, he wore a long, flowing white beard and was fanatically religious. He was in his fifties when he married his second wife Briendel, who had a son, Isaac Frucht, from her previous marriage. Together they had two young children, a girl named Chana and a boy named Yosef. Grandfather must have been about seventy years old in 1939 when the war broke out. He worked very hard, from six o'clock in the morning until ten o'clock at night, at his tailor's bench. There was no electricity in Gorzkow, so he worked by the light of a kerosene lamp. The farmers liked him because he was very honest and a good tailor. Before certain Christian holidays, the farmers would need clothes for the entire family, so they brought my grandfather and his sewing machine to their farms. Grandfather used to take his own cooking pot and utensils with him because he kept kosher and could not eat food at the farms unless he prepared it himself. The farmers would give him some potatoes or groats and beans to cook for himself. If he needed milk, grandfather would watch as it was milked from the cow directly into his pot. He had to make sure it was not poured from another container that was not kosher.

Most of the time, Isaac would go with grandfather to the farms. Sometimes he took me along too, and we would spend the entire week at a farm. He would trust me to watch the milk being milked for him. The three of us ate together. The farmer usually brought us back home on Friday afternoons, so that we would be home for the Sabbath. He would sometimes, as a bonus, give grandfather a little kasha, some beans, a little flour, or potatoes to take home. Very little money was paid for the tailoring work because the farmers did not have much, and besides there was fierce competition among the village tailors.

The daily meals at home consisted mostly of soup and bread, and herring once in a while. There was very little meat. However, come Friday, there was the baking of challah for the Sabbath and bread for the rest of the week. Chicken was a delicacy because there was not enough to go around, but with beef and a little fat, mother could make a wonderful meal.

It was a tradition to start the Sabbath meal with a piece of fish. Grandfather always had a piece of fish for the Sabbath. His wife was a wonderful cook. Our neighbor Sarah Finkelstein, known as Sarah Bashis, used to sell fish. She would deliver to the houses of her customers and then, if there was a big fish left over, she would sell it to my grandfather for a little less. Most of the time he would buy the smaller fish, which were cheaper.

The Sabbath was very important to the Jewish community. It allowed them to forget the weekly worries and struggles and to feel like kings in their castles. The same was true in our house. Financial and work problems were not discussed. Instead, the focus was on the children. Every Friday night after the Sabbath meal, the children would proudly recite the weekly Torah portions they had learned in cheder to the assembled family. My parents glowed with pride at such sessions. After the Friday night meal, my aunts and their children would come over to visit, and they would show off their children in similar fashion. One aunt once said that when her daughter grew up, she and I would marry. My father became very angry. He wanted to have his son marry someone very special and wealthy.

There was one big bathhouse in Gorzkow. Every Friday afternoon, in preparation for the Sabbath, all the Jewish males, men and boys, went to the bathhouse. The bathhouse was a separate building and was tended to by a man we called "Reuven the Bader." On Friday afternoons, when the bath was ready to be used, he would send out his teenage daughter with a frying pan and large spoon. She would walk around the village banging the frying pan as the signal that the bath was ready. My father would take me and my four brothers to the bathhouse. There were hot stones in the corner, which had been heated over a fire. Reuven the Bader would pour water on them, creating steam. People would sit opposite the stones on tiered wooden platforms that reached to the ceiling. An additional fee entitled you to a bunch of birch branches with leaves on them. The children would stay on the lower level, and the older people would go higher, as the higher you went the hotter it became. Then they used the branches on each others' backs as a massage. My father would hang our clothes on the ceiling rafters where it was very hot and steamy. When we were ready to leave after a few hours, any parasites that had been in our clothes would be gone.

At the end of the day on Friday, before sundown, Usher the Shamos would walk around the village and bang on the shutters and doors to announce that it was time to get ready for shul. All working activities then had to cease. There were some Jewish families that were so poor that they did not have food to celebrate the Sabbath. Some of the women in the village went to the more affluent families and collected food for the poor for Sabbath. When they delivered the food to the poor families, they always entered by the back doors of the recipients' homes. In this way, people did not know who received the food. The poor families were proud and did not want anyone to know that they accepted charity.

At sunset, all the males (men and boys) in the village went to shul for Friday night services. After the services, everyone returned to their homes for the Sabbath meal. The next day was occupied by morning services, followed by a day of rest according to religious mandate.

Our family life in Gorzkow was drastically altered when I was eleven years old. My mother had a miscarriage and afterward developed an infection. She was sick at home for a while, and then the doctors said she would have to go to the hospital immediately. She was taken on a Saturday by horse and buggy to the nearest hospital in the city of Krasnystaw, about seven miles away. Although Jews were normally not allowed to travel on Saturday for religious reasons, the rabbi allowed it because a life was at stake. My mother's twenty-two-year-old cousin, Zindel Honigman, drove her to Krasnystaw in his horse and buggy. My father walked behind the buggy all the way there, because it was the Sabbath and it was against his religious beliefs to ride on the Sabbath.

My mother was there for a short period, and the infection spread. There was nothing that could be done for her because there were no antibiotics available yet. The doctors in Krasnystaw decided she should be taken to a large Jewish hospital in the city of Lublin. She went by bus with my father to the hospital in Lublin, but it was too late for her to be helped. She died a few weeks later, on June 17, 1929.

A week before she died, father brought the three oldest boys, Meyer, Moishe, and myself, to mother's bedside so she could see us one last time. Meyer and Moishe went back to Gorzkow, and I stayed with my father until she died. She was buried at the Jewish cemetery in Lublin. I remember it being sunny and beautiful on the day of the funeral, and I remember I felt that it was the saddest day of my life. My mother was a very beautiful woman. Everyone in Gorzkow thought so, and she loved me very much, being her firstborn. At the time she became sick, she had been sewing a coat for me. The material was from a larger military coat, and she had cut it down so it would fit me. She used to sit in bed and sew that coat. She never finished it.

8
Remembrances of Life in the Big City

My mother had a brother, Uncle Shloime, who married a few years before my mother did and lived in the suburbs of Lublin. At the funeral, he suggested to my father that I stay with him for a while, and later it would be decided what I should do. At the time, I was not quite twelve years old. Uncle Shloime knew there were six of us children in the house, and that it would be hard for my father to take care of all of us without my mother. My father agreed to Uncle Shloime's suggestion. When my father left me in Lublin after the funeral, he was crying as he said good-bye. He was very broken up—he had just buried his wife and was about to lose his oldest child. I was crying too. I did not want to be left there, but in the end I was talked into staying.

Father also had two sisters in Lublin. They were still single and worked as domestics in the homes of wealthy people. They too wanted me to remain in Lublin.

My Uncle Shloime had a grocery store in Kosminek, an industrial neighborhood about three miles from Lublin. Kosminek consisted of an area of factories with enormous smokestacks, a railroad station, and a workers' residential area. I also remember a liquor factory and a yeast factory there. Kosminek was located between Lublin and Majdanek, where the Germans later established a concentration camp during the war. My uncle, his wife and two young children, his mother-in-law, and a single brother-in-law lived in the back of the store in a two-room apartment. I slept on a straw mattress on a board between two chairs. For the first year after the funeral, I got up early in the morning every day to walk to synagogue two miles away to say kaddish (prayer of mourning) for my mother.

My uncle and his wife were very nice to me, but his mother-in-law always looked for work for me to do. She ran the store, which was hers before my uncle married her daughter. Her only son was very learned, but very lazy. He did nothing in the store, and was very fat. I was the one who had to run errands for everyone. I missed my home very much. However, I was twelve years old, and a boy at that time was expected to learn a trade, start earning some money, and be able to fend for himself. My uncle promised he would find a place for me to work. In the meantime, I had to do chores around the house, take care of the children, and stay behind the counter in the store. The thing I disliked the most was having to put the children, a boy and a girl, to sleep. The boy would cry for hours before he went to sleep, and I had to rock him in his cradle. I grew very tired of this.

The thing I liked best was staying in the store. I learned very quickly. Within a month I got to know all the customers, mostly factory workers. They bought on credit and paid every two weeks when they received their paychecks. I would mark down their purchases in a book to keep track of the bills. I used to help myself to some treats when nobody was looking: a piece of cheese, a chunk of chalva candy, or a few sardines. The sardines came in a wooden box and were sold individually by weight. I was always hungry. My uncle used to take me to the city to buy groceries from a wholesaler, and I helped carry them home. Later, he would send me by myself, and I would bring as much as I could carry back with me.

Within a few months, I knew everything in the store, and my uncle would leave me in charge when he would go somewhere with his wife. I kept reminding my uncle that I needed a paying job. He did not pay me anything, just providing me with room and board.

The Jewish New Year was coming and I wanted very much to go home to be with my family for the holiday. I asked my uncle if I could go, and he gave me money for my bus fare home. My father, grandfather, brothers, and sister were all delighted to see me. I was very happy to be home, but things were different without my mother. Father had to limit his flour business considerably in order to find the time to take care of the children.

My younger brother Meyer was a big help to father in taking on the responsibility of caring for my three youngest brothers Moishe,

Irving, and Motel. That was a difficult job. Even when I had lived in Gorzkow, Moishe was a mischievous boy who refused to go to school. Meyer and I often had to carry Moishe to school, holding him by his hands and feet, while he screamed and protested. Once at school, of course, he was quiet for fear of the teacher's harsh discipline. Motel, on the other hand, was brilliant in school and did not pose any problem, quietly going about his studies. He rarely seemed to eat, being more interested in his schoolwork than in food. Irving was very good-natured even as a child, and liked to play tricks on grandpa. He seemed to spend much time visiting aunts and uncles to obtain treats, for he had a sweet tooth. Grandpa, of course, was very good to the boys and shared his table freely with them, despite the fact that he had his own two young children to feed. My father's sister, Aunt Sheindel, took my three-year-old sister Bella to live in her house. Aunt Sheindel took wonderful care of Bella, and her three young daughters made her feel very much at home.

There was nothing for me to do at home. The youngsters in town envied me for living in Lublin, a large city with more opportunities available than in Gorzkow. They all would have liked to have the opportunity to go to a big city. To go abroad was their biggest dream. Since that was impossible, they dreamed of the next best thing— going to a big city.

I stayed home for four weeks, but I knew that I had to go back to Lublin. I dreaded going back because Uncle Shloime's mother-in-law wore me out so. I especially hated that she made sure that I knew she was doing me a big favor by letting me stay there, but I had to go back. My grandfather finished sewing the winter coat for me that my mother had started just before she got sick. This was fortunate, because the winter season was coming soon.

When I returned, my Uncle Shloime spoke with a distant cousin in Lublin about getting me a paying job. This cousin worked for a wholesaler on Shpitalny Street dealing in iron bars. In the same courtyard as the wholesaler, there was a sweater factory, and he promised to talk to the owner about me. I went for an interview and the owner, Bairish Krempel, hired me as a floor boy. The pay was three zlotys (roughly the equivalent of three dollars) per week. I was very happy to have this opportunity to learn a trade. Knitting was considered a very good trade, better than tailoring or being a shoe-maker. My uncle agreed to keep me in his house, because three zlotys was not enough for me to support myself.

There were about twenty workers (male and female) in Mr. Krem-pel's sweater factory, with ten knitting machines and several woolen glove machines and spinning machines. I had never seen such machines before in my life. The machine operators made the sweaters in pieces and, as the floor boy, I carried these pieces in bundles to the homes of local women who sewed them together. I also carried the finished product back to our factory. In front of the factory, Mrs. Krempel operated a retail outlet where a small portion of the sweaters were sold. The balance of them were sold wholesale to other stores in Lublin. The Krempels lived across the street from the factory with their two sons, who were not much older than I was and who attended gymnasia (high school).

I walked the five-mile roundtrip every day from my uncle's apartment to work and then back again. Aside from carrying bundles to and from the shop, my job was to keep the place clean and to help the girls spin the wool from skeins onto spools. My goal, however, was to learn how to work the knitting machines, as that was a good trade with good pay. When Mr. Krempel hired me, he promised to give me the opportunity to learn how to operate these machines. Whenever I had a chance, I would ask a machine operator to teach me. I also learned from observation, and I tried the machines on my own, especially when one was not in use at lunchtime. After working there one year, in addition to other duties, I learned to operate a smaller machine that made parts for sweaters, like pockets, belts, collars, and also such items as scarfs. I asked Mr. Krempel for a raise, and he raised me one zloty per week, for a weekly pay of four zlotys.

Mr. Krempel used to send me to the post office for him, and I did a lot of clerical work. He sent me to the bank with very large deposits of cash. I was afraid to carry so much money because I had never seen such large sums before. For the Jewish holidays, I went home and the boys there envied me for being a knitter and living in the big city. I did not tell them I was making only four zlotys a week as a floor boy. After a year's work, I had only earned enough money to buy a suit, a shirt, and a pair of shoes.

Sometimes, when I came back from work my uncle would ask me to walk back to Lublin to pick up supplies for his grocery store. Life was not easy, but I looked forward to being a knitter—a man with a trade. When I turned thirteen years old, for my Bar Mitzvah Uncle Shloime took me on a Saturday to shul, where I was called to the pulpit to read from the Torah. There was no celebration and no relatives to share the occasion with me other than my uncle. It was nice of him to make the effort, but it served to remind me how much I missed my family.

Mr. Krempel was a very well-known figure in Lublin. He was a socialist, a leader of the Bund (the Jewish socialist workers' party) and a legislator in the Town Council, elected there by the Bund. On May 1, the socialist holiday, he would march in front of the May Day parade with a red flag. That was his public image. In private, in his factory, he was quite different. By my second year of work, I had learned to do everything that the knitters could do on the machines. However, he would not let me work as a knitter because he would then have to pay me a higher salary. I would have left his factory, but there was only one other sweater factory in Lublin. It would not hire me because I was too young.

I kept asking him for a raise, and his consistent answer was that the regular workers only worked during the short (two to three months) season. The rest of the year they did not earn anything, whereas I had a yearlong job. He knew very well that I had no alternative.

I went home again for the Jewish holidays when I was fourteen, and stayed for six months. I was tired of being taken advantage of by Mr. Krempel and Uncle Shloime's mother-in-law. Although there was poverty at home, my father appreciated my reluctance to return to Lublin and told me to stay as long as I wished. I knew a little about tailoring and helped grandpa with his work.

In the evenings back in Gorzkow, I went out with Isaac Frucht, my stepuncle, to his socialist club to listen to conversations and attend the dances there. I even learned how to play the violin a little. The club had different musical instruments which the members shared with each other. They also had a library, and I started reading books. The first book I read there made such an impression on me that I still remember it. It was written in Yiddish, translated from English, by the author Jay Jasinski, an American writer. The name of the book was *Nature and Science*. This book opened my eyes to the knowledge of how things in nature really worked, especially the process of evolution. I was fascinated by astronomy, how the earth revolved around the sun, and how technology developed through the ages. I was extremely interested in the book because, up to this time, I had been made to believe in the biblical version of creation. I read many books that winter and stayed in Gorzkow until just after Passover in the spring.

Each year, just before Passover, my father baked matzohs in my Aunt Henchie's house for the people in the village. She was one of my father's five sisters. Her house was much larger than ours and had a larger oven. Father would supervise the milling of the flour in a special section of the mill to make sure that it was kosher for

Passover. People bought a certain amount of this flour for their matzohs and my father would bake the matzohs for them, charging them according to the weight of the flour used. He organized a baking operation in assembly-line fashion. He hired fifteen to twenty girls to make the dough, divide it into small portions, and roll it out into round matzohs, which my father would then bake. Whenever possible, all the children pitched in to help. It was a big operation and hard work, and the baking started about four weeks before Passover. Father did this every year. After my mother's death, however, the holiday was never the same for me.

After Passover, I went back to Lublin to work for Mr. Krempel. One time, I delivered woolen socks from his factory to a major league soccer team, and the team gave me two tickets to their next game, which I shared with a friend. The game was between a major Polish soccer team named Polonia and a Viennese Jewish soccer team named Hakoach. I was thrilled to watch this game, especially since Hakoach won. The Polish audience almost rioted, not because Polonia lost but because it had lost to a Jewish team. They could not swallow that.

On weekends, I also played soccer on a local Jewish team. I played ping-pong in organization halls, and I attended frequent lectures by national Jewish speakers.

I worked for Mr. Krempel for about three years for the same four zlotys per week. I realized I had no future there. I was not given a machine to work on officially, but when a worker got sick I took his place. When it was very busy I also worked steadily at a machine. I knew Warsaw was the center of the sweater industry and I wanted to go there, but I had no money and did not know anyone there. However, I felt I could not stay in Lublin any longer. I knew my qualifications. I could work on many sweater machines, such as flat machines and P.D. machines. I also knew how to repair worn parts. These were foreign machines made in Germany and England and were very expensive. To get parts was very costly, so we had to know how to repair them and sometimes to rebuild an entire machine. I learned how to do this.

I quit my job, left Lublin, and came home when I was fifteen. I remembered we had a "landsman" (a person from my hometown) in Warsaw and asked my father to find out his address from his relatives in Gorzkow.

My cousin Zindel Honigman was an agent for a trucking company in Lublin. Cousin Zindel was an industrious, powerfully built man with a good sense of humor. Many stories were told about his great physical strength. For example, every spring young Polish military draftees would pass through Gorzkow on their way to their army induction in the nearby city of Krasnystaw. Typically, these young Poles would show their anti-Semitic feelings by beating up Jews as they passed through the village. One spring, Zindel was accosted by three such young men. He was by himself and the three draftees started baiting him by hurling insults at him. Zindel shot back the verbal abuse, which prompted one of the three to throw a punch at him. Zindel picked him up, swung him around, and knocked the other two unconscious to the ground. Afterward, whenever the draftees came through the village looking for Jewish targets to attack, Zindel had merely to walk down the main street to discourage this type of violence.

Zindel's job with the trucking company was to ensure that grocery items, like eggs, meat, and fruits, were picked up from suppliers and dropped off at retailers. Once my father found the name and address of our landsman in Warsaw, Cousin Zindel was able to arrange a free ride for me to Warsaw on a produce truck. I rode in the back of one of these loaded trucks and arrived in Warsaw the next morning.

It took me a long time to find our landsman, whose name was Sucher Borgenstein. He was a tailor and had a small shop in his house. He knew me and my family from Gorzkow, and I told him why I had come to the city. He was very nice to me, gave me food to eat, and told me how to find the knitters union. He told me that the government had closed their office recently, and so they conducted their business in the streets. Sucher and his wife invited me to come back in the evening and tell them how I had made out, and they offered to put me up. Sucher also told me about other people from Gorzkow who lived in his neighborhood. He made me feel that I was not alone in the big city. He then gave me the name of the knitters union agent and told me to ask around for him.

I found the street where the union was gathering that night. In Warsaw the streets were always full of people promenading in the evening, especially in the Jewish neighborhoods, where they would cluster around streets bearing names li e Zamenhofa, Nalewki, Gesia, and Pawia. People would walk back and forth and meet with landsmen and friends. At the corner of Gesia and Zamenhofa streets, there was a big street clock. People would make plans to meet at that spot. There were no cars in this section of Warsaw, as the people were too poor to have them. The only transportation consisted of the electric street cars.

I found the union agent. He told me to meet him the following evening and he would try to find a job for me. The knitters union, I found out, was highly organized and had several thousand members. The pay scale was very good. Most of the work was paid on a piece-work basis. Discipline in the union was very high. When the union called a strike there were no strikebreakers. Shortly after I first met the agent, the union was able to reopen its office.

The following evening I went to meet the agent and he told me to go to 37 Nalewki Street to a sweater factory owned by the Falk brothers. I was hired on the spot and immediately put to work on a machine with which I was very familiar. I was to be paid on a piece-work basis at the prevailing scale. The workday lasted twelve hours every day, which I did not mind because the longer I worked the more I produced and earned. At the end of the first week, I received my pay of close to one hundred zlotys. You can imagine my surprise —going from four to one hundred zlotys for one week's work! I could not believe my eyes when I was paid.

That week I slept in Sucher's house, and he was like a father to me in his generosity. Nonetheless, I did not want to abuse his hospitality, and I resolved to find my own living quarters. On Saturday, my first day off, I arranged to board with the Freedman family at 9 Pawia Street. Theirs was a poor household, and so they were happy to find a paying tenant.

The sweater factory, or shop, where I worked had ten knitting machines on the first floor of a commercial building. When I came to Warsaw in 1932, it was the beginning of the winter knitting season (normally August, September, and October), and the factory oper-ated two twelve-hour shifts per day. We started Saturday night and worked until Friday noon—a six-day work week. My first season in Warsaw lasted four months. The work was strenuous and I was very tired at the end of a shift, but at fifteen years old I was young and in good physical condition to handle it.

Nalewki Street was a long commercial thoroughfare bounded by factories and warehouses, where merchants from all over the country came to shop for their retail stores. The courtyard housing my sweater shop was off an alley connecting Zamenhofa Street with Nalewki Street. In this courtyard there were many manufacturing businesses that similarly attracted retail merchants seeking to stock their stores. Some courtyards specialized in hardware, others in textiles, and oth-ers in knitwear. My boss, Mr. Falk, had his living quarters and shop on the first floor of the building. His mother was a very old lady who lived in his apartment. She would come into the shop when I worked the night shift and tell us different stories. She told us about the squirrels who collected and stored nuts in the summer so they would have enough to eat in the winter. I knew that her stories were meant to teach us to be thrifty, to save our earnings, and perhaps to work harder. We all worked hard and produced, not only for Mr. Falk's sake, but for our own. For twenty-four hours straight, twenty workers, split into two shifts, operated the ten machines.

We alternated so that one week I worked the day shift and the next week I worked the night shift. The night shift was very tiring, and sometimes I had to sit down for a few minutes to close my eyes and rest. The machines were bolted down to heavy tables. They were the kind that were worked by hand, motorized machines being found only in the largest factories. I had to pull the knitting head of the machine back and forth by hand, and it was not an easy task. Across the table from me, operating another machine, was a man in his forties, named Lazar. He had a big scar on his face. While we worked, he would tell me stories about the aborted Russian revolution in 1905. While taking part in it, he was shot by a Tsarist soldier, which was how he got the scar. He was arrested and taken to Siberia, where he was imprisoned for twelve years. In 1917, the Bolsheviks freed him. I took to Lazar and I liked to listen to his stories. Although he was older and a more experienced worker, he could not produce as much as I did. He had to sit down and rest every few hours. He often said that he envied my youth and energy. Although I was only fifteen years old, I was earning more than he was.

I put some of my earnings into a savings account in the local post office, which served as a bank. I also sent my father some money, paid back my uncle Mortche for the money he had loaned me when I left for Warsaw, and bought some new clothes. I made a sweater and a hat for my little sister Bella from leftover inexpensive wool, and did the same for Aunt Sheindel and her three daughters who took such good care of her. I also bought warm underwear and sweaters for all four of my brothers, which I gave them when I went to visit the family for the Jewish High Holidays. I remember how beautiful my little sister looked in her outfit. She must have been six years old. All her little friends envied her. I felt very sorry for her though. Our mother had passed away when she was very young, and so she was living with relatives instead of her own family.

While home for the holidays, I learned that my brother Meyer had started peddling in Gorzkow. He would go out to farms on foot, buy produce, transport it on his back, sell it in Gorzkow, and make a few zlotys. Many local people earned money in this way. Two of my other brothers, Moishe and Irving, were learning to be tailors. My grandfather was teaching them, as he had taught my stepuncle Isaac. Motel was still too young to learn a trade.

This was my first time home after moving to Warsaw and getting my new job. I could tell that my father and the entire family were very proud of me. He told me he dreamed that some day I would become a sweater manufacturer and a rich man.

When I returned to Warsaw in October after the Jewish New Year in 1934, business was slow. I and many other people were laid off. The busy season would start again in July, but until then you had to eat and pay rent. Fortunately I had sufficient savings in the post office. I had heeded the story about the squirrels.

The long periods of unemployment in the sweater industry were boring and demoralizing. The knitting trade paid very well in comparison with others, but the busy season, which had lasted approximately three months in the past, became shorter and shorter as times became bad. Of course, I was not the only one affected, and the sweater industry was not the only one that was slow. All areas of employment in cities and towns were suffering from the economic depression gripping Poland. Thousands of unemployed Polish workers wandered city streets or roamed the countryside, hoping to find employment or perhaps just a meal to satisfy their ever-present hunger.

In order to alleviate the critical level of Jewish unemployment in Warsaw, different organizations tried to provide jobs. The American Jewish Joint Distribution Committee and HIAS (the Hebrew Immigrant Aid Society) obtained contracts from England, France, and the United States for knitted gloves, berets, scarfs, and stockings. Then these organizations would distribute these contracts among small manufacturers (called *chalupnikis*) who worked out of their homes, to alleviate some of the unemployment. The pay under these contracts was lower than usual, but the unions did not object to the low scale in this instance. I, and many other workers, benefited from these contracts, although they did not keep us busy very long.

In addition to these short contracts, I tried my best to find work of any kind. A friend of mine who made shoes got his work orders and materials from a jobber and took the work to his house. This work was only available in the spring, and did not last very long. He taught me at his house how to help him, and this kept me occupied for four or five weeks.

I went from one job to another in order to support myself because I knew that I could not expect help from anyone. My dream was to bring my father and brothers to Warsaw since I knew my father would have opportunities to better himself in a big city. I enjoyed living in Warsaw, despite the bad economic situation, poverty, and anti-Semitism. I had a place to live, and I managed to save money for the leaner times.

Rachmiel Freedman, in whose house I lived, wanted me to eat dinner at his house, but I did not want to become part of the family. Manya, his daughter, showed signs of liking me, and I thought it best if I did not eat there. I was young and not ready to get serious with a girl, although I liked her too. Sometimes I took her to the movies or for a walk in the park. Usually the streets were very crowded with young people walking and meeting friends. There were people in Warsaw from all cities and towns in Poland, and taking walks was how they met and made dates.

Sports activities were very popular among the Warsaw teenagers like myself. I liked to play soccer and ping-pong, and on Sundays a lot of young people participated in these sports. After a six-day work week, it was good to get outside and play ball.

There was a highly developed cultural life in Warsaw. I could get tickets to the movies for a fraction of the regular price at the Maccabi Club, a Jewish social organization. I used to see the latest movies from the United States, dubbed with Polish subtitles. Through the club, I also got tickets to the opera for matinees for a very small price. We took boating outings in the summertime on the Vistula River to the suburbs of Warsaw. Often during our outings, anti-Semitic insults were hurled at us by groups of teenagers. After a while, we got used to hearing, "Jews, go to Palestine" or "Hitler is coming and that will be the end of you," and tried to ignore the verbal abuse directed at us.

I liked to go out at night with girls to hear lectures by prominent speakers from different Jewish political parties. The popular place to go was Krasinski Park. The park was on Zamenhofa Street in a Jewish neighborhood, so it was safer for us there. It was quite different if we wanted to go to Saski Park on Marszalkowska Street. There was a guard at the entrance to this park. If the guard recognized you as a Jew, he would find fault with your attire so as not to allow you into the park. Unintentionally, he would be doing us a favor. If we gained entrance to that park, the chances of being beaten up by anti-Semitic gangs were very good.

In 1935, when I was seventeen, I finally succeeded in persuading my father to move to Warsaw. The children in our house in Gorzkow were getting bigger. The house was getting smaller for them, and the financial situation was not improving. I felt that, with his education as a religious scholar, he would be able to find employment in a big city like Warsaw, which had a large religious population. At first, he came alone, without my brothers, to try to get situated. I helped him rent a two-room apartment, but I could not live with him because I was not as religious as he expected me to be. I refused to wear a head covering at all times, and I rode the streetcars and played ball on the Sabbath. I also did not observe the kosher dietary laws. In Gorzkow, this type of behavior by a son of my father would have been unheard of. I did not want to hurt him, but I also could not live his lifestyle.

After a few months, my father brought two of my brothers, Moishe, then thirteen, and Motel, then nine, to Warsaw. By this time, Moishe had learned the tailoring trade from my grandfather and used his training to find employment in Warsaw. Motel was too young for a trade and was sent to yeshiva, which made my father very proud. Motel was a mathematical genius according to his teachers and had shown this great ability since early childhood. Meyer and Irving, who were then fifteen and eleven respectively, remained in Gorzkow with my grandfather.

My father used to visit me at the Freedmans' apartment and tell me how well Motel was doing at yeshiva. He was brilliant in his religious studies as well as his secular studies. Father was happy that at least one of his sons was going to fulfill his dream of being a scholar.

My father had had another son from his first marriage, before marrying my mother. This son lived in Warsaw and used to come home to Gorzkow to visit his mother for the Jewish holidays. During my childhood, when I would see him in the synagogue I would try to avoid him. This was due to the fact that kids would try to embarrass me by teasing me about his being my brother. From listening to family stories, I learned about my father's first wife.

When my father was a yeshiva student of about eighteen, he lived near my mother's family and was very much infatuated with her. However, being very religious, he was not permitted to have much contact with her or any other girls. Mother was considered one of the most beautiful girls in Gorzkow.

At that time, families in small towns would arrange marriages for their children, without the children first having an opportunity to meet their prospective spouses. For such a family, it was considered a successful match if their child married into a wealthy family. The next best thing, for a family marrying off a daughter, was to marry her to a boy studying to be a scholar. It was a status symbol to marry into a family whose members included a rabbi. If the potential groom was a religious boy and a scholar, he could marry a rich girl and continue his studies. In that way, he could be supported by his father-in-law for the rest of his life, or later take over the family business.

My father's parents agreed to such an arranged match for my father with a girl in the nearby town of Izbica. Without knowing his future wife, my father resisted this match. However, he could not disappoint his parents, as the wedding had already been arranged. The family traveled by horse and buggy to Izbica, about ten miles away, where the marriage ceremony was performed. I never learned many particulars about this marriage. I know that his wife was not pretty, and that my father was not happy since he was still in love with my mother. After being married less than one year, they were divorced. She gave birth to a son and continued to live in Gorzkow, and later remarried. The son from the short-lived marriage, named Beryl, was about ten years older than I. When he was a teenager, he moved to Warsaw, where he married a girl from a very wealthy family. Beryl never had any contact with my father while we lived in Gorzkow, but when my father moved to Warsaw, they got together and developed a very good father-son relationship. I got to know Beryl through my father. He was a nice man and very successful in his father-in-law's business. Father and I used to talk about him together, and these discussions often included fatherly advice. Father warned me not to get serious with Manya, as he wanted me to be successful in business first. He also urged me to be very selective in deciding on a wife. I think his advice was probably based on his own personal marital life.

Because of the anti-Semitic atmosphere of the time, young Polish Jews dreamed about emigrating from Poland, but there was nowhere to go. Many had relatives in the United States who had left Poland before the First World War. The only relative we had in America was grandfather's sister in Chicago, D'vora Diamond, who used to send him five dollars every Passover. After she died around 1935, he never heard from her family.

The only way for a young man to get to America was to go as the husband of an American woman. There were women who came to Warsaw from America, looking for a husband. Some young men would grab at the opportunity, even though the women were much older than they, or had other visible faults. A twenty-five-year-old man who worked with me married a much older woman who had come to Poland from the United States for the purpose of finding a husband. He left with her to go back to America. There were many such instances.

Some young Jews tried to leave for Palestine, but it was very difficult to get an immigration certificate from the English. Following the British White Paper of 1937, the number of certificates to Palestine were severely limited. Some young men even tried to smuggle themselves to Russia, but they were often caught, sent back to Poland, and then arrested for crossing the border illegally.

In 1937, Aaron, the oldest of the Freedman children, decided to smuggle himself into Palestine by way of a train that was going from Warsaw to Trieste, Italy. He planned to go by boat to Palestine from Trieste, although he had no ticket and no money. He hid under a seat in a train car, and the young people who had British-issued certificates covered him with their coats. He stayed hidden under the seat for the entire trip. However, he was caught in Trieste by a guard as he tried to board a Palestine-bound ship. He was arrested and sent back to Poland on foot. He was walked by a guard from town to town, and country to country. Each town sent its own guard to the next town with him. When he reached Katowice, a city in southern Poland, he was put in prison for several months. Upon his release from prison, his parents sent him money to come home to Warsaw. The entire trip back home from Italy took Aaron more than six months, and when he returned we could not recognize him. He was dirty, his clothes were reduced to rags, and he was emaciated. Despite stories like Aaron's, young Jews continued to try to escape the country. That is an indication of how desperate they were to get out of Poland.

The Germans Invade Russia

All these memories of Gorzkow and Warsaw flooded through my mind as I sat in the woods near Lubien, watching the animals graze. And I was happy to be far away from the Germans, at least for the time being, even if I was a slave for Stephan.

Being a shepherd was not my only job, and it was not one of my major responsibilities. Stephan took me into the fields and showed me how to plow and ready the fields for sowing different grains. The furrows had to be straight. I had to walk behind the horse and direct it in a straight line—especially for the first line. If the first line was not straight, all the others would follow the same curved path. I had to hold the reins and plow handles in both hands and be careful to keep the plow at a certain angle so it would not jump out of the ground. When the job was finished, one could tell if it was done by a sloppy or neat farmer. It was not easy to learn, but after a few days of practice with Stephan he trusted me to plow the fields by myself. At the end of each full day's work, I could hardly wait for Marfa, his wife, to give me my meal. Afterward, I would go to the barn and immediately fall asleep in the hayloft. Harvest time was also very hard work. I had to learn to hold a scythe straight in order to cut the wheat.

The hardest and most backbreaking work was potato digging. This was normally considered women's work, but I was put to work doing that too. One had to bend close to the ground to dig the potatoes and fill the baskets, which were later picked up by a wagon. The women were used to doing this type of work, as they did it all their lives. Each one took three rows to dig. At first, I could only do one row in the same time it took for them to do three, and by the end of that one row I thought that my back was broken. Eventually I could work as well as they did. I did not want them to think that a Jew could not work as hard as a Polish farmer. I did not want to reinforce commonly held misconceptions in Poland about Jews.

The food was usually better around harvest time, although the work was harder. Stephan would slaughter a large pig and every part of the carcass was used. All kinds of delicacies were made from it. Even the blood was used to mix with kasha to make sausages.

Months, and then seasons, passed by and I was kept busy laboring on Stephan's farm. I did not mind the hard work. I felt a sense of satisfaction that I could work as an equal with the other farmers. I began to feel a little secure in a way, because on a farm I was not visible to the Germans. I hoped that if things got worse for the Jews, I would still have a hiding place on Stephan's farm.

I wanted to visit Manya, who worked as a farm hand for a farmer in the neighboring village of Zamolodycze. I often wanted to ask Stephan for permission to go there, but I was so tired after work that I could only think of going to sleep. I did manage to see Manya once every two weeks or so. It was a one-hour walk each way. She was the perfect picture of a farm girl, with her blonde hair and blue eyes, and wearing working clothes that the farmer gave her. Like me, she worked for nothing and hoped that in this way the farmer would keep her from the Germans.

On Sundays, there was no work in the fields. Some of the younger farmers went to church. The older folks would take their horses to pasture to give them a rest, as the balance of the week they were needed in the fields. While watching the horses they would socialize and gossip. The main topic, of course, was the war, which they hoped the Germans would win. They were all Ukrainians and members of the Russian Orthodox Church. They were happy that the Germans had conquered Poland, because of the history of Polish repression of the Ukrainian religion, language, and culture. Although the Germans were another foreign occupying force, they were viewed in a positive light because they had lifted this repression of the symbols of Ukrainian nationalism.

On Sundays, I would take the cows and horses to pasture and listen to the older people talk. They were a different breed from the

Polish people. They were less anti-Semitic. They religiously read and adhered to the Bible, and believed that God would someday mete out punishment for the atrocities that the Germans were inflicting on the Jews.

They knew the Jewish people in the neighboring towns and villages. They did business with them. They knew the names of the Jewish storekeepers, doctors, and tailors and were familiar with them as individuals. When these farmers came into town and heard that a Jew they knew had been killed by the Germans, they claimed to feel bad about it. At least that is what they said to me.

Although the local farmers hoped the Germans could win the war, they were angry at the Germans for imposing produce quotas. More than half of all the Ukrainian farmers' products were taxed for delivery to the Germans. The penalty to a farmer for cheating was death.

I knew them all and listened to their stories. All the while, I evaluated which ones I could trust to go to if there was an emergency.

One day, Stephan had to deliver his produce quota to the Germans in nearby Wlodawa. He took a wagon filled with sacks of grain. When he returned and sat down to supper, he told me what he had heard in town. "Hershku," he said to me, "you have no idea what the Germans are doing to the poor Jews." He told me that the Jewish stores were closed. He also told me about the local Jews he knew who had been killed in the streets of Wlodawa by the Germans. Jews were starving and being forced to live in a ghetto in Wlodawa. They were not allowed to leave the ghetto. The penalty for leaving was death. "You are very lucky that we keep you here," he said. I looked closely at him, trying to figure out what he meant—whether he wanted to chase me out or whether he wanted me to work harder. I told him I was thankful for his keeping me.

Then he took out a small box and asked me if I was a connoisseur of gold. He pulled out a woman's watch from the box and asked me if it was real gold. I looked at the watch and told him that I never had handled gold, but that it looked like a nice watch. He said he got this watch from a Jew in exchange for a few pounds of flour. I did not know anything about gold, but it was a beautiful and expensive-looking watch. He gave it to Marfa to wear.

Stephan was very friendly with the village soltys (or elders), and if anything was happening he was one of the first to hear about it from them. One evening, Stephan instructed me to get up earlier than usual the next morning. I was to take the animals out to pasture, and not bring them back to the farm until he came and told me it was all

right to do so. He had heard that the Germans were coming to
Lubien the next day, and he did not want me to be on the farm in
case the Germans searched the area. I did as I was told, and when
dusk fell Stephan did not come out to the pasture. The animals were
ready to go home and they looked at me nervously, as if they were
asking for the reason for the change in routine. They became noisy,
and the dog started barking, trying to tell me to take them home.
Finally, after dark, Stephan rode out on his horse and led us back to
the farm. He told me that about twenty German soldiers and Ukrainian policemen had gathered the Lubien farmers together. They told
the farmers that they were not fulfilling their quotas, and that they
would punish the ones who were cheating. Then they accused one
farmer of cheating and shot him in front of the gathered crowd, to
hammer home their message.

With the spring planting completed, I helped Stephan get the barn
ready to receive the soon-to-be-harvested crops. We changed the
wagon sides from low to high to be able to pile up more bundles of
grain. We sharpened the scythes, and Marfa prepared delicacies
from a slaughtered pig to take to the fields for the busy harvest
season.

It was the beginning of the summer of 1941. German troops
started pouring into the area on trucks, motorcycles, tanks, and all
kinds of mechanized transports. They were quartered in every house,
every barn, and every available shelter. Thousands of them came into
the area, and they flooded the surrounding villages. The local people
felt something big was going to happen, but did not know what.
Lubien was about ten or fifteen miles from the Bug River, which was
the Russian-German border. Stephan asked me what I thought was
going to happen. He thought that, as a Jew and city dweller, I knew
more about current events than he did. I told him I did not know
what was brewing, but I was aware of the fact that the Germans and
the Russians had signed a nonaggression pact. He told me that with
so many Germans around, it was dangerous for me and dangerous
for him to have me around the farm.

One evening, he told me to take the animals early to pasture the
next day and also to take an extra blanket. He would then come out
to me in the evening and bring the animals back himself. He came
when it was getting dark and brought some food for me. He took the
animals back to the farm, leaving me alone in the woods. I spread
one blanket out near a tree and covered myself with the other blanket. I tried not to fall asleep, as I was afraid of the wild animals in the
woods. All I had for protection was a big clublike stick. Early the next

morning, Stephan returned with the animals. He blew a previously agreed code whistle and I whistled back. He told me that more Germans were coming into the area, and that the farmers were afraid to go to the fields and leave their households unattended. The farmers knew the Germans would help themselves to anything they wanted, but felt that if the farmers were present in their own homes there might not be as much plundering.

No one knew what to expect, and Stephan would not let me go back to his farm. I spent four days and nights in the woods, and on the fifth night, just before dawn, I felt the ground shaking. Thousands of artillery guns had opened fire somewhere toward the east, in the vicinity of Wlodawa. Soon afterward, as dawn broke, squadrons of planes began flying overhead. The sound the planes made reminded me of when they had flown over Warsaw and bombed the city. The sound of planes flying overhead lasted for several hours, and I could hear their bombs exploding far away. When the bombardment started, my first thought and perhaps wish was that the Russians were attacking the Germans, or perhaps England, France, and America had started fighting them. With renewed fighting, I hoped that Poland would be liberated from German occupation.

Toward daylight, Stephan showed up with the animals and brought me food. He informed me that the previous evening, just before sunset, all the military units had pulled out from the villages and headed toward the Bug River to invade Russian territory. He told me that it was quiet now in the village, and that if he did not return for me in the evening I should bring the animals back to the farm myself. When I came back in the evening, I saw the farmers standing in the fields, looking eastward where the horizon was red with the battle. Everyone was certain that the Russians would be victorious and would soon start chasing the Germans back. The only thing they were concerned about was that there could be fighting in their villages, which might destroy their homes and endanger their families.

When I ate supper that night with the family (I often ate this one meal with them in the house), Stephan, Marfa, and her mother were especially nice to me. Stephan kept talking about how bad the Germans had been to the Jews. He said he felt sorry for the Jews and was glad that he at least could give me shelter. After supper, Stephan and I sat outside on the porch and he told me he was certain the Russians would win and chase the Germans back. Everyone in the village, he said, wanted the Red Army to win. After all, they were their "Russian Orthodox brothers." He asked me whether I thought the Red Army would come to Lubien, and I told him that no one could tell what would happen. I felt he wanted me as insurance, so that if the Red Army came and was told that Stephan had sheltered me against the Germans and had been good to me, this would show he had not cooperated with the Germans. He asked me what I would tell the Russians. I told him that, of course, I would tell them that he had been good to me.

A few days later, news trickled in that the Germans were winning. Stephan changed his tune. He said that no one could fight like the Germans and that soon they would take Moscow. He said that then the Germans would establish a Ukrainian state. He told me not to worry, however, because the Ukrainians would treat the Jews better than the Germans had. From listening to him talk like this, I became suspicious and did not trust him anymore. He was a good friend with the village soltys, who collaborated with the Germans. I lost the superficial feeling of security I had developed and felt that he would denounce me to the Germans whenever convenient. In the meantime, however, I knew he needed me on the farm. It was harvest time, and all hands were busy in the fields. Even his elderly mother-in-law came along to the fields to help with the bundling of grains.

The weather was good, and so was the harvest. The animals were taken care of by the neighboring shepherd, so that I could go into the fields every day with Stephan and work alongside him. He told me many times that he would not have believed that a Jewish boy from the big city could work so hard on a farm. He also told me about the victories the Germans were having, driving deeper into Russia. He based this news on the bulletins that the Germans posted in the village, with maps showing how far their army had advanced into Russia.

One night, I was awakened in the hayloft from a sound sleep by the barking of the village dogs. The next day, Stephan told me what had happened. The Germans had captured hundreds of thousands of Russians as they advanced into Russia. Some of the Russians managed to escape and take shelter in the woods. At night they would come into the local villages, asking for food. The previous night, a group of ten escaped Russian prisoners of war had come to Lubien. The Germans searched the village the following day and found the ten Russians hiding in the Russian Orthodox church. They marched the Russians outside and made them dig their own graves, forcing the local villagers to gather around to watch. The Russians were told to take off their clothes. The Russians knelt and begged for mercy, but the Germans shot them all.

The village people were crying and terribly upset. Stephan's mother-in-law was so upset that she could not eat that day. Even Stephan had tears in his eyes. He and the other farmers identified with the Russians as followers of the same church. He said that, for such a terrible thing to have happened, the world must be coming to an end.

I kept thinking that thousands of Jews were being killed every day and the farmers did not lament that. I was always wondering what Stephan thought of me. There were no orders from the Germans forbidding Jews from working on farms. No one, not even Stephan, knew that I was a runaway from a labor camp.

One evening shortly after this incident I visited Manya. She was one of the spectators the Germans had gathered in the village to watch the massacre of the Russian prisoners. She was crying, thinking of what had happened to her family that she left in Warsaw. I could appreciate her feelings of despair, as I had been wondering what had happened to my father in Warsaw and my two brothers who had walked to Gorzkow, as well as what had happened to the rest of the family there. Of course, we also wondered what would happen to us.

10
Ominous News from Warsaw

After we finished with the grain harvest we started digging potatoes. It was backbreaking, but I was used to it already and kept up with the others.

Potatoes were the staple food for us, as well as for the animals, and were stored to last until the next year's crop. We stored them in large dugouts in the fields and covered them with straw and earth, so that they would not freeze in the severe Polish winter. On top of each potato mound was a narrow wooden flue for ventilation. This type of storage place was called a *copiec*. In the wintertime, we went to the *copiec* whenever we wanted potatoes. There were seven or eight such mounds scattered on Stephan's farm, each holding about a thousand pounds of potatoes.

It was the fall of 1941, and it was time to thrash the grain we had harvested. Stephan got his neighbors to help, and when we were finished we assisted his neighbors with the same chore. It was a good harvest that year, but the farmers said that most of it would go to the Germans. Every two weeks Stephan had to bring his quota to the Germans in Wlodawa, according to the orders of the village committee. This included grains, meat, and other produce.

Around this time, one of Stephan's cows got sick and died. She had swallowed a piece of metal and choked to death on it. It was a big loss for Stephan. He had to bring the dead cow to Wlodawa and show it to the Germans because they maintained an inventory of each farmer's animals. They wanted to make sure the farmers did not kill the animals for their own use. Most of the time I went with Stephan to the railroad station in Wlodawa to help unload his wagon. I was dressed like a farmer and no one paid attention to me.

Manya's mother, Chaia Freedman, somehow got out of Warsaw and made her way to her relatives' house in Hola. A short time later, Kornila, the Hola Freedmans' neighbor, passed through Zamolodycze bound for Wlodawa with a wagonload of farm produce for the Germans. He made a point of stopping at the farm where Manya worked to give Manya the news of her mother's arrival in Hola. Manya immediately came to Stephan's farm and asked me to go with her to Hola to see her mother. I got permission from Stephan to walk Manya to Hola the following evening.

It was a two-hour walk to Hola. Along the way, we spotted a man chasing a runaway cow. He was hollering and cursing the cow in Yiddish. From far away, his Yiddish accent identified him as a Jew from Warsaw. The cow was in another farmer's wheat field, and he was trying to chase it back where it belonged with his herd. Like me, he was also dressed like a farmer's helper in coarse linen clothes. As we came closer, I recognized him as a taxi driver from Warsaw named Moniek. I knew him very well. He used to park his taxi on the corner of Pawia and Zamenhofa streets, close to where I lived. I remember when he beat up an anti-Semitic doorman in Warsaw who had refused to allow him to park his taxi in front of the doorman's building because Moniek was a Jew.

Moniek recognized me, and Manya and I helped him chase the cow back to his herd. We were very happy to see each other. We were both in the same situation, working for farmers in order to survive. Like me, he also had escaped from Warsaw and had been caught trying to cross the Russian border with his girlfriend. They were captured on the western side of the Bug River by the Germans. His girlfriend tried to run away when they were caught, and the Germans shot her. They imprisoned him in Wlodawa, beat him, and kept him for two days without food. Then they let him go.

We reminisced for a while, and I found out that Moniek was now working on a farm in Hola. He began to cry when he described the death of his girlfriend and how he missed his family back in Warsaw. After talking with him for an hour or so, I had to continue on to Hola with Manya. I was saddened to leave him—he reminded me of the "good old days" in Warsaw.

When we arrived in Hola and entered the Freedman farmhouse,

Manya could hardly recognize her mother. She was haggard, had lost a lot of weight, and looked like an old woman. She told us that the Germans had killed her oldest son Aaron for trying to escape from the Warsaw ghetto. Manya's father Rachmiel continued to work in the soap factory and looked like a skeleton for lack of food. She said Jews were dying from hunger in the streets of the ghetto. Every so often, the Germans would take thousands of Jews out of the ghetto to the train for "resettlement" to the east, but no one knew where they were sent. There were rumors that they were being taken to concentration camps where they were being put to death. She could not tell me anything about my father, as she had not seen him in the Warsaw ghetto.

When Chaia Freedman finished relating the tragic news from Warsaw, everyone in the house sat in silence for a long time, as though in mourning. I looked around at the family members, remembering how they had looked not so long ago before the war—a well-to-do Jewish family, owners of a farm and mill. There was Shimon, who was alive then, his wife Shifra, and their two young boys, and Chaia's brother Lazar and sister Ziesel. I remembered when I lived in Warsaw with Manya's family. They always talked about their "rich" country relatives in Hola. When the poverty was bad in Warsaw, Rachmiel would be laid off from his job in the soap factory, and they would rely on the help of their relatives on the farm. They often received packages of food and sometimes of money. In the summer, when the heat became intolerable in Warsaw, Chaia would take Manya to visit her sisters on the farm for a few weeks of fresh air and good food.

Now the situation was hopeless for everyone. Shimon was dead, and the remaining Freedmans felt that the Germans would not let them stay on the farm much longer. After spending a few more precious hours with her mother, Manya and I walked back to our farms that same night.

It was the time of the Jewish High Holidays. For Rosh Hashanah and Yom Kippur, we gathered at David Turno's shul to pray. Here, we heard the news from Jews in the neighboring towns and villages. In nearby Parczew, an entire Jewish family had been slaughtered by the Germans. The father of the household had been a horse trader, and a farmer owed him money for a horse he had bought from him before the war. The farmer falsely told the Germans that the Jewish man had threatened to kill him if he did not repay the debt. The farmer had friends in the Polish police. The Germans took the entire family (husband, wife, and four children) and shot them.

The High Holiday services were conducted as if it were Tishah

B'Av (the holiday of mourning to commemorate the destruction of the Temple in Jerusalem). David Turno was praying and crying. Lieb (the cantor, rabbi, and melamed all in one) tried to console the people by saying that it was time for the coming of the Messiah. People were worried about what tragedies the next days would bring. Their only hope was a turn in the war or a miracle. Their prayers consisted of pleadings to God, asking why this was happening to the Jewish people. It was a very sad time.

Not long afterward, on a Sunday, I went to visit Manya with Stephan's permission. I had not seen her for several weeks. She was in the farmhouse, making a straw mattress to put on the floor for her to sleep on. When I arrived, she was very nervous and after a while she told me why. She did not mind the hard work, but the farmer's son had recently become a police officer in nearby Wlodawa. He began making advances toward her every time he came home to visit his parents. She told the farmer about it and he told his son to behave. She was scared the farmer's son would denounce her to the Germans if she continued to resist his advances. I realized immediately that she was in a perilous position and decided to take her away from the farm. I told her farmer that her mother was very sick and that I had come to take Manya home. I told him she would return soon. We walked the ten miles from Zamolodycze to Hola that night, and i left her with her relatives there. She never returned to that farmer.

By the time I made my way back to Stephan's farm in Lubien, it was almost daylight. The dog was very happy to see me. He licked me and jumped all over me in his excitement. He had not seen me go to sleep in the barn the previous evening, so he was happy to see me now. The cows were mooing noisily. They wanted to be let out to pasture. Marfa brought my bag of food to the usual place in front of the barn, and I went out for another day with the animals.

I found another farm in Lubien where Manya could work. The farmer's name was Vasil, one of the people I had met on Sundays while grazing the animals. He was an elderly farmer with a wife, but no children. He had told me that he felt sorry for what the Germans were doing to the Jews, and he agreed to take in Manya. Stephan allowed me to take the horse and buggy to bring Manya to Lubien from Hola, as it would have been a considerable walk. Manya's mother, now living in Hola with her relatives, was not happy to see her only daughter go to another farm. Her hope was that Manya would stay with her in Hola. However, she realized that many other Jewish youths were similarly working for local farmers to avoid the Germans.

11
The Winter of 1941–42

It was the fall of 1941 and, with the completion of the harvest, we were busy on the farm getting everything ready for the winter. We repaired the roofs and collected wagons full of dried leaves, which we used for insulation in the walls of the buildings. We laid narrow vertical strips of wood between the roofs and the ground, leaving about a ten-inch space between the outer wall and these strips. Then we packed leaves in tightly between the strips and the outer wall. The insulation was relatively effective in keeping the cold out of the buildings and was refurbished every fall.

The onions, beets, and other vegetables were taken in from the garden and stored for the winter in Stephan's basement. The garden was taken care of by the women, but I helped with it too, and Marfa liked me for that.

With the field work taking less time, I spent more of my time taking the animals out to pasture. As the animals grazed, I listened to the farmers as they watered their livestock and told stories of seeing escaped Russian prisoners wandering in the woods. Once while tending to the cows, I saw three men coming toward me. I figured they must be escaped Russian prisoners. Their clothes and shoes were torn, and they were very thin. Their attitude was not threatening, and they asked me in Russian, which I understood, if I had some food I could give them. I gave them all the food I had in my bag. I did not tell Stephan about it because I thought he might not like my giving away the food. After this incident, I frequently saw Russian soldiers who had escaped from the Germans, wandering in the nearby woods. Whenever I saw them, I gave them my food, as I felt sorry for them and I knew I could feed myself back on the farm. It was getting colder, and some of the Russians dug holes deep in the woods and covered these dugouts with branches and dirt. They were very well camouflaged, so that you could not find them unless you knew where they were. Sometimes, the Russians planted little trees on top of their hideout, which they called a *ziemlanki*.

A *ziemlanki* was a long, narrow underground tunnel. There was an entrance on one side, camouflaged with branches. On the opposite side was an opening for fresh air. This hiding place could hold about five or six people, tightly packed against each other without any room to move around. The Russians stayed in their *ziemlankis* when it was too cold to be outside. I did not know much about these *ziemlankis* then, but we found them useful later on when I and others had to hide in the woods.

The Germans conducted several raids on the local villages and the surrounding woods, searching for escaped Russian prisoners. A shepherd sitting with me in the woods one day told me that some Germans had discovered a few Russians in Lubien. The Russians ran into an empty barn in a field to hide. The Germans surrounded the barn and ordered the Russians to come out. When they refused, the Germans set the barn on fire. One of the prisoners threw a grenade at the Germans and killed several of them. Then, the prisoners jumped out of the burning barn and ran in all directions. One got away, but the Germans killed the others.

The winter of 1941–42 was very harsh. I was kept busy cutting the hay and mixing it with bran for the cows, and taking them out to the water trough. I also prepared the food for the pigs and fed them as well as the horses. I often helped Marfa milk the cows, and I chopped wood for the house. I was constantly occupied with the farm chores.

When it got too cold to sleep in the unheated barn, Stephan allowed me to sleep in the house. I made a mattress from a bundle of straw, placed it on the kitchen floor near the oven, and slept there. I got up before daylight, while everyone else slept, in order to start my chores, which had to be completed early, as the days were short.

The snows came, and some mornings the snow was piled so high from the night before that I barely got out of the house. Then I had the additional chore of digging a path to the barns. Sometimes the snow was higher than I was, and it was freezing cold. I heard rumors that the Russians were coming from the woods to the farms at night, begging for food. The Germans issued an order that any farmer who let a Russian onto his farm would be punished by death.

I often could not sleep at night, as I heard many of the dogs in the village barking at wandering Russians. I wondered how the Russians could exist outside in the woods and withstand the terrible cold weather. I figured that they must be very strong people. I thought perhaps I too would have to hide in the woods some day, and I wondered if I would be able to survive in this kind of winter weather. I could tell by the barking of the dogs which farmers let the Russians into their houses. If they let the Russians in, the dogs would stop barking. If they did not, the dogs would continue barking as they followed the sound of the Russians moving to the next farm.

Stephan secured the doors and windows of the house with hook and eyes, so that they could not be opened from the outside. This was despite the fact that no one knocked on Stephan's door. I began to wonder if the Russians knew of a reason to stay away from Stephan's house. A few nights later during a big snowstorm, we heard a knock on the door. Nobody answered the knock, and the village dogs attacked the Russians outside. We heard them pleading, "Let us in, in the name of God, we are freezing to death." No one answered. The prisoners left, and I heard Stephan tell his wife that he was sorry for them. Stephan's mother-in-law crossed herself, unhappy to have turned the Russians away. She said that, after all, they were their Christian brothers in the eyes of the church, and uttered: "May God help them." I wondered if there might come a time when I would knock on their door, as the Russians had, and they would similarly turn me away. I tried not to think about the possibility. In the meantime, I was thankful to have a roof over my head.

A few weeks later, I traveled with Stephan to Wlodawa to deliver a wagonload of grain to the Germans. It was freezing cold, and I was dressed in a long coat with a high collar and a hat over my ears, so that my face was hardly visible. When we approached Wlodawa, we passed an open field enclosed by barbed wire. In the enclosed field, what seemed to be thousands of Russian prisoners were standing in the bitter cold, hopping up and down and beating their arms to keep from freezing. Some of them put their hands through the wire toward us, begging for food. Many were on the ground, already frozen to death.

Stephan wanted to show me how compassionate he was, or perhaps he wanted to atone for not letting the Russians in on that stormy night. As we passed the barbed wire, he took the bag of food Marfa had prepared for us and threw it over the fence. The prisoners instantly descended upon it as we drove on. A neighboring farmer who delivered his grain to Wlodawa a week later told Stephan that, when he drove by the barbed wire, half the prisoners were lying frozen on the ground.

The news we received about the war was not good. The Germans were smashing the Red Army, taking one Russian city after another. We knew they were getting close to Moscow. I usually heard the war news at dinnertime from Stephan, as we sat at the table.

Whenever I wanted to visit Manya, I had to ask Stephan for permission. As Manya was now living nearby in Lubien, I would visit her once or twice a week. We often reminisced about life in Warsaw. She also told me about other young Jews from the villages who, like us, were hiding out on farms. The Germans at that time did not pay much attention to the few Jews in the villages and on the farms. Even as they were busy on the Russian front, the Germans concentrated on the Jews in the larger cities.

Several times during the winter, Manya and I walked to Hola to visit her relatives and her mother. Her father remained in the War-saw ghetto. Her younger brother Shmuel worked on a farm in Hola like us. Manya still could not get over the news that her older brother Aaron had been killed in Warsaw by the Germans.

12

Betrayal at the Hands of the Hola Farmers

In the spring of 1942, we started the farm work in the fields, as we had done the previous year. By now it was easier for me, because I was experienced. Stephan did not have to help me and did not stand over me to tell me what to do. He trusted me to handle the horses without his help. The barns had to be cleared of manure from the accumulation of the winter, and then the manure had to be hauled to the fields and spread. This job alone took me about a month. The animals were cared for during this time by the neighboring shepherd. We worked all summer long, and harvest time was much like it had been the previous year. Life continued and was filled with work. Stephan rode to Wlodawa with wagonloads of grain, but I did not go with him. This was because, in the summer, I could not be bundled up and would have been recognized as a Jew. Besides, there was much work to be done on the farm in the fall of the year.

Since Stephan had to pay the neighboring shepherd for watching our animals, he would send me with the animals to the woods whenever he could spare me from the farm work. While there, I met some former Russian prisoners who had escaped. Knowing Polish and Hachlacki, it was relatively easy to understand their language. Some of them had weapons. I asked them where they got these weapons, and I offered to buy a gun from them. They told me that the villagers from the Russian side of the Bug River had given them the guns, but they refused to sell one to me. I offered what little money I had, but money meant nothing to them. They also told me that there were many escaped Russian prisoners, living in the woods near Parczew, who had formed armed partisan units.

Stephan would tell us at the dinner table what he had heard in the village from the other farmers. They told him all kinds of horrible stories about what the Germans had done to the Jews in the neighboring towns, how they were being rounded up into ghettos and then loaded onto trains to unknown destinations. The farmers told Stephan that all the Jewish merchants from the neighboring towns of Wlodawa, Parczew, Sosnowica, and Ostrow Lubelski, with whom the farmers had dealt for years, were no longer there. Some of their businesses had been taken over by non-Jews. The rest were just closed up. When I heard this news, I knew that the temporary security I had on Stephan's farm could not last much longer.

One day during the fall of 1942, after a day of work in the fields, I came back to the barn. After I fed the horses and put them in the barn, I headed toward the farmhouse. Before I could walk in, Stephan and his family came out to the porch. I knew immediately that they had bad news for me. He gave me a nice melodious Ukrainian "Good Evening," called me in for supper, and then gave me the bad news. A new order had been issued by the Germans that Jews were no longer allowed to work on any of the farms. All Jews from the neighboring villages were to assemble in the village of Hola, on Manya's relatives' farm. According to the order, the assembled Jews were to be transported by horse and buggy to the Wlodawa ghetto. Effective immediately, if a Jew was discovered in a village or on a farm, the punishment was death, both to the Jew and the farmer who sheltered him. Stephan told me that he could not risk his life and the lives of his family by keeping me any longer. He said that he was very satisfied with my work, and that the whole family liked me and considered me one of the family. However, I could no longer stay with them. His wife Marfa prepared a package with two loaves of bread, a piece of pork, a pair of extra warm pants, and a warm undershirt. I ate my supper but could hardly swallow the food. I was a little puzzled and suspicious of their behavior. I wondered why they were trying to be so nice to me. Perhaps they were intending to betray me in some way. I worried that there might be Germans waiting to kill me as soon as I stepped out of Stephan's yard.

That night, I took my bundle and started walking to the farm where Manya worked. Stephan walked me part of the way. Before he said good-bye, he stopped and volunteered that, if he were I, he would not go to the Wlodawa ghetto. He told me he knew what the Germans did to the Jews there. He said that, from Wlodawa, Jews were sent to the Sobibor death camp. He had learned this from his trips to Wlodawa to deliver grain to the Germans. He advised me to hide in the woods, since I knew the surrounding territory. He reminded me that the Russian partisans were in the woods. He suggested I might find and join them, and maybe I could survive that way. He did not know that I had had this possibility in mind for a long time.

Stephan told me that if I ran out of food, I could come to him in the middle of the night. However, I should pick a dark night and use a signal knock on the window, consisting of two short and two long taps. He told me before he left me that, if I found the partisans, to tell them how good he had been to me. He was trying to insure himself against both the Germans by sending me away, and against the Russians by having me tell them that he had been good to me so that they would not rob his farm. I did not think that he was a friend of Jews in trouble, but I felt he was sorry for me as an individual. I had worked for him for over two years without pay, and he liked me. I was genuinely moved by the friendly advice he offered. I had also noticed tears in the eyes of Marfa and her mother when I said good-bye to them.

I stopped at Vasil's farm, where Manya worked. She had gotten the news from Vasil and was prepared to leave immediately. We started out for Hola on foot. It was a cold autumn night, and we walked in silence. After a while, I broke the silence and told her that I had decided not to go to the Wlodawa ghetto, but to go to the woods instead. She was undecided about joining me in the woods and first wanted to find out what the rest of her family was going to do. However, she said that she probably would go with me.

As we approached Hola, an old lady who lived on the outskirts of the village met us while carrying two full buckets of water. Her name was Polashka. She knew us because she was friendly with the Hola Freedmans. As soon as she saw us, she put down her buckets and crossed herself. She told us she had heard about the German order regarding the Jews, and wondered what the world was coming to. She told us we would survive because she had greeted us with two full buckets of water, and that this was a sign of luck. I could not see how two buckets of water could help us, but it was good to hear some encouraging words.

When we came to the "Srulke farm" (so named after Manya's grandfather Srulke), we discovered that her family had been dispossessed from the farmhouse by the Germans and was living in a nearby shack on the farm. Approximately forty Jews from the surrounding villages and farms were huddled inside the shack. Some were old, some were young, and there were some young couples with children. I knew most of them from meeting them on holidays at David Turno's shul, when I had first come to Hola from Warsaw. Manya's mother and brother, Shmuel, were in the shack. Her Aunt Shifra, now a widow, and her two little boys, along with her Aunt Ziesel and her husband Moishe Yohel and their four-week-old baby, had left Hola the night before. No one knew where they had gone. As we entered the shack, we found the occupants sitting around with their belongings, waiting for morning, when they were to be taken to the Wlodawa ghetto. It was a sorry sight.

I felt compelled to tell the assembled group that I planned to go to the woods instead of the ghetto. I urged them to come with me. I told them that I knew well what to expect in the ghetto. Jews in the ghetto were being starved, killed, and transported to the Sobibor death camp. They also were aware that this was happening to the ghetto Jews.

I had anticipated the skeptical response my suggestion drew. Several in the group questioned how they would be able to survive in the woods, especially with winter approaching. Others doubted that they would be able to hide from the Germans. I told them that escaped Russian prisoners lived in the woods and that I had seen them there. I pointed out that the Russians had been able to survive the previous winter and at the same time avoid detection from periodic German searches. However, I did not want to mislead anyone. I told them I felt that our chances of survival in the woods were very slim, especially for people with families and for older people, but I had to give them the choice and let them know my decision.

About fifteen people decided to follow me to the woods instead of going to the Wlodawa ghetto. They included Manya, her mother and her brother Shmuel, my friend Moniek the Warsaw cab driver, a few older people, and some young men from nearby Sosnowica who, like me, had been workers on farms in the vicinity. The rest waited to be taken to Wlodawa in the morning.

I advised those people joining me to take blankets, warm clothes, food, eating utensils, and knives. I still had my military shoes that I had gotten from the bombed-out military ordinance warehouse in Warsaw. I had been careful not to wear these shoes on the farm, so they were in good condition. I also wore a warm jacket and carried a hunting knife.

We started out for the woods before dawn. We walked for several hours, about ten miles, deeper into the woods in the vicinity of Hola. When it became light we stopped in a very dense part of the woods so as not to be seen or heard by anyone. Lazar, an elderly Jew from Sosnowica, took out his prayer shawl and said the morning prayers. I asked him to pray for all of us.

We had something to eat and after a while it started to drizzle. A sixteen-year-old boy from Sosnowica, who had worked on a farm like me, decided to build a shelter. He was a very enterprising and talented youngster, and we all pitched in on this project. We had a very large heavy gray sheet with us. This boy chopped down some saplings, cleared them of leaves and branches, and made a very good tent with the sheet. It was not large enough for everyone, but the women and elderly were kept from the rain. The rest of us sat on the ground in the rain. This boy was a big help to the group in other ways. He collected dry wood to make a small fire to cook something. It was hard to find dry wood for fire, but it was important, as it made less smoke than the wet wood. We did not want to be visible to anyone.

Later that day Moniek, Manya, and I left the group and went deeper into the forest, hoping to meet up with some Russians who might give us weapons or some other assistance. I told the others to stay alert and, in case anyone spotted them, to move away from that area deeper into the woods. We walked a few miles from the group and did not meet anyone. We came back to the group and stayed there almost a week. Every day three of us went deeper into the woods in different directions, without success.

The nights were very cold, but we expected that. Lazar, who prayed every day, tried to keep up our courage by telling us that God would help us. For safety reasons we decided to move deeper into the woods. We went about four miles further away from Hola. Each day in the woods, our food supply dwindled. Finally, we finished all the food we had taken with us when we left Hola.

We were facing the prospect of slowly starving to death in the woods. I remembered Stephan's offer should I run out of food, and decided to take him up on it in order to alleviate the group's hunger. Manya, Moniek, and I started out for Lubien late one night. We arrived at Stephan's farm in the middle of the night. The dog recognized me and showed his happiness by jumping all over me and barking excitedly. Moniek and Manya stayed hidden behind the barn while I went up to the house and tapped on a window with two long and two short knocks. Stephan came outside and I told him I needed some food. He was surprised to see me and told me to wait in the barn while he went into the house to get food.

While waiting for Stephan, I searched the barn for his old Polish army rifle. I knew where he kept it hidden, but it was no longer there. I looked in other places in the barn and tore away some boards that could be hiding places, but did not find it. Stephan finally came out and called me into the house.

When I entered, I saw that Stephan was holding the rifle. He gave me a bag containing two loaves of bread, some kasha, a piece of pork and another pair of pants. Then he told me to take the bag and never come back again. He told me in a firm tone that if I came to him again he would kill me, and motioned threateningly toward me with his rifle. He said he had nothing against me, but his life was dearer to him than mine. He told me to leave the area because the Germans and local farmers had organized groups to hunt down Russians and Jews. Each village had a few persons, acting as guards, who walked around the village perimeter at night to make sure that no Jews or Russians would try to sneak in to get food. He also told me that in a neighboring village the local guards had caught a Jew on a farm and killed both the Jew and the farmer.

We began our trip back to the group with the food from Stephan. Before we could make it back, daylight broke. We were afraid to be spotted, so we settled in a dense place in the woods and waited for night. After sunset, we walked back to where the group had been, but nobody was there. We ate one loaf of bread and saved the rest of the food for the group, hoping to find them nearby. We walked around for several days searching for them, and finally decided we would have to ask someone. The only person I could trust was the old lady, Polashka. She lived on the edge of the woods, away from the village, and we headed for her house one evening.

When Polashka saw us she almost fainted, and then she crossed herself. She called out our names in a surprised voice and said that in the village they had told her we were all dead. Then she told us what had happened a few days before. (We figured out that it was the day after we had left our group, while we were in the woods with Stephan's food and waiting for nightfall so that we could come back.) A large group of about fifty villagers (without any Germans) went into the woods, armed with clubs and pitchforks. They surrounded our group, forced them to march to Sosnowica, and then turned them over to the Germans. There they were all shot. This roundup had been organized by the Hola village elders. The villagers told Polashka that we were also among those murdered, so when she saw us she thought we were ghosts. She thanked God out loud that we were alive, and advised us to leave the area quickly for our own safety. She also told us who the two leaders of the raid had been. One was a man named Vasil (not the same Vasil as the farmer Manya had worked for in Lubien). The second was a man from Hola, named Timofi, who was the brother of the village mayor. The men who participated in the raid were all local villagers who had lived together all their lives with many of the Jews of our group. They knew in advance what the Germans would do to the Jews they rounded up. Like Stephan, Polashka also warned us about the village guards, who walked around the village perimeter at night to keep out Russians and Jews.

Upon hearing Polashka's news, Manya began crying bitterly. She continued sobbing uncontrollably for a long time. Her mother and brother had been shot with the others. Of our group of fifteen who had chosen the woods over the Wlodawa ghetto, twelve were dead. If not for the fact that the three of us had waited for night to fall before returning to the group, we would have been shot too.

The Zamolodycze Raid

Manya, Moniek, and I left Po-
lashka and reentered the woods. We still had one loaf of bread left
and a piece of pork, but none of us could eat. We decided to go much
deeper into the woods than we had previously. I remembered that,
while shepherding for Stephan, I had met some Russian partisans
who told me about a very dense forest where they had spent the
previous winter. The forest was in the area of Zamolodycze, west
of Lubien. There was a small stream running through it, and the
Russians told me they had made a dugout to hide in near the
stream.

We started walking in the direction of Zamolodycze. Manya kept
crying, and nothing we said could console her. We walked the entire
night and found the stream. We sat down to rest near it and took a
nap. I awoke at daylight and roused the others. We could hear dogs
barking in the distance and figured the noise must be coming from
the village of Zamolodycze.

We walked for several days in the Zamolodycze woods. There were
many wild animals in the forest, such as deer and wild boars, and on
several occasions we were attacked by boars and wolves. We only had
big sticks and knives to defend ourselves, but these were enough to
fend off attacking animals. Our dream was to get our hands on a
gun. One night, while not far from the stream, I heard a noise. I

alerted Manya and Moniek, and we all listened without moving a muscle. We heard someone walking in the distance, and it did not sound like an animal. We walked away from the stream into the woods and waited to see who it could be. Soon we saw two young girls walking toward the stream. We wondered who could be walking in the middle of the night in the wilderness. When they came closer, we heard them speaking in Yiddish, and we recognized them. They were two daughters of David from Hola, whose son, Moishe Yohel, had recently married Ziesel, Manya's aunt. They carried two buckets to get water from the stream. We did not want to scare them, so we started talking loudly in Yiddish so they would hear us. We approached them, and they recognized and embraced us.

They took us to their hideout. It was not far from the stream, in a very densely forested area, where young fir trees spread their long branches very low to the ground. We had to crawl on all fours in order to get into the dugout that the Russians had told me about. There were four families there, totaling eighteen people in all. We sensed that they were not anxious to see us, as the dugout was already very overcrowded.

Hiding in the dugout were David from Hola, his wife and three daughters. Two of his daughters had lived and worked in Warsaw, and had come home because of the war. Also in the dugout were Isa from Hola, his wife, two daughters, and a son, David. Another son of theirs had left for Russia in 1939, when people were still able to cross the border. There was also Zelik from Zamolodycze, a shoemaker. With him was his wife, his daughter Faiga, and son Mendel. Also in the dugout were Moishe Yohel (David from Hola's son), his wife Ziesel (Manya's aunt), and their four-week-old baby. The final occupant of the dugout was Yosel Barbanel from the village of Maryanka. He had stayed with the group because his girlfriend was Pearl, Isa from Hola's daughter. Pearl was a very striking dark-haired girl, famous in the area for her beauty.

The dugout was so well camouflaged that, even if you were very close to it, it was not visible. Several small trees were planted on top of it. On the end opposite the entrance, there was a hole for air, which was also camouflaged with trees. Inside, the ceiling of the dugout was so low that one could not stand. It was dark and damp and like laying in a grave. There was not enough room in it for the entire group, and so some had to sit outside the dugout nearby.

I knew all these people. They used to get together in Hola on Manya's family farm when I first arrived in Hola from Warsaw. They had found a very well-camouflaged dugout. The problem was that the dugout was only designed for two to four people, not for such a large contingent.

The second problem I saw related to Ziesel's baby. The baby was hungry and cried all the time. Ziesel had no milk to nurse the baby, and there was no food to feed it. It was very important not to make any noise because there were open fields nearby where cows were grazing. The fields were close enough that, at times, we could hear shepherds talking to each other.

After a few days in the vicinity of the dugout, I decided that this was not a safe place for us. I tried to persuade Yosel Barbanel that we would be better off in smaller groups. I knew from my recent experience in the Hola woods that large groups would more likely attract attention. Yosel agreed with me, but he wanted to stay with his girlfriend Pearl. She, in turn, refused to leave her parents, who wanted to remain with the others. That is why they stayed together. Unable to convince Yosel to leave, Manya and I postponed our departure.

The people in this group had left Hola the night before Manya and I came to Hola from Lubien. They had gone directly to this hiding place, which Zelik from Zamolodycze had known about. Ziesel had wanted to take her sister Chaia (Manya's mother) and Chaia's son Shmuel (Manya's brother) with the group, but Chaia had insisted on waiting on the family farm for Manya.

Ziesel's and Moishe Yohel's baby continued to cry from hunger. Everyone, including its parents, knew the noise endangered the entire group. A few days after joining the group, I woke one morning to find the baby was dead. No one asked how it happened—we all realized how difficult it must have been for Ziesel and Moishe to have smothered their baby. Since we did not have a shovel, we buried the infant in a shallow grave. David, the baby's grandfather, murmured the ritual kaddish over the grave. The parents cried, and we all cried with them.

A few days later, shortly after dawn, we heard a commotion all around us. We heard the sound of many feet crunching through the underbrush, coming closer and closer. We knew we were surrounded. The approaching voices spoke Ukrainian. They were the villagers from Zamolodycze. They yelled toward the dugout, "Jews, get out of there."

They crawled in through the heavy underbrush on all sides of us. There were at least seventy of them, carrying sticks and pitchforks. One of their leaders was Vasil, a young man from Zamolodycze, who carried a rifle (he was not the same Vasil who had helped round up the Jews in the Hola woods). I knew him from when he used to come to the mill to press linseed to oil, and I could tell that he recognized me also. Now he was a Ukrainian policeman in Wlodawa. He was visiting his hometown of Zamolodycze when he took part in this raid.

When they reached the dugout, most of us were already outside it. The villagers knew all of us by name and immediately realized that Zelik was not among us. Two of them crouched at the entrance to the dugout and shouted into the hole: "Zelik, come out!" When Zelik did not appear, the two crawled into the dugout and dragged him out.

I looked around at our captors and did not see any Germans— just a mob of villagers. I asked one of them whether there were any Germans accompanying them, and I was told no. It appeared that they wanted to get us away from the dugout. They took us out of the heavy growth of small fir trees into a little clearing, not very far from a larger forest. Then they started to march us in the direction of Zamolodycze.

Although there were no Germans there—only Vasil with his rifle —I sensed they meant to do us harm. I took off my heavy coat and draped it over my arm. As soon as we got close to the larger forest on our left, I yelled in Yiddish as loudly as I could: "Everybody run!" Moishe Yohel and Ziesel, who had just lost their baby a few days previously, were standing next to me. I heard them say: "We are not running. Let them kill us. We have nothing to live for anymore."

I grabbed Manya's hand and we started running as fast as we could. I hoped that everyone was doing the same thing. I heard the villagers shouting: "Catch them!" I turned left toward the woods, and when I looked back I could see that the rest of the group had scattered and were running in many directions. I heard a shot from a rifle, and then a second shot. I also sensed a man running after us. We were running very fast, but he caught up with us after about a mile and grabbed me by the coat I was carrying. I let go of the coat in the hope that he would stop pursuing us, but he dropped it and kept chasing us. I pulled out my hunting knife as I ran. When he caught up with us again, I suddenly stopped, turned around and stabbed him in the chest with all my might. He dropped to the ground without a sound, and we continued running. I heard the villagers hollering from a distance, but no one pursued us anymore.

We entered the woods and continued running for about another half hour. We came to a road, but we were afraid to expose ourselves by crossing it. We might be spotted by the villagers. At the edge of the road were small fir trees, with long branches growing down to the ground. We threw ourselves down on the ground and rolled under the branches, well hidden. We were gasping for breath from running, to the point where we could not talk to each other for a while. It started to rain. I had lost my hat and coat. My face was cut and bloody from the branches whipping by while we ran, and I was shivering from the cold and from fear. Manya was in equally bad shape. She had lost her kerchief. We were soaked from the rain and hungry.

We decided to stay in our hiding place under the branches until dark, in case some of the villagers were still searching for us, and then cross the road. After lying there about two hours, we heard a detachment of German soldiers riding on horseback down the road in our direction. When they came closer, I saw a big dog following them. I knew the Germans could not see us, but I was afraid of the dog, which was crisscrossing from one side of the road to the other. As the dog approached, we held our breath for fear of detection. Luckily, when the dog reached a point parallel to us, his crisscross pattern took him to the opposite side of the road. He did not sense us. The Germans passed by and we started to breathe again as the sound of their horses' hooves gradually retreated in the direction of Zamolodycze.

About an hour and a half after they had passed, we heard shooting in the distance. It appeared to be coming from the direction of Zamolodycze. I counted about thirty shots, and then it was still. We stayed hidden under the branches. After a while, the same Germans on horseback with the dog came back on the same road. Once again, they passed us uneventfully. We lay under the branches until darkness fell. We were wet, cold, and hungry and did not know where we were. We were afraid to go into a village for fear of being spotted.

I decided we should go back to Stephan's farm, although he had warned that he would kill me if I ever returned. I knew his character, and I did not believe he would do it. The going was rough, walking that night back to Stephan's farm. Manya was sick, shivering and running a high fever. She could hardly walk. I had to support her, and we had to stop to rest many times.

We approached the village of Lubien late at night and entered from the back of the village to reach Stephan's house. Stephan's dog was once again very happy to see me and started licking and jumping all over me. I tapped on the window with two long and two short knocks, but no one answered. I knocked again louder and announced my name, saying that I was hungry, but there was no movement in the house. I remembered the escaped Russian prisoners from the

winter before—how they had knocked on the door begging for food
and the door had not been opened for them either. We finally went
away and walked to Vasil's farm in Lubien where Manya used to
work. Here Manya knocked on Vasil's window, but the same thing
happened. No one answered.

We walked back in the direction of Hola. It was a cold December
night, and we were soaking wet. As we approached Hola, we saw
Polashka's house at the edge of the woods and decided to try her
house. We knocked on the door. She opened it, surprised again to
see us, and invited us in. I remember her crossing herself as we
entered. I explained that Manya was sick and we both needed something to eat. She immediately undressed Manya and dried her with a
towel. As she did this, she kept talking to herself: "In such a cold
night people shouldn't have a roof over their heads? My God!"

Her house consisted of one room with a low ceiling. There was no
furniture, just two little wooden boxes in the middle of the room.
The oven took up half the room. In one corner was a small box with
a kerosene lamp on it that provided very little light. The sole decora-
tion was a crucifix on the wall.

The only place to sleep was on top of the baking oven. Polashka's
husband was sleeping there when we arrived. He was not normal.
Everyone considered him crazy. He had a permanently fixed smile
on his face. He seemed oblivious to the world around him and never
worked on his farm. His wife did all the farm work.

Polashka was a generous, warm-hearted woman, and she gave us
everything she had, which was not much. She gave Manya some old
dry clothes to wear. She gave me her husband's torn jacket and an
old hat. She warmed up a little pot of milk and found a piece of
bread and fed us with it. All the while, she talked to us in the tone of
a mother talking to her little children.

She told us the story that she had heard from the local villagers
regarding what had happened to the Jews in Zamolodycze. In relating this story, she was unaware that we had been part of that group.
She told us that the farmers had gone out to capture all the Jews
hiding in the woods and had marched them all to Zamolodycze. Once
there, they locked them in Zelik's house. One of the villagers then
rode on horseback to Sosnowica, about five miles away, to bring the
Germans. The Germans arrived on horseback. They took the Jews
out of the house one by one and shot them all.

The villagers of Zamolodycze watched in a crowd as the killings
took place. They knew all these Jews. They had grown up together,
and done business together. They knew the parents and grandpar-

ents of these people as well. Zelik was the village shoemaker, who made the shoes for most of the villagers and their families. His son, Mendel, had tried to escape. He jumped out of an attic window and started to run away, but the villagers caught him and the Germans shot him also. Once all the Jews were killed, the villagers dug a hole in Zelik's yard and buried all the bodies. "How could they do that?" Polashka exclaimed. "It's the end of the world, and God will punish them!"

Polashka could tell that Manya was very sick. Her fever continued unabated, and she could not stop shivering. Since I saw that Polashka was so good-hearted toward us, I asked if Manya could stay at her house for another night. By then, I hoped she would be better. I told Polashka I would go out to the woods and come back for Manya the next evening. She agreed, and promised to hide her in the attic. Polashka gave me a piece of bread, and I put on her husband's torn jacket and went out into the Hola woods. The sun was already coming up.

I walked alone in the forest all day, never staying in one spot for more than a few minutes to rest. At nightfall, I returned to Polashka's house. Manya felt a little better. Her temperature was gone. Before daylight, we left Polashka's house for the woods, expressing our gratitude for her kindness.

We started back toward the Zamolodycze forest. We had had an understanding with the people in the dugout that, if for any reason we had to scatter because of an ambush, we would come back late at night to the dugout to see if there were any survivors. I reasoned that since we had gotten away, some of the others might have also. I was hoping to find at least a few members of the group left. I also remembered that Moniek was not with us at the time of the raid. He had left us the night before to steal a goose from the farmer for whom he had worked. There were many geese on the farm, and he knew where they were kept at night. At the time, I had suggested to him that he not catch geese because they make too much noise, and instead get a chicken. I had hopes that at least Moniek would be alive.

We wandered for two days in the Zamolodycze woods and finally found Yosel Barbanel and Faiga, Zelik's sixteen-year-old daughter. Soon, we found Moniek with a goose under each arm. Yosel had had a revolver at the time of the raid. When we all scattered and ran, he was chased by a farmer. He shot and wounded his pursuer and escaped.

We stayed a few more days in the area of the woods, hoping that someone else might have also escaped and would be looking for us.

Yosel could not forgive himself for not being able to save his beautiful girlfriend Pearl. He kept hoping that maybe she was not among the dead and insisted that we remain in the area in case she was still alive.

I told him what Polashka had related to Manya and me. I told him about Faiga's brother Mendel, and how he had escaped through the attic window but had been caught and shot. I told him how they had taken each person out of the house, one by one, and shot them. Polashka had told us that the farmers were ordered by the Germans to watch the executions. When they brought Pearl out of the house, the village women were crying—she was so beautiful. When I told Yosel and Faiga the story, they broke down in tears, but I felt they should know what had happened.

Shortly afterward, we found wandering in the woods Isa's youngest son David, who was Pearl's brother. Of the twenty people in the dugout at the time of the raid, six had survived—Faiga, Yosel, Moniek, David, Manya, and myself. The rest had been executed in Zamolodycze.

14

I Lose Manya
in the Skorodnica Forest

It was getting very cold. Moniek had his two geese, but we were afraid to make a fire to cook them for fear we would be spotted by someone.

Yosel suggested that we leave the Zamolodycze woods and head toward the nearby village of Maryanka. That was his hometown, and he believed his family was somewhere in the Maryanka woods. His father, Rachmiel Barbanel, had been a successful cattle merchant before the war. He and his wife had four sons—Chaim, Yosel, Symcha, and Chanina—and three daughters. Their ancestors had lived in the area for many generations and, as a result, they had many relatives in the neighboring towns of Sosnowica and Wlodawa and in the surrounding villages. When the Germans ordered all Jews to the ghettos, Rachmiel and his family went to the Maryanka woods instead, and all of his relatives from the area joined them. Altogether, Rachmiel's immediate family and close relatives in the woods numbered about fifty people. I had met Rachmiel for the first time at David Turno's shul in 1939. Among his family, he was treated with the respect of a king. His son Yosel had chosen to go to the Zamolodycze forest because his girlfriend Pearl and her family were there.

As we neared Maryanka, Yosel explained that the farm on the outskirts of the village near the woods belonged to a farmer named Pakula. He was a fervent Polish patriot and a very decent man. He was also an old friend of the Barbanels. When the Germans came to Maryanka, Pakula was a big help to the Barbanel family.

We stopped at Pakula's house, seeking information on the where-abouts of Yosel's family. It was the middle of the night. Yosel went into the house by himself while we waited in the woods. It was cold and raining, and we were shivering. We waited for quite a while until Yosel came back and brought us into Pakula's house. Pakula was about thirty-five years old and lived with his wife and two young daughters. The house was warm and smelled of freshly baked bread. When we came in, the warmth and smells enveloped us, and it was as if we were drugged. We became dizzy and sleepy. Moniek sat down on a box in the corner and fell asleep immediately. Pakula's wife cut up the freshly baked bread and gave everyone a piece. We tried to wake Moniek so he could eat, but we were unable to rouse him. Faiga and Manya still were sobbing with grief over the loss of their families. Pakula had heard about the massacre in the Zamolodycze woods and tried to comfort them. Drawing upon an old saying, he told us: "Before it gets light it must first be dark, and there will be an end to the German rule also."

I was amazed at Pakula's friendliness. I was not used to it. I called him aside and asked him if he knew where we could get some weap-ons from the local farmers. I had been lucky enough to survive the farmers' raids twice—once in the Hola woods and once in the Zamo-lodycze woods. I told him that these experiences had taught me that without weapons we could not survive in the woods. We were hunted both by the local villagers and the Germans. Without weapons, it was also impossible for us to get any food. He explained that many villagers had guns, and that they often kept them buried in the ground. He told me he even knew of a farmer who had buried an entire Polish air force plane in his field. In September 1939, a pilot had run out of gas and had landed his plane in the field of the farmer, who then proceeded to bury it intact. Pakula went on to answer my question by saying he did not know who had weapons but that he would try to find out for us.

Pakula told us that he did not know where Yosel's family was, but every once in a while Yosel's brothers would stop at his house for some food. He advised us to go to his barn to sleep, and return to the woods before daylight. He suggested that for the next several days we stay nearby in the woods during the day and return to him each night. Perhaps by that time one of Yosel's brothers would make contact with him.

Keeping vigil, I slept very little that night. I peered out of the barn through cracks in the wall, and saw that Pakula could not sleep either. He kept walking back and forth between the barn and his house. I sensed he was keeping guard over us in a protective way. I noticed that he wore a heavy black coat. It made me wonder how we would survive in the oncoming heavy snows and freezing weather.

I woke up everyone before dawn and we went into the woods again. We spent three nights and two days in this manner, alternating between the woods and the barn. Pakula woke us in the middle of the third night to tell us that Yosel's two brothers had arrived. We walked into the house and there stood Symcha and Chanina. They had heard about the massacre in the Zamolodycze woods. When they had come to Pakula, the first thing they asked was whether he had heard anything about Yosel. Pakula did not say anything to them. Instead, he just brought us in, and they were very surprised and happy.

Pakula gave us several loaves of bread, kasha, and other food. His wife surprised us by cleaning and cooking the two geese for us that Moniek had taken from his farmer in Hola and had been carrying around for several days. We took the food and thanked them. Then we left with Symcha and Chanina for the Skorodnica forest in the vicinity of the village of Skorodnica, near Maryanka.

We left after midnight with Chanina, a tall twenty-year-old in a long army coat, leading us. Although he knew the area very well, fresh snow had just covered the ground, and he became disoriented. I watched him as he turned his head from left to right and listened, and I knew that we were lost. The forest we were in was very dense, and it was easy to become lost. We were looking for a broken branch at which we were supposed to take a turn. There were no pathways. We walked for miles and apparently kept missing the spot where we were supposed to turn.

It was almost daylight when we noticed we were not far from Zamolodycze, which was opposite the direction where we had intended to go. We were afraid to risk being spotted by traveling in the daylight, so we moved into a denser area of the woods and waited for nightfall. Manya was so tired from walking all night that she dropped to the ground before we could collect some branches to sit on. The ground was wet from the snow and we were chilled through and through.

After dark, we started out again, this time with Symcha leading. He was a little shorter than Chanina, but he took longer strides, and Manya and Faiga could not keep up the pace. I told Symcha to slow down and he obliged.

Toward daylight we came to the area where Yosel's family was encamped. We could see the smoke from their cooking fires while we were still a distance from the camp. I heard them chopping wood as we came closer, the sound echoing through the forest. When we arrived, we saw several different groups of people sitting around their fires. I immediately wanted to get away from there. I told my group not to join them but to sit down a distance from them. Symcha agreed with me. They were close to seventy-five in number, and a group that size was likely to attract attention.

Rachmiel was overjoyed to see his son Yosel. He had feared that Yosel had been killed in the Zamolodycze massacre. Of course, the entire group was happy to see him. They were all related, and that was why they were staying together. In addition to Rachmiel's family, we met Chaim Weisman, his wife and five children, also from Maryanka. We also met Hershel from Skorodnica, his wife Hannah, her mother and their two-year-old baby girl, and many others.

I was extremely tired from walking all night. After being introduced to many people, I moved about fifty yards away from the group to rest. I sat down on the ground, leaned against a tree, and fell instantly asleep.

I do not know how long I slept, but the sound of automatic weapons fire woke me. I jumped up and looked around. The group was no longer there. I started running away from the direction of the shooting and came to the edge of the woods. I saw the entire group running out of the forest into an open field, toward the left of where I was. I quickly turned to the right and ran along the edge of the woods. The automatic weapons fire was part of a trap set by the Germans to chase the people out into the open. There was water on the field, making it muddy and slippery. On the other side of the field the woods started again. I glanced to my left and saw people slipping and falling in the field, and then getting up and running again as the firing continued. Some fell and did not get up. Some of them were carrying their bedding over their heads, seeking protection from the bullets.

As I ran along the edge of the woods, I fell into a swamp up to my neck. Then I saw a little boy, about ten years old, who was running after me. He fell into the same swamp. He held onto the overhead branches to keep from drowning. He was from the area and knew the woods there. He told me not to run any further because the main highway was a few yards ahead. We could hear the shooting continuing for a long time, becoming more and more sporadic.

We remained there, up to our necks in the water, for the entire day. We could hear the Germans talking to each other, combing the woods for Jews. They were very close to us, but the swamp kept them far enough away that we were not detected. In the evening, we heard the sounds of moving trucks. The Germans were leaving the area via the highway just in front of us.

After dark, we climbed out of the swamp, returning to the place where the massacre had started. Small groups of people came back, looking for the others. I could not find Manya, and nobody else had seen her either. After several anxious hours, she finally returned. She had hidden under the low branches of a fir tree. The Germans had passed right next to her, but miraculously they had not seen her. On the way back to us, she had gotten lost and that was why she had been so late. Chaim Weisman survived the same way. He had hidden under a bush close to where the group had originally been sitting. He had not run with the group. The Germans did not notice him and he was saved. His wife and five children also came back and were extremely happy to find him alive. Rachmiel Barbanel, his wife, one of his daughters, and many of his relatives had been killed at the edge of the woods while running into the field. One other daughter had been wounded. His four sons survived.

Among the other survivors were Vigdor and his wife, Hershel and his wife Hannah, and his mother-in-law and baby, and Motel Barbanel (Rachmiel Barbanel's brother) and his wife Chanche. About thirty people had been killed in the attack. The rest of us buried the dead and moved to a different location in the woods about five miles away.

This time we were more careful. We sat in small groups, mostly five to six people, about 125 yards from each other. For food, we went only to friendly villagers. Hershel and his wife Hannah went to his hometown village of Skorodnica, to a neighbor with whom they had left some of their household belongings. They came back with a feather bed cover. Chaim Weisman went back to his village of Maryanka to get some bedding. The winter cold was upon us.

It was the end of 1942. The weather was getting very severe, and at night we lay in a circle with our feet toward the center of the circle, under the one feather bed cover that Hannah had brought back. There were about ten of us in our group, all trying not to freeze.

We were now constantly on the lookout. We were deep in the woods, many miles away from any roads. One day a group of about forty Russian partisans arrived in our area. This was in January 1943. They all had weapons. Their leader's name was Fioder, an experienced military man. They came from the Makoszka forest in the area of Parczew, about forty miles west of us. The Germans had surrounded and attacked them there. The Russians had broken through the encirclement, but with heavy losses, and had come to our area. They told us there were many Jews who had refused to obey the Germans' order to go to the ghettos and who were wandering in the Makoszka forest. Many of them, they said, were being killed by the Germans in raids.

The Russians settled near us in the Skorodnica forest and stayed for a few days. This was a very undisciplined group of marauding fighters. As they had done in the Makoszka forest, as soon as they settled near us they started to rape the young Jewish women in our group. Although we protested, they were armed and we were not, so there was little we could do to stop them.

A very heavy snowstorm had fallen just prior to the Russians' arrival, and the Germans simply had to follow the footprints of the Russians to find them. A few days after the Russians had arrived, the Germans attacked. They came in a very large force and started firing at us, but at first they did not come very close because the Russians returned their fire. We scattered in different directions. The shooting went on all day throughout the woods. Many Germans were killed, but many of the Russians also were killed. In the course of the battle, a number of our people were also lost. Fortunately the days were short, and when it started to get dark the Germans pulled out.

When the shooting started we all had tried to run away, as we had no weapons to fight with. As I was running I saw Hannah's mother, hit by a bullet, fall on top of Hannah's little two-year-old girl, whom she had been carrying. I turned aside and fell into a deep snowbank. I was completely covered and lay there until the shooting stopped.

Later, when we returned to our base after dark, I could not find Manya. I went to everyone I could find to ask if they had seen her. Someone said they thought they had seen Manya fall after being hit by a bullet. I was grief-stricken. Manya had been my girlfriend for a long time. Ever since leaving Warsaw in the fall of 1939, she had thrown in her lot with me. We had lived through many experiences in the woods, and I felt responsible for her. I could not get her off my mind and continued to hope that somehow she had survived.

The Russian partisans left, including among them many Jewish partisans from the Makoszka forest. Our small group was again alone. The Russians would not let us go with them, as they would not take anyone without weapons.

The Hunt

It was the winter of 1942–43, and we were camping in the Skorodnica forest near the village of Wyryki. We were scattered in small groups, totaling about forty people, and only very few of us had guns, which had been purchased from the local villagers.

The cold was unbearable. It was so cold that the birch trees were splitting from the low temperature. The crack of the trees splitting rang out like rifle shots in the forest. Some birds sitting in the trees froze to death and fell to the ground. It was impossible to sit through the night without a fire. We made small fires and sat around them. Our fronts were warm but our backs were so cold that the backs of our coats, wet from the falling snow, were frozen stiff as a board. Our faces were black from the smoke, and so were our hands, which we kept near the fire for warmth. Our clothes were full of holes from the sparks that jumped out of the fire, and the points of our boots were burned from keeping our feet so close to the flames.

We could not stand in one place and had to move around to keep our feet from freezing. On very cold winter days, the early morning hours just before sunrise were the coldest time of the day. The constant fear and the biting frost were terrible. Those of us who had a weapon felt a little more courageous. When we went for food, we were sometimes able to get some warm clothes for members of the group.

Early one morning, we heard the loud sounds of trumpets from far away in the forest, followed by distant shooting all around us. We deserted the fires and the little food we had and started running. First the elderly and the unarmed left, and then the ones who had weapons (about five people) retreated more slowly to cover them. It was hard to orient ourselves as to which direction to run, because the shooting seemed to come from all around us. Besides the rifle shots, we heard the barking sound of many dogs. The echo of the dogs' barking made us feel that the noise was coming from behind each tree. We became totally disoriented as to which direction to run. I noticed while I was running that the sound of the barking was not like the barking of the village dogs, but more like that of wolves.

We kept running and soon saw animals running in packs near us. There were wild boars, foxes, wolves, deer, and other animals running in the same direction we were. Then we heard shouts in Polish: "Catch them! Catch them!" We did not realize at the time that the shooting was not aimed at us. What we later learned was that the Germans, together with the local Polish nobility, had organized a hunt in the forest. As part of that hunt, they had mobilized many villagers from that area to help chase the animals in one direction. Among the chasers were also about fifty Jewish prisoners from Adampol, a German forced labor camp near Wlodawa, which was under the command of German SS Officer Graf Zelinger. They were watched by a special detachment of Germans, who were also hunting.

We were trapped like the wild animals being hunted. The five of us who were armed started firing at the oncoming Germans, trying to put up enough of a resistance to give the unarmed ones a chance to scatter and escape.

Then a miracle occurred. As we were running, a very severe snowstorm came suddenly upon us, with hurricane-like winds. The sky turned pitch black. The noise from the wind was frightening. Many trees crashed to the ground in front of us. We were blinded by the heavy blowing snow. The Germans could not continue with the hunt under these conditions and withdrew. We were later told by the villagers that some high German officials from Berlin had participated in this hunt. The storm saved both us and the animals from the Germans.

Toward evening, the storm abated. We returned to our encampment of the previous night, as we always did after being forced to scatter in a raid. Some people did not return until morning, at which time we began to search for the others. We found more than a dozen people from our group, frozen stiff exactly as they had fallen during the storm. We carried them all back to a dugout in our area, which some of our group had used previously for shelter. This dugout had been tunneled by Russians during the prior winter. We used this dugout as a mass grave, but we could not put all the bodies in the dugout. Some were frozen in such a position that they would not fit in the tunnel, so we laid them on the ground and covered them with a mound of snow.

Among the dead was David, Isa from Hola's young son. He had been one of the few to escape the Zamolodycze massacre with me. Now he too was gone. His grave was under the snow.

16
Taking the Offensive

The dirt, the lice, the cold weather and hunger, and the losses of loved ones made many in our group think that they might be better off in the Wlodawa ghetto. Wlodawa was the only town in the area where Jews still remained in the ghetto. All the other Jewish ghettos in the neighboring towns had already been liquidated, their occupants having been transported to concentration camps.

I felt that the Germans kept the Wlodawa ghetto still functioning, with a lot of Jews living in relatively bearable conditions, for a reason. The Germans wanted to induce Jewish people hiding in the surrounding woods and other places to come to the ghetto. This way, they could more easily liquidate all the Jews in the area at one time. I felt it was a mistake to go to the Wlodawa ghetto instead of remaining in the woods, and I voiced this to the people who wanted to go to the ghetto. However, they said that they could not survive the severity of the cold winter in the woods.

Chaim Weisman, who had lost his wife and four of his five children in a German raid, decided to go to the ghetto with his youngest daughter, Bebale. Chaim Barbanel and his wounded sister Esther, the "tall" David from Sosnowica and his sister and brother-in-law Moishe Shivak, and many others, perhaps twenty people in all, went to the ghetto. They promised that if they could survive through the winter in the ghetto, they would return to the woods in the early spring.

The departure of the bulk of our group to the ghetto left only six of us who preferred to remain in the woods. The group remaining consisted of Moniek, Faiga, myself, and the three Barbanel brothers, Yosel, Symcha, and Chanina.

We learned from Pakula, who had heard through the village grapevine, that Russian partisan groups were still operating in the Makoszka forest in the vicinity of Parczew. We knew we could not remain in our area for long. It was difficult to get food from the villagers and we had very few weapons. We decided that in order to survive we had to get more weapons and join a larger group in the Makoszka forest.

At this point, the only weapons we possessed were Yosel's revolver and a rocket gun that Chanina had found in a field near Maryanka in 1939. The rocket gun was not a deadly weapon. It was only good for firing flares to light up the sky at night, but it looked like a pistol.

I decided to go to Stephan to try to get his rifle. Before doing that, we found a friendly villager who was willing to sell us a sawed-off shotgun. We paid him a very high price, but we were glad to get it. Because it was so short, we could carry it under our coats without its being noticed. It belonged to Symcha.

The six of us walked to Stephan's house in Lubien. We reached his house at dusk through the back of the village. I knew that at this time of day I might find Stephan milking the cows, as that was his usual routine.

Symcha, Yosel, Chanina, and I walked to the front of the barn. Moniek and Faiga remained behind the building. Stephan's dog saw me and started jumping up and licking me. As always, he was happy to see me. I noticed a light coming from the kerosene lamp in the barn. I had Yosel's revolver, Chanina had his rocket gun, and Symcha had his shotgun. The three of us walked quietly into the barn, followed by the dog. Stephan was milking a cow, and as we came in I pointed the revolver at him. "Hands up!" I hollered. Stephan turned, looked at me, and asked, "Hershku, you're going to kill me?" I said, "No, I won't kill you," but I kept the gun right to his head.

Chanina and Symcha, standing next to me, kept their weapons ready. I said: "What I want from you is your rifle, and I will give you two minutes to get it. Otherwise you will be dead." He said: "But, I don't have a rifle. Will you kill me?" "You will be dead in another minute, where is the rifle?" I demanded. He realized from my tone that I meant business. He told us that the rifle was in the other barn.

The dog could not understand what was going on, although he could sense the tension in the air. He looked from Stephan to me, not knowing what to do, so he started running around growling.

We all went to the other barn, and I asked Stephan where the gun was. He wanted to get it for me, but I would not let him. He told me it was hidden in a corner of the ceiling rafters. I found the rifle and next to it a box of bullets. This was the rifle he had held on me when I came begging for food the previous winter. Before we left him, I told him that we were part of a large group of Jewish partisans in the woods. I warned him that if the villagers were to catch and kill a Jew, our group would return to burn down the village. Then he offered us some food, which we accepted. This showed the power of being with an armed group. He told me not to forget to tell the partisans that he had been good to me.

We left for the woods, and about fifteen minutes later we heard the clanging of the Lubien church bell sound the alarm in the village. Each farmhouse had an outside alarm, either a bell, a triangle, or some sort of piece of metal, and after those were rung the church bell would start ringing. I was certain it was Stephan who had put out this alarm.

We left the Lubien area, and I now carried Stephan's rifle. We walked to Maryanka to see our friend Pakula. He told us he knew a farmer who had a rifle, and he told us where to find him. This farmer was known as a German collaborator and a friend of the Wlodawa police. We knew we would have to use force to get a rifle from him. We rested up in Pakula's barn for a few nights. During the days we stayed in the woods.

A few nights later, around midnight, we started out for the farmer's house, which was in the center of Maryanka. We knocked on his door, but no one answered. A large dog attacked us, and I hit him with the butt of my rifle. He did not bark anymore. Then I said to my companions in a very loud voice: "Get the kerosene and we'll burn down the house." This made the farmer open the door immediately. Symcha told him to turn over his rifle or he would kill him. The farmer swore that he did not have a rifle. We took him out to the barn, while Yosel guarded the door to ensure that no one left the house. We roughed him up until he disclosed the whereabouts of his rifle, which we gave to Moniek. It was a brand new Polish military rifle, with the packing grease still on it, and with it we found a box of bullets. Now we all had weapons, except for Faiga.

We decided to go to Zamolodycze to take revenge for the massacre that had taken place there the previous year. Faiga, Zelik's daughter and the only person left from her entire family, and in whose yard all the slaughtered Jews had been buried, led us. It was a Sunday night. We came in, as usual, through the back of the village. From far away we heard the sound of music. As we came closer, Faiga realized that the music was coming from her house. Faiga, who did not have a gun, was carrying an axe she had picked up as we entered the village. She was furious as we came closer to her home, remembering how the villagers had herded her family back to Zamolodycze to be shot.

We charged into the house. There was partying and drinking going on. I recognized Vasil, the leader of the villagers who had forced the Jews to march to Zamolodycze and had turned them over to the Germans. He ran for the window, but we shot him before he could escape. Faiga recognized one of the men who had dragged her father, Zelik, out of the dugout in the woods. He was wearing her father's boots. We shot him also, and Moniek took his boots. I recognized Moishe Yohel's boots on another villager and told him to take them off. We shot him too. The others begged for mercy.

Faiga was enraged, like a wild animal. She knew each of the partygoers by their first names. She ran around her house, breaking everything with her axe and calling out their names as she did so. We were planning to burn down the house, but the people who ran out sounded an alarm, and soon we heard the bells of the church ringing. As we left the house, we saw a mass of villagers coming toward us, and we heard one or two rifle shots. We started shooting back. Chanina fired his flare gun into the air. This lit up the village and scared the villagers, who stopped advancing toward us. Then we retreated into the woods. We were elated that the villagers had seen armed Jews who had come to take revenge. We hoped this would deter them in the future from hunting down and killing Jews in the area.

We walked to the Hola woods. Now there was no problem getting food. We were armed. Out of fear, the villagers would give us food, and if they refused, we took it ourselves.

The six of us stayed in the Hola woods for a while. In order not to be detected, we were careful not to stay in one place for more than a day. Because of the deep snows, we walked backward when crossing a road, so as to camouflage the direction from which we had come.

At one point, we stopped at Polashka's house on the edge of Hola. We wanted to find out whether there were Germans in the vicinity. She was surprised and glad to see us. She had heard of the revenge we had taken at Zamolodycze, and she blessed us and told us that we would survive with God's help. She was a very religious woman. She asked about Manya, and I told her that she had been killed. She cried and said she was sorry that such a nice girl had been lost. She gave us food to eat and told us she could not get over the fact that we were armed. She wished us luck and we left her.

A Short Stay
in the Makoszka Forest

Some nights later, we went for food in the vicinity of the village of Krupiwiec. Such a food-foraging expedition was called a *bombioshka*. The Russian partisans had used that name when they went to ask for food. If the villagers refused our requests for food, then we took it ourselves using the threat of our weapons.

I knocked on the door of a house, and a man with a gun opened it. He looked as though he might be Jewish so I asked: "Amchu?" the Hebrew word for "our people." This was used as a password among Jews. He answered with the same password. We entered the house. There were three men in the house—two Jews and a Russian—all with guns. We learned they had become separated from Fioder's Russian partisan group when they and we had been attacked by the Germans in the Skorodnica forest. They too had come to this house looking for food. The Russian's name was Vashka. A short man, he was an experienced partisan and very friendly. One of the Jews, from Ostrow Lubelski, was named Shainche. The other, from Warsaw, was named Harry. He had come to this area after the war broke out to stay with relatives who had lived near Parczew. We called Harry the "Americanietz," because he had lived in America for ten years. He had come back to Poland to visit his sick mother, just before the German invasion, and had been unable to return to America. We invited them to join our small group, and they welcomed the idea. Now we were nine strong, and all but Faiga were armed.

They told us about Fioder's group, which included many Jews. Anyone who had a gun could join them. Harry felt that, following the German attack in the Skorodnica forest, the group had probably broken up into smaller units and these probably had gone back to the Makoszka forest near Parczew. I suggested that now, since we had guns, we should join them. My reasoning was that they were a larger group, and we would have a better chance for survival with a larger resistance group.

These three men knew the Makoszka forest well, since they had come from there. They told us that in the forest many unarmed Jewish groups were in hiding. According to them, the Makoszka forest was a safer place to stay than the Hola woods because there were more armed partisans there.

In the back of my mind was the thought that, perhaps, Manya might not be dead. Perhaps she was with the Russian partisans. I had not seen her fall, and no one had found her body. I had been told thirdhand that someone thought he had seen her fall from a bullet. But perhaps she had escaped with the Russians and was with the partisans in the Makoszka forest.

The group accepted my suggestion, and we headed for the Makoszka forest. After walking for some time, we noticed that two of our group were not feeling well. Yosel was suffering from frozen toes on one foot, but he had not told us until that point. It happened when he was running from the Germans during the last raid in the Skorodnica forest, when so many in our group had been killed or froze to death. His foot was hurting him, and it was hard for him to keep up with us.

Shainche also did not feel well and looked very pale and drawn. He kept coughing but did not complain. On the first day of our journey, everyone kept up the pace. On the second day, Shainche started feeling worse and could not walk very well. Yosel also could not keep up with us.

Chanina, Yosel's brother, made a crutch for him from a branch he broke off a tree, and that was of some help. But Shainche was hurting badly, and we had to slow down for him. Finally, we had to stop when he fell to the ground and could not get up. I knelt down over him to feel his forehead and could tell he was burning up with fever. I asked him what was hurting him, but he could hardly talk.

We had been walking along the edge of the forest, and we noticed a sled drawn by two horses coming toward us on a nearby road. The farmer noticed us too and started whipping his horses to escape. We yelled at him to stop, and Chanina fired a warning shot. The farmer immediately stopped his sled and started pleading with us not to kill him. He wore a very worn-out coat, and his face was white from the frost. He told us he had not done anything wrong and begged us to let him go. We explained that we needed his sled because we had two men who were sick and unable to walk. We told him to drive us, and we would tell him where to go. He said the horses were very hungry as he did not have any food for them, and they could not go very far. We replied that he had better do what we told him, and we all got onto the sled. He saw he could not resist us, so we started out.

Shainche was burning up and asked for a drink of water. Faiga held some snow to his lips. After several hours it began to dawn. We were nearing the Makoszka forest, but Shainche could not make it. He closed his eyes and died quietly on the sled. We could not bury him, as the ground was frozen as hard as a rock. All we could do was to lay him next to a tree and cover him with snow. His friend Harry said the ritual kaddish prayer. The farmer took off his hat and crossed himself. Harry told us that Shainche had been a very brave partisan.

We rode for another few miles on the sled and then stopped and got off. We told the farmer to go on his way. We were close to our destination. With Harry leading, we entered the Makoszka forest. Faiga now carried Shainche's rifle.

We walked for a few miles in the forest. Harry knew the way to the area where Fioder's group had previously been based. Suddenly, a man pointing a rifle jumped out from behind a tree and ordered us to halt. Harry recognized him immediately. "Bochian!" he hollered. That was his nickname. Most of the Jewish partisans in the woods were known by nicknames, not by their true names. Bochian was very well known in the Makoszka forest. He was a Jew from Parczew. He was middle-aged and bowlegged. All his life he had worked as a baggage handler at the Parczew railroad station. When the Germans tried to empty the Parczew ghetto of Jews by sending them to the Sobibor concentration camp, many escaped to the nearby Makoszka forest, including Bochian and his family. He told us about the raids that the Germans had conducted on the Jews in the Makoszka forest, in which many Jews, including his entire family, had been killed.

After talking with Bochian for a while, we realized the big difference between the situation of Jews in the Hola woods and the situation of those in the Makoszka forest. In the Makoszka forest, under

Fioder's leadership, the escaped Russian prisoners had organized themselves earlier than our group and had weapons. There were many escaped Russian prisoners concentrated in the Makoszka forest, and their presence made the Jews in the forest feel a little safer. Additionally, many of those Jews were also armed.

The Jews there had their share of problems with the Russians, however. The Russians demanded whiskey, they robbed the Jews of money and weapons, and they raped Jewish women. They lived according to the law of the jungle, especially in the beginning before the Jews organized themselves, obtained more weapons, and resisted their lawlessness.

Bochian was a very lively and talkative fellow. He took us to where the Jews were based, which was called a Tabor (camp). There were about two hundred people there, mostly women, children, and elderly men, and they were spread out in small groups. Mostly, they were from Parczew. Some were from local villages such as Kodeniec, Zahajki, Pachole, and Krzywowierzby. Many of them I already knew. I had met them at Manya's family farm when I first came to Hola. I recognized some of the Jewish teenagers from different villages, who used to come to Hola on Saturdays to socialize.

We were a little disappointed when we got there, intending to meet up with Fioder's Russian partisan group. Fiodor's unit was gone. We asked how large a group Fioder had and indicated that we wanted to join it to organize a larger force to fight the Germans. They had pulled out a week before, and no one knew their whereabouts.

The individual camps consisted of small groups. Most of them had dugouts, and some of them had weapons. Some Russians had stayed behind because they had Jewish girlfriends. Early on, before the Jews had organized and armed themselves, many young Jewish women chose to pair off with individual Russian soldiers to avoid being attacked and raped by other Russians. The Jewish woman would then live with her Russian in his dugout. We were told the story of a Russian soldier whose small group, consisting mostly of Jews, had been surrounded by Germans and had exhausted their ammunition. The Germans ordered the group out of their dugouts with their hands up. Realizing the situation was hopeless, the Russian quickly dug a shallow trench into a wall of his dugout, placed his Jewish girlfriend in the trench and covered her with a thin layer of dirt. He then emerged from the dugout and was shot immediately by the Germans. His girlfriend survived undetected.

Despite the difficulties some of the Russians created, the Jews felt safer with them around. This was due to the fact that the Russians had weapons, and the Germans knew that they were armed. The Germans were more cautious in attacking when they knew there would be resistance. When an attack occurred and was met with resistance, the cautious advance of the attackers permitted unarmed people to scatter.

I went around to every small group in the Tabor, holding out a faded, wallet-sized picture of Manya and asking if they had seen her. Some people knew her as "Manya, the pretty blonde girl from Warsaw," but no one could recall seeing her in the Makoszka forest. I had to accept what had first been told to me—that she had been killed on that freezing day when the Germans had attacked us in the Skorodnica forest.

We stayed in the Tabor for about two weeks. Yosel started to feel worse. He slept under trees in the freezing cold, and his frozen toes bothered him more and more. Most of the Jews there knew Yosel and his entire family from before the war. He had been a very popular boy, was good-looking, and was the best dancer at all the Jewish gatherings. He was also very popular with all the girls.

It was February 1943, and the cold weather did not let up. It was difficult for our group to get food, as we were not familiar with the area or the local villagers. We did not want to take the chance of going to an unfamiliar farmer who might inform the Germans about us. The other groups had food because they went back to the nearby villages they had come from. However, they were unwilling to share with us, and we were starving.

The only logical thing for us to do was to return to our area in the Skorodnica forest, where we knew the local villagers and could successfully forage for food. Our problem was Yosel. He definitely could not walk far, and the trip back would take two days and two nights. A family that was a distant relation of the Barbanels, and who had their own dugout, agreed to take Yosel in with them. They assured us that whatever happened to them would happen to him. His brothers left them some money so they might buy some food from a friendly farmer.

We felt very bad about leaving Yosel there. We knew what could happen in the event of a German attack, although their dugout was in a separate area and very well camouflaged. We hoped that, when the cold let up in the spring, we could return and take him back to our area.

At nighttime we started the long journey back to the Skorodnica forest. The night was very cold, and we had to stop to make a small fire in order to keep from freezing to death. Moniek, who was the most experienced in keeping a fire going, looked black from smoke on both his face and clothes. Only the whites of his eyes could be seen. He was an expert at searching for dry firewood, which was a problem to find as everything on the ground was wet from the snow. The wet wood would take longer to ignite, and then it made a great deal of smoke, which we were afraid someone might see. Moniek used to stand up and rub his back against a tree trunk to scratch himself, cursing the lice with very colorful expressions. It was one of the few things that made us laugh. With his ragged clothes and blackened face, he looked like a circus clown.

18

Our First Attack Against the Germans

little boy had hung around our group in the Makoszka forest where we left Yosel. He was an orphan, about ten years of age, named Itzik. He took a special liking to me, perhaps because I brought him food and warm clothes obtained during our *bombioshkas*. When we decided to return to the Skorodnica forest, he pleaded with us to take him along. Faiga took pity on him, as he had no relatives. Like Faiga, his entire family had been wiped out. He looked into my eyes and said, "Uncle Hershel, I won't be a bother to you. I will get a gun too, and I can run very fast." He reminded me very much of my little brother Motel. Motel was about the same age when we had parted in Siedlce. He and Moishe had gone home to Gorzkow, and I had continued on to Hola.

We decided to take Itzik with us. Eight of us headed back to the Skorodnica forest: Harry, Vashka, Moniek, Faiga, Symcha, Chanina, Itzik, and myself. While walking back, we saw an isolated house and decided to stop there to ask for food. It was late at night. We knocked on the door and announced that we were partisans. A man opened the door and saw our group of armed men. He gave us two loaves of bread and some sausages, and was friendly toward us. We asked him if there were Germans in the area. He said they were in the nearby village of Sojka but toward evening they had left for Parczew. We told him not to mention to anyone that we had been there, and he promised he would not.

We walked single file in the woods. Chanina, who was more familiar with this area, led the way, and Itzik kept up with us. After two nights of walking, we arrived at the Skorodnica forest.

Once back in the Skorodnica forest, we tried to attract as little attention as possible. We did not stay longer than one day in any one place. When we left a spot, we erased any signs that we had been there, so as not to be followed. We tried to forage for food in distant villages rather than local ones. We did not rob the farmers, but asked for food and tried to win their sympathy. We also sought to establish a network of trustworthy local villagers, who would inform us of the whereabouts of the Germans. We hoped we might survive until the cold weather eased up, and then locate a partisan group to join. We were only seven people and a little boy and hoped not to be spotted by the Germans or anyone else. We also hoped that, once it got warmer, the people who had left our group earlier in the winter for the Wlodawa ghetto would rejoin us.

One evening, we were in the woods not far from Hola when we met six armed Russian partisans. They were camping and making a fire to warm themselves. It was freezing weather, so when we saw their fire and heard them speaking in Russian we came closer. They heard us approaching and aimed their rifles in our direction. They asked us who we were, and we answered: "Friendly Jewish partisans." Vashka, the Russian who had come with us, was very happy to meet some fellow Russians, and we were glad too. I suggested that we join together into one group. That would make us thirteen adults and a little boy. They agreed.

The Russians were very tall people, all from the same area in the Caucasus Mountains. Their leader's name was Sergei. They told us they had been taken prisoner by the Germans near Kiev at the outset of the German invasion of Russia. They had escaped from a prison camp near Chelm, where thousands of Russian prisoners had died from starvation and cold. The six of them were part of a large group of prisoners that escaped, but they had gotten separated from their group in the Parczew area when they had been attacked by Germans.

While we were in the forest near Hola, we stopped at Polashka's farm. I went in with a few of the others to ask whether there were any Germans in the area and also to get some food. She told us she had heard there were ten Germans in Hola that were staying at Timofi's house, in the center of the village. She gave us some food and warned us to be careful.

Timofi was one of the ringleaders of the group which had hunted down the Jews who had left Hola with me. These were the Jews who had gone into the woods with me in the fall of 1942, disobeying the German order to assemble in Hola for transport to the Wlodawa ghetto. Timofi's group of villagers had taken the captured Jews to Sosnowica, where they were shot. Manya, Moniek, and I had survived only because we had gone to Stephan's house for food the previous night. Polashka had told me that Timofi was one of two leaders of the villagers who had organized this roundup. The other was named Vasil (who was not the same Vasil we had killed in our retaliatory raid on Faiga's house in Zamolodycze).

From Polashka's house, we returned to our group in the woods and told them about the ten Germans in Hola. The whole group became excited. Symcha, who was always ready to go into action, was the first one to suggest that we attack the Germans, and the Russians were of the same opinion. I wanted to make sure that there were not more of them in the village. Not far from Polashka's farm was the old farmer Kornila, who lived across the road from what had been Manya's family's farm. He had been a very good friend of Manya's family and had given Manya and me a ride in his wagon to Hola in 1939 for the final leg of our trip from Warsaw. In fact, the wedding of Manya's Aunt Ziesel to Moishe Yohel in 1940 was held in Kornila's house. He had offered his house because he had one very large room. Many times during that winter, when I had gone to his house to ask for food, he had shown his hospitality.

I decided to go to Kornila and ask him about the Germans in the village, in order to compare the information he had with that of Polashka's. Kornila was surprised to see me. He told me he had heard in the village that there were ten Germans in Timofi's house. He said they often came into the village to drink and have parties, and then they would return to their garrison in Sosnowica, only a few miles away. He suggested that, for our own safety, we leave the area and not make any trouble.

We decided to attack the ten Germans. We went back to the woods and walked along the edge of the forest until we neared Timofi's house. There were a few hundred yards of open field between the woods and the back of his house. From a distance we could hear singing and the playing of a harmonica. Each of our Russians had grenades, in addition to their rifles. Our group had three grenades, one each for Symcha, Chanina, and me. Our plan was to get close to the house, throw a grenade in, and then shoot the Germans as they ran out. Although it was dark, we noticed as we got closer that there was an armed guard walking around the house. In order for our plan to work, we had to eliminate the guard. To distract him, we sent

Faiga, who looked like a Ukrainian farm girl, to talk with him. We hoped he was not German, because Faiga could not speak German, but she could converse with a Ukrainian in his own language. Fortunately he was Ukrainian, and she started a conversation with him. While he was distracted, Moniek slipped up behind the guard, grabbed him by the throat, and silently choked him to death. Our group was right behind Moniek. Symcha reached the house first and threw in a grenade. Sergei threw in the second one. They made two tremendous explosions. The Germans started jumping from the windows and running out the door just as we had planned. We started firing our rifles, trying to pick them off as they sought to escape. They did not have a chance to get their weapons.

Little Itzik started running toward the house, but I held him back because there might still be some Germans hiding in the house. I jumped to the side of the house and tossed in another grenade. At that moment, we heard the firing of rifles and machine guns from the other end of the village. This weapons fire came from other Germans in the village who were holding a party in a different house. The house we attacked was completely devastated. I spotted one German running in the dark, and I shot him. Little Itzik took his rifle. The shooting from the other end of the village began to get closer. We decided to pull back into the woods and go far away from Hola. We knew the Germans would conduct an intensive search of the area. Itzik's German rifle was too heavy for him to carry, so we took turns carrying it for him. He was very proud of it.

We later found out from friendly villagers that we had killed six Germans and several villagers, including Timofi. I believe that Polashka and Kornila had not lied to us. It was likely that the other group of Germans had arrived in the village shortly before our attack.

This was the first offensive action we had taken against the Germans as a group, and the villagers knew that "Hershku" from Hola, the boy who had worked for Stephan, was among the partisan group. It was a tremendous uplift to our morale to be able to hit back at the Germans. It was also important to us to show the villagers that Jews, once armed, would strike back. We pulled out toward the Wyryki area, deeper into the woods and closer to Wlodawa.

19

March 1943

After a few weeks, our six Russians decided to travel east to the other side of the Bug River, to join up with other Russian partisans. We did not go with them. We decided to wait for the return of the people who had left our group for the Wlodawa ghetto earlier in the winter. We hoped that Pakula could make contact with them in the spring.

It was early March 1943, and the weather was still very cold. One day a terrible snowstorm hit. It was impossible to start a fire, and the cold was unbearable. We decided to make a tunnel in the snow. We put branches on the ground and packed snow on top of them to make a roof. Then we dug a tunnel under the branches. We left an opening on one side for air, and all eight of us lay in that tunnel. We had learned this practice from the Russians we had seen the previous year. It was very warm underneath the snow. Itzik could not understand how it could be warm with all the snow around us. We stayed in this tunnel for two days, and it snowed the entire time. The surface of the earth was covered with snow. As long as no one left this hiding place and made footprints in the snow, it was impossible to tell that anyone was underneath the snow. This was the safest two days, without fear, that we experienced during that time. The only bad thing about our bodies being warm was that the lice became more active. Moniek was especially bothered by the lice, and he kept turning and cursing and waking us.

Finally, we decided we had to leave the safety of our tunnel to find some food. I suggested that we go to Stephan's house. It was a very difficult journey, with the snow up to our waists. It took a long time and a lot of energy to reach Lubien. We all went together and knocked on Stephan's window as before, and as before there was no answer. I announced that it was Hershku, and that I was with a group of armed partisans. Then the light came on and he opened the door for us. He tried to appear friendly. He saw that all of us were armed, and he told us he had heard about the partisans' attack on the Germans in Hola. He also told us he had known that I was one of them. I guess he felt he had better be friendly. He asked how we could stand the cold weather in the woods, and said that he was glad I was alive. His wife and mother-in-law crossed themselves and asked us if we were hungry. We said we were, and Stephan told Marfa to bring us some food and a drink of bimber (homemade vodka).

I could see that Stephan was scared of us. I asked him to bring some straw into the house so that we could sleep for a few hours in a warm place. I also told him we were part of a large group of partisans and that the rest of the group was in the forest. I went outside to stand guard, and the others lay down on the floor. Stephan came outside with me. He gave me an old heavy coat to stay warm and kept me company. He reminded me he had told me not to go to the ghetto, and said I would be dead by now had I gone. I told him that I remembered his advice. I also said I remembered that when I had come to him earlier in the winter for food he warned me he would kill me if I came back again, and that he had mobilized the villagers with his alarm to be on the lookout for me. He explained that he had been afraid because the Germans had killed many villagers for helping Jews and Russians. He then put his hand in his pocket and pulled out a little box containing a woman's watch. He asked me if I remembered him showing me this watch when I had worked for him. I did remember it. He had said previously that he had bought the watch in Wlodawa. Now he told me that he had been given the watch in exchange for a loaf of bread from a Jew in Wlodawa. He handed it to me and said he wanted me to keep it because it had belonged to a Jew. But I felt he was trying to bribe me and refused to take it. I told him that the Jew he had gotten the watch from needed the loaf of bread more than he needed the watch, and I did not need it either.

I told Stephan I wanted him to know that we were fighting the Germans, and that they were the enemy of both the Jews and Poles. The difference was that the Germans were killing the Jews, while they wanted to keep the Polish and Ukrainian people alive as slaves to feed them and work for them. Eventually the Germans would probably kill the Poles and Ukrainians also. I asked him if he had heard about the beating that the Germans were receiving on the Russian front. "Yes, Hershku. We are praying for the Russians to win," he said. "We are doing more than praying," I said. "We are helping the Russians to win."

After a while I went into the house with Stephan and told Vashka to relieve me so I could get a little sleep. I warned him to keep an eye on Stephan so that he would not have a chance to alert the village that we were in his house. I napped for a while. Stephan did not go to sleep. Before dawn, we prepared to leave, and Stephan gave us some more food to take with us. Faiga got a warm coat to replace the rag she had been wearing, and we took off for the woods in the direction of Maryanka.

The weather started to turn a little warmer. It was the end of March 1943. When we got deep into the woods we sat down. I told Moniek to make a fire, take off his clothes, and hold them over the flames to delouse them. We all did the same. This did not help for long because this method could not get rid of them completely. If the clothes were rid of the lice, they were still in our hair or in our skin. We very seldom had a chance to wash or change clothes, so we had to live with the lice.

Later in the year, we came to the house of an elderly villager for food. The old man noticed that Moniek was scratching himself. He knew what was bothering him. To get rid of the lice, he described for us a formula of mercury mixed with an egg white. A strip of heavy felt was dipped into this mixture to absorb it and then left to dry. The felt strip was worn diagonally across one's chest, and after a while it was switched to run in the opposite diagonal direction. This formula took care of the lice not just temporarily, like the flame of the fire, but also eliminated the lice eggs so that they did not hatch. This was a tremendous relief for us. This old man told us he had learned about this formula in the First World War when he was a soldier in the Russian army. They had had the same problem then. He said they would have to lay in the trenches and be unable to change their clothing for weeks. A pharmacist had told them to use this formula, and it had helped them. Now he was passing it on to us. We told others about it, and eventually all the partisan groups in the woods used it. At first we had a problem getting mercury, but our good friend Pakula obtained it for us from a pharmacy in Wlodawa.

Although the weather was a little milder in March and the biting frost was not eating into our bones as it had in January and February, we still needed a fire at night to cook and warm ourselves. The food we ate was always obtained from a village that was not in the vicinity of where we were camping. We never went for food to the villages close to our base, so as not to lose the sympathies of the local people. Moniek would steal chickens, which Faiga would cook for us. Little Itzik liked chicken soup very much.

Itzik told us stories about his home. On Friday nights, his father would come back from synagogue, the whole family would sit around the table, and his mother would serve them chicken soup. The smell of the soup in the forest reminded him of Friday night dinners with his family. His mother, father, brothers, and sisters were all dead now. The entire family had been taken by train, together with the other Jews in his village, to the death camp at Sobibor. His mother had pushed him through a small opening they had made by breaking off a board from the moving cattle car. The place Itzik had landed was not far from Parczew. A Jewish family there took him in. The family had three children close to his age. Two weeks later, the Germans ordered all Jews from Parczew to be "resettled to the east." The Parczew Jews knew that resettlement to the east meant transport to a death camp. Many of the Parczew Jews, including the family that took in Itzik, escaped to the Makoszka forest a few miles from the town. One morning, however, many of these Jews were rounded up and killed by the Germans, including the family that had adopted Itzik. At this round-up, the Germans had encountered severe resistance from armed Russian and Jewish partisans, and many Germans were killed. Itzik had survived after losing his own family and his adopted family. Later, he found us when we came to the Makoszka forest, and he adopted us as his third family.

After Itzik had been with us for a while, we noticed he was limping. He had an infected big toe on his right foot. His foot started swelling, and he could not keep up with us. He was in a great deal of pain. I talked this problem over with Symcha and Chanina, and we decided the only way to save him was to find a permanent hiding place where he could recuperate.

I suggested we leave him with Vasil of Hola who, we were told, together with Timofi had led the roundup of Jews in the Hola forest in 1942. This was the first group of Jews who had left Hola and had gone with me to the forest instead of to the Wlodawa ghetto. (He was not the same Vasil who had led the group of villagers who had rounded up the Jews from the dugout outside Zamolodycze and marched them to Zamolodycze to be shot. We had killed him in our retaliatory raid on Faiga's house in Zamolodycze.)

We went to Vasil's house late at night. Chanina and I went in and told him that we were Jewish partisans. By this time, the villagers were afraid of our group of Jewish partisans because we had taken revenge in several villages against people who had caught Jews in the woods and handed them over to the Germans. Now when Jewish partisans approached at night, the villagers no longer sounded the alarm.

I told Vasil we knew that he was one of the leaders of the group which had rounded up the Jews in the Hola woods the year before and had taken them to Sosnowica to be shot by the Germans. But, I said, we had not come to take revenge. I informed him we had a young boy who was sick. We wanted Vasil to hide the boy in his barn until he got better. We told him that Itzik had an infected toe and a swollen foot, and that he should try to get some medicine to help him. We promised to come for Itzik once he got better.

Vasil swore he had not participated in the raid on the Jews outside Hola, but we said we had reliable information to the contrary. We also told him that he had better do what we asked, and that we would check up on him from time to time. If anything happened to Itzik, we warned, he and his wife would pay for it.

I felt that Vasil, given his leading role in hunting Jews in the Hola woods, would be the least suspected of any villager to be harboring a Jew. Yet he would do what we told him because he was afraid of us. Itzik was unhappy and scared to be left with this farmer, but we had no choice. We were afraid that gangrene would set in.

Vasil lived at the edge of the woods, and we assured him that no one had seen us come to his farm. Otherwise, he would have had to report to the Germans that the "bandits" (that is what the Germans called us) had been there. Then they would probably come for an investigation and perhaps a search. Vasil gave us some food, then took Itzik to the barn and promised to make him comfortable. We felt this was the safest place for Itzik, as only Vasil and his wife lived on the farm.

20

Rescuing Jews from the Wlodawa Ghetto

Symcha remarked that, now that it was getting a little warmer, the people who had left us early in the winter to go to the Wlodawa ghetto would come back to the woods if they were still alive. Among the people who had left for the ghetto were Chaim Weisman and his daughter Bebale, and Symcha and Chanina's brother Chaim and their wounded sister Esther. The understanding between us when they left was that, when they returned in the spring, the best way to find us would be through Pakula.

We started out for Maryanka to ask Pakula whether any of that group had shown up. Symcha and Chanina were very anxious to get their brother and sister back to the forest. Pakula had no news for us, but he said he was going to market day in Wlodawa the following week. Market day was on Thursdays, and villagers from the surrounding areas came to do their purchasing and selling. Pakula offered to smuggle one of us into Wlodawa, hidden under a pile of straw in the back of his wagon. He would then let the person off at the end of town, where the Jewish ghetto was located.

We spent the next week in the forest around Maryanka. Then Chanina decided to take Pakula up on his offer. We came to Pakula to tell him that and, when we walked into his house, standing there was Chaim Barbanel along with another man who had come with him from the ghetto. It was such a surprise that Symcha started crying, and everyone began embracing one another. However, our joy was tempered by the news that Symcha's sister Esther, who had been wounded in a German raid during the previous winter, had died in the Wlodawa ghetto.

Chaim was the oldest and the tallest of the four brothers and three sisters in the Barbanel family. He did not look the same as he had when he had left for the ghetto earlier in the winter. He was very pale and extremely thin. We were very happy to have him with us. Now Pakula did not have to risk his life by smuggling Chanina into the ghetto to look for Chaim.

Pakula, in whose house our joyful reunion with Chaim took place, was like a father to us. He was very patriotic, and he hated the Germans just as much as we did. He helped us in any way he could, but we were careful not to endanger him. We came to his house only when absolutely necessary. Chaim got back his good Polish rifle that Pakula had held for him when Chaim left for the ghetto. Pakula gave us all some food and brought in some straw so that we could lie down on his floor for a few hours' sleep. Before dawn, we headed back into the forest again.

Once in the forest, Chaim described to us the life of the Jews in the Wlodawa ghetto. The people were dying of starvation. The Germans often selected Jews to be sent to the death camp at Sobibor, a few miles south of Wlodawa. Many people in the ghetto hid, like moles, in the ground. They dug hiding places under toilets, ovens, in closets, and other places, and camouflaged these spots so that the Germans would not discover them.

Despite their desperate situation, life still went on in the ghetto. They prayed together, they traded among themselves, they smuggled people out to the surrounding city of Wlodawa to buy food, and they even managed to conduct weddings. Chaim told us that some of the more religious people had even baked matzohs for the upcoming Passover holiday.

Previously while traveling through the Maryanka woods, we had come upon two Jewish men in the forest. One had a gun. We invited them to join our group, and they accepted. They told us they had just come all the way from the Makoszka forest, nearly forty miles away. They had escaped from a German raid there. At the time of the raid, there were no armed Russian partisans in that area, and the Germans attacked all the hiding places and dugouts where the Jews were, meeting little resistance. We asked them about Yosel and the people he stayed with, but they had not heard of them. However, they said that the Germans had thrown grenades into all the dugouts, and we felt that Yosel must have perished then. Now, with Esther and Yosel gone, of the seven Barbanel siblings there were only three brothers left—Chaim, Chanina, and Symcha.

The man who had come with Chaim from the Wlodawa ghetto was a little older than the rest of us. His name was Moishe Lichtenstein, and we learned that he had served in the Polish military before the war. He was better dressed and looked healthier than Chaim. Chaim told us that this man was organizing the young people in the ghetto to prepare for an escape into the woods. The Germans were aware of Moishe Lichtenstein's activities and were looking for him, and they had even posted a reward for his capture.

Chaim also told us about the tales of bravery that were circulating in the ghetto about our Jewish partisan group in the woods. They knew every one of us by name, and they hoped we would someday come to rescue them from the ghetto. They knew that if we did not, they would eventually all die in Sobibor. After Chaim finished briefing us about the situation of the Jews in the Wlodawa ghetto, we all decided to try to get as many Jews as possible out of the ghetto and into the woods. Rescuing Jews who had been earmarked for death would be the best way to fight back against the Germans.

Because of his military training, Moishe liked to give us orders. For those of us who were proven partisans against the Germans and had suffered through life in the forest, this was irritating. He continued to give us orders in the style he had acquired in the Polish army, but we ignored him.

Moishe told us about his preparations in the ghetto. He had organized about fifty young men who were ready to come out to the forest. He had bought warm coats and boots for them. Donations had been collected from the wealthier Jews in the ghetto for this purpose. He had also bought and smuggled into the ghetto several weapons, which had cost him a great deal of money in Wlodawa.

The day after we had come upon Chaim and Moishe, we decided that Moishe should go back to the ghetto immediately. Since he knew the terrain of the ghetto, we hoped he could quietly bring out as many Jews as possible. We planned to go back to the ghetto many times, but did not want to alert the Germans to the fact that Jews were escaping. We were also concerned that there might be Jews who were informers, and we had to be careful of them. The next night, the entire group went with Moishe toward Wlodawa and camped in the nearby woods. Moishe went into the city and entered the ghetto.

While we waited in the woods, Chaim mentioned that this night was the first seder of Passover. Faiga jumped up and exclaimed: "Oh, it's the first seder night, and we didn't even know!" "And what would happen if we would have known?" challenged Moniek. "Would you have stopped to prepare matzohs and chicken soup for the seder?" I told them we should not delay our mission because of Passover. Just the opposite. Helping the Jews escape from the Wlodawa ghetto was like taking the Jews out of Egypt. Everyone agreed, even Vashka the Russian, and he did not know anything about the exodus of the Jews from Egypt.

We waited for Moishe at the appointed place, in a wooded area not far from a road. There was a full moon—a Passover night moon. No one talked—each one of us was deep in his own thoughts.

I remembered Passover at home as a child. I recalled how clean and how nicely painted the house was. The table with the special tablecloth was set with different dishes used only for Passover, with a cup of wine for each child and an extra cup for the prophet Elijah. There was matzoh, fish, and chicken soup. It smelled so good. I got to ask the traditional four questions during the seder service, and we could hardly wait for father to finish reciting from the Passover Haggadah so we could start eating. We stood in this cold naked forest, not like hardened partisans who were resisting the German forces, but like little children dreaming about a holiday we knew would never again be the same.

We waited for more than three hours. Moniek, who kept watch at the edge of the woods close to the road, finally heard people approaching. He called out in Russian: "Stop! Who's there?" The rest of us raised our weapons in frozen silence. "It's Moishe Lichtenstein," came a whispered voice. He had brought out fifteen people.

Moishe told us that, while some of the Jews were in their ghetto hideouts reading the Passover Haggadah, he and his group had climbed over fences, run through alleyways, and finally found their way to us. They were all young, in their early twenties. They told us that the concept of Jewish partisans had only been a fantasy to them, and here they were looking at us, heroes with guns and grenades— real soldiers. Of course, we did not wear uniforms like soldiers, as Moishe Lichtenstein would have liked. Moishe was dressed like an officer, in a long military coat with a wide belt around his waist and a revolver at his side.

We were very happy to see them all. Chanina recognized Yankale, whom he had known before the war. Chanina used to come to Yankale's father's general store in Wlodawa for supplies. They were so happy to see each other that they embraced. Another man in Moishe's group was Moishe Peshalis (that means that his mother's name was Pesha), a very tall man with a round face and ruddy complexion, who had been a butcher before the war. He was very strong and athletic, and respected for his great strength. It was said that before the war the non-Jews had given him a wide berth. They often beat up Jews, but never started up with Moishe Peshalis. Shmuel Stul was also in Moishe's group, a young man who was so thin he looked like a skeleton. Moishe Lichtenstein, their leader, had two lieutenants, Motel Rosenberg, a tall lean man who had also been a soldier in the Polish army, and Chaim Tencer. The group looked well dressed. They were organized and had been well prepared to leave the ghetto. The only ones with weapons were the three leaders —Moishe Lichtenstein, Motel Rosenberg, and Chaim Tencer.

We all started out together toward the Skorodnica forest near Maryanka. On the way, we stopped overnight at Wyryki, a large village. We knew a friendly farmer there, a relative of Pakula. His farm was close to the woods, and we went to him to find out if there were Germans in the village. He told us there were none. Since he was a poor farmer according to Pakula, we did not take any food from him.

We went into several other nearby farmers' homes to ask for food. Now that we were a larger group, we needed more provisions. The group from the ghetto stayed outside while we went into the houses. The villagers had become used to our requests. Most of the time they were cooperative, but if they said they did not have any food or if they refused to open their doors, we threatened them and helped ourselves to any food we found in the house. This was a new experience to the ghetto group, and they started to learn how we existed in the woods.

We left the village and continued toward the Maryanka woods, which formed a part of the larger Skorodnica forest. We set up a base in the woods not far from Maryanka, a territory with which our group was familiar. We made a fire in the evenings and baked potatoes. Moniek sometimes brought some chickens, which he was good at catching in the dark, and Faiga, the only woman in the group, would cook them. She would cook some kasha, potatoes, or whatever we had. There was no shortage of meat, but since bread was always scarce, we substituted for it with potatoes.

I could sense the uneasiness and fear of the ghetto people by the way they looked around them. All they could see were the trees in the darkness and the stars in the sky, and they could hear the far-off sounds in the forest of wild animals. I tried to lift their spirits a little by explaining that the woods were very large and that here they could feel freer than in the ghetto. In case of a German raid, one could always escape farther into the woods. Besides, we had some weapons, and we would get more to allow them to defend themselves. I reminded them that spring and warmer weather were approaching, and that it would not be like the previous winter with freezing cold and deep snows. I also explained that, since a few of us had gotten weapons, we could now go into the villages for food and not be afraid that they would hand us over to the Germans. The farmers respected and feared us now. Finally, I told them that we had brought them from the ghetto on the night of the first seder, when we traditionally read from the Haggadah: "Slaves you were in the land of Pharaoh. From now on you are free." They understood my message in citing this passage and listened intently to my words of encouragement.

We decided that before we took more Jews out of the Wlodawa ghetto, we should try to obtain weapons for them. This way they would be armed and could defend themselves and be an asset to us.

In the meantime, we went to Pakula for information. He told us about a German newspaper he had seen when he was last in Wlodawa, and which he had brought home with him. He showed it to us, as he could not read German. I could make out from the paper that the war was not going well for the Germans. I had to read and reread it several times to understand that the paper was praising the heroism of the German soldiers at Stalingrad. The paper said that for strategic reasons the German army had had to regroup, but the Führer promised to renew the offensive and to take the city.

The villagers also sensed that the war was not going well for the Germans. The Germans no longer displayed maps in the village squares showing the advance of their army into Russia, as they had done at the beginning of the Russian invasion. The villagers were now not certain that the Germans were going to win the war. Some villagers started sympathizing more openly with those of us who were fighting the Germans. They pointed out to us collaborators who had caught Jews and handed them over to Germans and farmers who had hidden weapons.

We were informed that two farmers in the village of Mosciska had weapons buried in the ground. All of us who were armed, consisting of our original group along with Moishe Lichtenstein, Motel Rosenberg, and Chaim Tencer, prepared to leave on an expedition to Mosciska. Moishe the butcher also came with us. Although he did not have a gun, he was big enough to scare you without one.

We left at midnight to find the first farmer. When we located him, we brought him out to his barn. We told him we knew he had hidden weapons, and we wanted them. We said we were fighting the Germans for his country and his freedom, so he should cooperate with us. He denied that he had any guns, but we knew he was lying. Moishe the butcher grabbed him and with one punch knocked him to the ground. He continued to deny he had any guns. Then Moniek took a stick, told the farmer to pull down his pants, and started giving him lashes on his behind. After that the farmer decided to cooperate. He took us to the back of the barn and dug up a wooden box containing six new Polish rifles and several hundred bullets. That was a very fortunate find for us. We took off quietly from the area and returned to our base by daylight, after having walked the entire night.

A few days later, the same group set out to find the second Mosciska farmer who was hiding weapons. Motel Rosenberg wore a long army coat with a wide belt and revolver at his side, impressively uniformed just like Moishe Lichtenstein. We also took Yankale, who looked very, very skinny but was like a demon when he got angry. We arrived at the second farmer's house in Mosciska after dark. He also denied having any weapons. Yankale became enraged and threatened to kill the farmer on the spot if he refused to cooperate. Afraid for his life, the farmer admitted he had been lying. He had only one rifle hidden in the barn, which he gave us.

Another time we got lucky. We went to a farmer in the village of Maryanka. Motel Rosenberg was with us. He looked very impressive in his long military coat with his revolver at his side. The farmer kept staring at him. I took the farmer aside and whispered to him that this tall man had just flown from Russia and had been dropped in the area by parachute. Motel said we had to have weapons to beat the Germans and that we knew the farmer had a rifle. The farmer called us outside and without further persuasion handed Motel a rifle from the barn. We thanked him, and before we left he gave us a bottle of bimber and a few loaves of bread. This was the easiest time we ever had getting a gun.

A week or two after Moishe's group joined us, and having obtained more weapons, we decided to return to the Wlodawa ghetto. The entire group walked through the night, covering about fifteen miles. When we approached Wlodawa, we stopped in a wooded area near a road. Moishe Lichtenstein and a few other ghetto people, along with Chaim Barbanel, went ahead to try to enter the ghetto undetected, while the rest of us waited for them.

We knew that a lot of the ghetto people wanted to come out to the woods. Moishe Lichtenstein tried to dictate whom to take and whom to leave behind. He chose only his friends and young people. But the people he favored had parents, brothers, sisters, uncles, and aunts in the ghetto, and they too wanted to come out. This had created many arguments in the ghetto that spring. After several hours, he came out with about twenty people.

A few days later, our original group, the Maryanka group (which we had called ourselves because most of our group had come from Maryanka), together with some of the men we had previously taken out of the ghetto, went to rescue more people without Moishe Lichtenstein. Twelve of us entered the ghetto through back alleys. We told anyone who wanted to come with us that they would be welcome. We did not limit our invitation to young men of fighting age. Those who chose to come were mostly people who had relatives with us in the woods. In total, we took about twenty-five people of all ages. We undertook this third trip because we felt that the Wlodawa ghetto would soon be liquidated and its occupants sent to Sobibor. All the ghettos from the neighboring towns, such as Lubartow, Parczew, and Leczna, had already been liquidated much earlier. Only the Wlodawa ghetto still existed. We told this third group that we could not guarantee their safety in the woods. However, in the woods they always had a chance to escape and defend themselves once we obtained weapons for them. In the ghetto they were like mice in a trap.

Shortly after this third trip to the Wlodawa ghetto, Moishe and his men went in one last time and took out more Jews. In all our expeditions into the ghetto, we took out more than one hundred people. Among those were Motel Barbanel (uncle of the Barbanel brothers) and his wife Chanche and their little girl, Chaim Weisman and his little daughter Bebale, Vigdor from Skorodnica, David "the tall one" from Sosnowica, and his sister and brother-in-law Moishe Shivak. In May 1943, a week after our last expedition, the ghetto was liquidated. The Germans surrounded it and took some of the people to the nearby Adampol labor camp. The rest were either killed by the Germans right on the spot or taken to the Sobibor concentration camp.

Our group now numbered about 120 people, and all we had among us was about twenty rifles, several revolvers, and a few hand grenades. With that amount of weaponry, we considered ourselves a significant force against the Germans, but we needed more weapons for the rest of the group. We felt we were strong enough to ambush a small German convoy in order to obtain those weapons.Many German convoys passed on the main road running from Lublin through Parczew to Wlodawa. Our Maryanka group proposed to Moishe that we ambush one of these convoys.

About twenty of us, all armed, walked to a spot on the main road.

near Parczew, about thirty miles from our base. We hid in the woods at the edge of the road for hours. The Maryanka group stayed together, with Moishe Lichtenstein and his men in a group beside us. We lay flat on the ground, motionless, and watched the road. Moishe Lichtenstein was to give us the signal to attack, and we were to keep our heads down until then. A few convoys passed by, but they were too large for us to take on.

Late in the afternoon, we spotted a military jeep approaching at high speed, followed by a truck carrying German soldiers. We were very tense and eager to attack, but Moishe held off giving the signal. Finally, when the jeep was right in front of us, he signaled to us and we opened fire.

Symcha threw a grenade on the jeep, and Vashka threw another one under the truck. The vehicles' occupants tried to run, but in a few minutes eight Germans lay dead on the road. One escaped into the woods. There was a German girl riding in the jeep with an officer who was killed. She jumped out and was captured. Moishe the butcher captured a tall German soldier with a long, giraffe-like neck. He grabbed the German soldier by his hair and growled: "This one's mine." The German was crying and begging for mercy, but all we could see in our minds were the Jewish women and children whom the Germans had killed, crying and begging for mercy. Moishe took his German and Moniek took the girl into the woods and shot them. This was the first time that the ghetto Jews who were with us saw dead Germans. Until that point, all they had seen were dead Jews in the ghetto.

We obtained nine rifles and four pistols, along with several grenades and a lot of ammunition, from this attack. We knew we had to get out of the area quickly. Later we learned that, in response to our ambush, the Germans had ordered that all roads in the area be cleared of nearby trees. For five hundred feet on either side of the road, all trees were chopped down so that the area would be less dangerous for convoys.

A big celebration took place when we returned to our base in the Skorodnica forest and told those who had remained behind about our success. The news of the ambush also spread quickly to the surrounding villages. We felt we had to move out of the area because we expected a German reprisal. The entire group now had a substantial amount of weapons and ammunition, and everyone felt a little more secure. We walked in the direction of Hola.

From villagers we obtained news of the war, which was not going well for the Germans, and we were happy to hear that. We also learned about the Warsaw ghetto uprising, which had begun on Passover and lasted several weeks. The Germans had to use artillery and tanks before they wiped out the few remaining Warsaw Jews and burned the entire ghetto. Many Germans were killed in putting down the uprising.

The weather was getting warmer as the spring of 1943 blossomed around us. The trees in the woods were filled with new foliage, and it was easier to hide from the enemy. We felt a little more hopeful, although we still felt like animals in the woods, surrounded by people who wanted to kill us all. But our morale was much better now than it had been during the winter months, when the weather was murderously cold and we lay in the woods with few weapons and little food, hunted by both the Germans and the villagers. Many of our close friends had been shot before our eyes, and many had frozen to death during the terrible winter months.

I tried to convey my more optimistic thoughts to our group, and especially to the newcomers from the Wlodawa ghetto. Many of them had left friends and relatives behind in Wlodawa, and when the ghetto was liquidated they had probably been sent to the Sobibor concentration camp. I wanted to make them realize that they were fortunate to be free in the woods, instead of being confined in a concentration camp.

21

We Join Chiel Grynszpan's Partisans

In the course of our wanderings in the woods we stopped in the Hola area many times. When we did, we always made it a point to visit Vasil's house to check up on Itzik and see how he was progressing. Itzik had a good hiding place in the barn. Vasil fed him well and obtained all kinds of medicines for Itzik's frozen toes. He was slowly improving. Often, when it was very cold, Vasil took Itzik into his house to sleep, where it was warmer.

Whenever we stopped to check on him, Itzik implored me to take him with us. He said he had a rifle and wanted to be a partisan and kill Germans. However, we felt he should remain there until his foot was completely healed and the weather was warmer.

When we returned from the area of the convoy ambush, we stopped at Hola and went to see Polashka first to find out what was going on in the area. Polashka told us the bad news. A large number of Germans had come into the vicinity a few weeks previously, looking for partisans and Jews. They searched the woods, the farmers' homes, and all the buildings in Hola, Zamolodycze, and other nearby villages. They went from farm to farm, and when they came to Vasil's house where Itzik was hiding, Vasil had become very nervous and frightened. When the Germans went to search his barn, Vasil ran after them screaming that there was no one in the barn. Then he stood in front of the barn door, as if to block them. One of the Germans shot him where he stood. The Germans searched the barn but found no one. They noticed that a board from the back wall of the barn had been broken loose, and they found foot marks in the wet ground behind the barn leading to the nearby woods. They searched the woods but could not find anyone. We did not know what had happened to Itzik.

Food continued to be a big problem. We now had over one hundred people to feed but could not obtain provisions for so many people from the nearby area villagers. I and several others from our group left the Hola area and proceeded to the Karolin settlements on a food-foraging expedition. This was in the Maryanka area. Each settlement had only a few farms, not enough to be called a village, and they were scattered a few miles apart. It was a very dark night. We intended, as always, to knock on the door and ask for food. It did not occur to us that in such an isolated area Germans would be inside the house we approached. They had posted a sentry outside, but we had not seen him in the dark. However, he saw us and fired a warning shot. The Germans ran out of the house and started shooting. They had a machine gun. We answered their fire with one volley from our rifles, and in that exchange Vashka, our Russian, was killed. It was our mistake for not being careful enough, and we paid the price. Vashka was a good fighter and a good friend.

We scattered and ran in the direction of the woods. The Germans continued shooting but did not pursue us, because it was pitch black and they could not tell how many of us there were. I found myself near Chanina, Chaim, and Symcha Barbanel, but we did not know what had happened to Motel Rosenberg or Moniek. We walked in the woods for several hours until we reached our base. It was still dark. I would not have found it had it not been for the Barbanel brothers, who knew the woods in the area even in the dark. We were worried about Motel and Moniek, but they finally returned much later in the morning. They had become lost in the woods.

Later in the spring of 1943, we met a group of Polish and Russian partisans in the Skorodnica forest. Their leader was named Vanka Kirpicznik. When I looked at Vanka I felt I knew him from somewhere. Then I realized I had met him in the woods while caring for Stephan's animals. At that time he had asked me if I was Jewish. I told him that I was. Then he had asked me if I knew where there were any escaped Russian prisoners of war. That was in the fall of 1941, shortly after the Germans had attacked Russia and thousands of Russian prisoners of war had escaped from German captivity into the woods. Vanka thought that as a shepherd in the fields and in the woods I would know their whereabouts. He told me that he was from the Polish underground and wanted to organize the former Russian prisoners into a partisan force to fight the Germans. He said the Germans would eventually lose the war, and Poland would become an independent country, and that that would be good for the Jews too. I told him I had seen Russians in the woods, that they had approached me as they had the other shepherds to ask for food, and that I had given them what I had. However, at the point in time when Vanka approached me, I did not know where the Russians were. When I first met him, Vanka appeared to be about forty years old, with gray hair, a round face, and a thick nose. He wore high boots laced up to his knees. He spent some time with me, and when he left he said that if we both lived, he hoped we might see each other again. Now here he was—the leader of a large unit of Poles and a few Russian partisans.

We both seemed to recognize each other at the same time. He asked me if I was the shepherd from near Lubien. "Yes," I said, and we shook hands warmly.

We discovered that there were some Jewish men from the Makoszka forest in his group. I also recognized Fioder from among the Russians in Vanka's unit. He had been the leader of the Russian partisans who had come to our forest during the previous winter. He had lost many of his men when the Germans had attacked his group and ours. This was the attack in which Manya was lost.

Fioder's group had stayed with us in the early winter of 1942–43 for several days prior to the Germans tracking them down, so I knew Fioder reasonably well. He knew Manya, and I asked him about her. He said that during the battle he could not save the unarmed people because many of his own men were perishing. Many people died from the frost, if not from the German bullets. The cold had been terrible.

Vanka proposed to us that we join his group and become one partisan force. We could not decide. Our original group, together with those taken out of the Wlodawa ghetto, numbered more than one hundred people. I felt it would be to our advantage to unite with a large fighting unit. However, some of the ghetto Jews were reluctant to take this step. Vanka's unit was affiliated with the leftist Polish resistance, and many of the ghetto Jews were reluctant to get involved with a leftist organization. I argued that we should be more concerned with survival and with inflicting damage on the Germans than with political affiliations.

Vanka appreciated the disagreement within our ranks. He told us

Zindel and Betty Honigman with their daughter Fella in eastern Poland shortly after liberation in late summer 1944. Zindel escaped from a work detail at the Sobibor death camp, together with two other camp inmates, by killing two guards and slipping away in the woods. On a moving train bound for Sobibor, Betty pushed her four-year-old daughter through a crack in the cattle car, then followed her and was hidden by friendly farmers in Gorzkow until liberation. Photograph courtesy of Betty Honigman.

Wallet-size photograph of Manya Freedman taken in 1939, which Harold Werner carried with him throughout the war and showed to people in the woods in his unsuccessful search for her.

Symcha Barbanel, Dora Grynszpan, Abram Grynszpan, and Velvale the Patzan. From the archives of the YIVO Institute for Jewish Research.

Jewish partisans posing for a Russian photographer in German-occupied Poland in late 1943. *Foreground from left:* Shenka from Wlodawa, Abram the Patzan, and Chanina Barbanel. *Standing from left:* Harold Werner,

The Hornfeld family in Gorzkow in 1933. Sitting in front *(left to right):* Faiga Hornfeld, daughter Judith, and Falick Hornfeld. Standing *(left to right),* the other children: Mordechai, Tova, Dina, and Shlomo. Parents Falick and Faiga Hornfeld smuggled themselves, along with Dina and Shlomo, to Israel (then Palestine) in 1936. In 1938 they arranged to have Mordechai and Judith join them. Tova remained behind in Poland, was married in August 1939, and, together with her husband and infant son, was killed by the Germans. Photograph courtesy of Shlomo Hornfeld.

Chanina Barbanel *(left)* and Leon from Warsaw (nicknamed "Atleta" by the Germans) in their Polish police uniforms in Lodz, Poland, on May 19, 1945. Leon joined in the October 14, 1943, mass uprising of camp inmates in the Sobibor death camp, was picked up in the surrounding woods by the Jewish partisans, and fought with their unit until liberation.

Velvale the Patzan in a Polish police uniform, around 1946.

Left to right: Harold Werner and two of his partisan colleagues, Chanina Barbanel and Hershel from Skorodnica, pictured in 1946.

Photograph taken in Poland in 1946. *In front:* Betty and Simon Honigman. *In back:* Harold Werner in Polish police uniform and Velvale Honigman (a cousin).

In front from left: Harold Werner and his brothers Meyer and Irving. *In back from left:* Simon and Abraham Honigman. Picture taken in Germany in 1946.

that in the Ochoza forest near Zahajki there was a group of Jewish partisans operating under the leadership of Yechiel ("Chiel") Grynszpan. He suggested we might go there and perhaps join forces with them. He described that area as being safer than the one we were in, since it was large and swampy. The Germans could never penetrate there in a large-scale attack. The ground would not support them.

Moishe Lichtenstein was not enthusiastic about joining another group. He wanted to be the leader. Nonetheless, our Maryanka group, together with some of the ghetto people (about twenty-five of us in all), decided to travel to the Ochoza forest to look for Chiel Grynszpan's group. It was agreed that the rest of our group, with Moishe, would wait until they heard from us. Vanka gave us one of his men, Yanek, to guide us to the Ochoza forest.

It was now the late spring of 1943. Our entire group of twenty-five, heading toward the Ochoza forest, was armed. Early in the morning, after a full night of walking, we were still a distance from the village of Zahajki, at the edge of the Ochoza forest. We decided to rest near the side of a road. While we were resting, we noticed two horse-drawn wagons rapidly approaching us, carrying about a dozen Germans. We silently looked at each other and instinctively knew we should attack them. Now that we were armed in sufficient numbers, there was a very strong feeling within us to start taking revenge against the Germans. Chaim Weisman broke the silence and yelled, "Germans are coming!" Luckily, the Germans were still sufficiently far away that they did not hear Chaim's outburst.

When the wagons came alongside of us, we were well hidden in the bushes and we opened fire. As we did so, the Germans jumped off the wagons and ran in all directions. They were caught off guard, but they answered with rifle fire. Some of the Germans were thrown off when the wagons turned over.

The exchange of fire lasted about fifteen minutes. When it was over, four Germans lay dead on the road, and the rest had scattered into the woods but kept shooting in our direction. We decided not to pursue them into the woods, so as not to risk the lives of any of our people. Our group picked up four rifles and disappeared deeper into the forest. It was a successful ambush, even though we had not planned it.

When we got further into the forest, a few miles from the ambush, we sat down to rest. Chaim Weisman and his daughter Bebale, together with Hershel and his wife Hannah, sat near me. Chaim was about forty years old and came from the village of Maryanka. He and his family had gone into the woods with the other Maryanka Jews instead of going to the Wlodawa ghetto. During that first winter in the woods he lost his wife and four of his five children in different German raids. The only member of his family he had left was his youngest daughter Bebale. She was about ten years old but cared for him as if she were an adult. Because of these tragedies, he had taken Bebale back to the Wlodawa ghetto for the winter, and there he had witnessed many German atrocities against the ghetto Jews. We had brought him out of the ghetto in the spring. Understandably, he had become very jumpy from his experiences. He saw Germans around us even when there were none. Bebale would try to calm him down and tell him not to scare people. She was afraid we would throw him out of the group. But this time when he had yelled, "Germans are coming!" he had not been imagining things.

We walked for the rest of that day and the following night. Toward daybreak we came to a swampy area and sat down to rest. I was keeping watch at the time. We were very near the village of Zahajki. Vanka had told us that many of the Jewish partisans with Chiel Grynszpan had originally come from the villages surrounding the Ochoza forest. We thought that if we sat in this area for a while, we might encounter some partisans going to the villages for food or news of the Germans. We later learned that many of the villagers in this area were sympathetic to the partisans.

It was still early morning when in the distance I heard people walking. The crumbling of the leaves under their feet could be heard from far away. I alerted the group, and everyone silently stood up with rifles ready. When they came closer, we realized they were partisans, and we called to them, "Amchu?" They answered back, "Amchu," and we relaxed.

The approaching partisans consisted of Chiel Grynszpan and five of his men, all armed. Chiel, who was not a tall man, had very broad shoulders. He wore a German uniform and a long military coat with officer's boots and a hat. I did not recognize him at first because of his German uniform, although I had seen him in 1942 with Fioder's group in the Skorodnica forest. He remembered me. With him were two brothers from Zaliszcze, Mortche and Yurek. Two other members of his small band were Yosel, whom everyone called Yefim, and his cousin Hershel, both from the village of Kodeniec. I knew Yefim and Hershel from Hola, when they had come to visit and socialize with the other young people at Manya's family's farmhouse during the Jewish holidays.

Chiel had been a platoon leader in the Polish army before the outbreak of hostilities in 1939. Like many other Jews from the area villages, he had escaped to the woods when the Germans began rounding up the village Jews for transport to the ghettos. I learned later that it was not only his military training that made him well equipped to be the leader of his partisan unit. He also possessed good judgment about situations and about people, and he was able to instill confidence among the group that his decisions were usually the best course of action.

Chiel was surprised and happy to see us. He knew most of our people from before the war. He came from the town of Sosnowica, which was a few miles from the villages of Maryanka and Skorodnica. I and Moniek, who came from Warsaw, were the only ones not from that area. Chiel slapped me on the shoulder, saying he was impressed with what he had heard about our activities against the Germans in the Skorodnica forest and about our rescue of the Jews from the Wlodawa ghetto. He told us he was very glad we had come.

We started out toward Chiel's base. In order to get there we had to go through swamps. In some places we could only proceed by swinging from one tree branch to another, like monkeys, in order to avoid sinking into the mud. The woods in that area were full of swamps, in the middle of which were small islands with clumps of trees growing on them. In order to reach the island where the partisans were camped, we had to be careful not to fall into the surrounding swamp.

Following Chiel, we all made it. Even little Bebale jumped and swung like she had been doing this all her life. She encouraged her father to hold onto the tree branches tightly as he swung, and not to be scared. She was a very brave little girl.

We arrived at the base, which consisted of several islands close to one another. Chiel's people came out to greet us, and we knew many of them. They had heard about our activities, and specifically about the people we had taken from the Wlodawa ghetto, the ambushes of German convoys we conducted to obtain weapons to arm the people from the Wlodawa ghetto, and the way we had punished informers and those who had murdered Jews.

Avram "Bochian" recognized me from my short stay in the Makoszka forest during the previous winter. He hugged and kissed me. He was the cook for Chiel's people and invited our group to eat. They had not expected us, but they shared whatever they had with our group.

By nature Bochian was a very jolly fellow, especially when he had an audience. He was a forty-year-old Jew from the city of Parczew and had worked all his life as a baggage carrier at the Parczew train station. He would pantomime how he carried the heavy suitcases for the passengers, how they bought tickets, how they got them stamped, and how the whistle blew when the locomotive started. That was his favorite number. He was our entertainer, and he was very amusing to watch. His comic antics were a psychological cover for his recent ordeals, having lost his wife and children to the Germans in the Makoszka forest.

Our unit stayed with Chiel's people for about a week. Then we walked back to the Skorodnica forest to find Moishe and the rest of our group to bring them back to Chiel. We walked for two nights to reach the Skorodnica forest. We found Moishe and his group and led them back to the Ochoza forest. Once united with Chiel's unit, we were a group of about two hundred Jewish partisans, most of us armed.

Besides Chiel's group of armed men, a group of older people, women, and children lived on a separate nearby island. Some of these were the parents and relatives of Chiel's partisans. Most of these older people, women, and children, along with Chiel's armed men, were from the surrounding towns and villages. When they were ordered by the Germans to the Wlodawa ghetto, they chose to run away to the woods. Originally they had gone to the Makoszka forest. There had been a big German raid there, in which many people were lost, as had happened to my group in the Skorodnica forest. They then chose to move to this swampy area of the Ochoza forest.

The island where the older people, women, and children were located was called the Tabor (the Russian word for camp). Some of the people in the Tabor who came from the nearby area returned at night to their former neighbors to ask for food. The older Jews of the Tabor felt they could risk this type of exposure because the villagers were aware of the activities of Chiel's armed partisans and of the revenge taken by his partisans against villagers who caught Jews and turned them over to the Germans to be killed. When we joined with Chiel's force, we placed the older people and children from our group in the Tabor.

Despite the efforts of the older Jews of the Tabor, supplying food and clothing for the hundreds of people in our base was a constant problem. The partisans shouldered the major burden of satisfying these needs. We sent out two or three teams, several times a week, on *bombioshkas* to gather food. These expeditions were almost always conducted at night and were directed to distant villages so as not to antagonize the neighboring villagers. Because of the distance to be traveled, the *bombioshkas* sometimes took two full days. Between our *bombioshkas* and our military missions, much of the time most of our partisans were away from the base.

Usually, one or two partisans who were from the targeted village would lead us there and would point out the wealthier farmers. We always tried to make our requests of the wealthier farmers, rather than poor farmers or friendly ones. The farmers we approached could not resist armed partisans but nonetheless did not want to give away their food stocks. Their response was to hide their livestock, bread, sausage, and produce. We were usually not interested in taking a cow because beef spoiled quickly. We preferred to bring back a pig, because we could store parts of it, and the pork kept longer. Under the circumstances, there was no question of trying to keep kosher.

The villagers were aware of our preference for pigs. They would try to hide them in barns and cellars, and even carved dugouts in the ground for them behind their barns to try to keep us from finding them. Our partisans used all kinds of tricks to search out hidden pigs. Often, they would walk around a farmer's yard making pig noises, which many times provoked an answer from a hidden pig.

Once we found a pig, we would kill it on the farm, quarter it, and transport it to the base by wagon. Most of our group who were from the villages knew how to cut up a cow or pig, and some of them had been butchers before the war. They also knew how to make sausages, which were considered a special treat. The best sausage makers were Sucha Korn and his brother Itzik.

When we slaughtered a pig, we would cut off slabs of the back fat, about three or four inches in thickness, called "slonina" in Polish. Then we sliced it into pieces, salted it, placed it in burlap bags, and buried it in different spots in the woods. Even though I and a few others in Chiel's camp kept a rough diagram of where these caches of slonina were buried, it was sometimes hard to locate them. We resorted to these caches for food in emergencies, when they were very much appreciated. The sliced-up pieces never seemed to spoil. Even after being buried for an entire winter, they remained edible. The best part was that it did not need to be cooked. We ate it raw, and it tasted very good.

We did the same thing with barrels of whiskey as we had with the pork. When we destroyed a spirits factory, we would save one barrel for ourselves and bury it in the woods. The spot where it was hidden was known only to Chiel and me, so that the men would not help themselves at an inopportune time. Whenever we were in that vicinity, we doled out the liquor to the men.

The food we did not store was quickly distributed. Each island had someone who was a good cook. The Tabor people would apportion the meat throughout the islands in our base. The partisans kept plates attached to their belts and had their own spoons and knives. Eating utensils were kept in one's shoes at all times, so that they would not be lost in case of a sudden emergency. For the same reason, we always slept with our shoes on.

A second problem we faced, in addition to the constant need to seek out food supplies, related to the former Russian prisoners of war. They often roamed the woods in unorganized bands, terrorizing Jews who in the beginning had very few weapons with which to protect themselves. These Russians would disarm those Jews with weapons, demand money or whiskey, and rape the Jewish women. Our group in the Skorodnica forest had also experienced this problem. In the early days in the Skorodnica forest, we were not armed and so could not very well protect ourselves against the Russians.

A few days after our group joined with Chiel's, a few of us were walking around the perimeter of the base when we saw a Russian chasing a Jewish girl from the Tabor. We ran after them and caught the Russian. We gave him a good beating and told him that if it ever happened again we would shoot him. We protected the women and older people from being harassed and tried to enforce a certain degree of order in the woods.

Most of our group became fully integrated into Chiel's unit. However, Moishe Lichtenstein was unwilling to do this. He and a small portion of the people who had come out of the Wlodawa ghetto set up a base on a separate island not far from us.

In addition to Chiel's group and the Russians who roamed the area, a group of about fifty Polish partisans under the command of Vanka Kirpicznik operated near us. This was the first Polish resistance group in our area affiliated with the left-wing Guardia Ludowa ("Peoples' Guard"). Later, when it became a larger group, this movement changed its name to the Army Ludowa ("Peoples' Army"). Vanka took orders from the Army Ludowa, the Polish resistance movement headquartered in Moscow.

There were other Polish resistance groups in addition to the Army Ludowa. The Army Krajowa ("Land Army") also operated in our general area, but at considerable distance away from us. They were hostile to the Jewish partisans and to Jews in general, and also to the Army Ludowa. They took their orders from the Polish government-in-exile, headquartered in London.

Another group of Polish partisans called themselves the Batalione

Chlopsky ("Farmers' Battalion"). Their members were drawn exclusively from farms and rural areas. Their leader was a man named Mikolajczyk, who was based in London. They were more liberal than the Army Krajowa and did not threaten us or threaten the Army Ludowa people. Sometimes they cooperated with us in military activities.

There was also a smaller group called the NSZ, which stood for Nationalny Szily Zbroiny ("National Armed Force"). The NSZ consisted of ultraconservative Polish fascists. These were the same people who, before the war, had joined the Endecia. Then they used to beat up Jews, break windows in Jewish synagogues and business establishments, and stand in front of Jewish stores so as not to let customers enter. Luckily, their membership was small in our area, and they were not much of a threat to us.

In one of our meetings with the Army Ludowa group, Vanka Kirpicznik suggested that Chiel's group join with his to form a larger unit under Vanka's direction. We hesitated, and then told him we would think it over.

Afterward, we had a meeting among ourselves to discuss Vanka's proposal. I told Chiel I thought we should join Vanka's group. We would have a better chance of survival as part of a larger fighting force. Since we had many enemies besides the Germans, size was important. The Army Krajowa and the members of the NSZ were hunting down Jews, just as the Germans were doing. Additionally, we would have a chance to get more weapons if connected with Vanka's group.

Many people, including Chiel, were of the same opinion. The older Jews from the Tabor also felt we would be better off in a larger force. It would give us a greater chance to protect ourselves and also make us able to fight the Germans more effectively. We could always plan and carry out our own activities independently when necessary.

A group of us went back to Vanka and told him we would be willing to work with him in carrying out actions against the Germans. We emphasized, however, that we wanted to remain an independent Jewish fighting unit under Chiel's leadership. Vanka was happy to accept our offer.

Moishe Lichtenstein was opposed to joining with Vanka. He said he would never trust a Polish organization, and that all Polish people were anti-Semites. Many of the Wlodawa ghetto group camping with him on his island agreed with him. We tried to argue with him, but were unsuccessful. Vanka spoke with him several times, explaining that the Army Ludowa was not anti-Semitic and wanted to join with the Jews in fighting the Germans, our common enemy. The old people from the Tabor also went to Moishe to try to persuade him.

From Moishe's behavior, I and many others concluded that he was power hungry. He just wanted to be a leader. He could not even get along with Chiel. Chiel was a mild-mannered man whom everyone liked. He commanded without throwing his authority around. Chiel was a good leader and respected by all of us.

Many of the partisans acquired nicknames in the woods. For example, the name "Bochian" was a nickname meaning "stork" in Polish. I had been actively involved in persuading our partisan unit to become affiliated with the Army Ludowa and afterward became Chiel's primary liaison with the Army Ludowa. For this, Chiel gave me the nickname "Politruk," which means "political commissar." That name also recognized the fact that, having been educated in political affairs through my union in Warsaw, I was more politically aware than most of our partisans in the woods. Many of the partisans who joined Chiel's unit after our affiliation with the Army Ludowa knew me only as Hershel Politruk.

22

Rescuing Jews from the Adampol Labor Camp

An estate called Adampol was located about eight miles from Wlodawa. This estate was part of Count Zamoyski's holdings, which comprised hundreds of thousands of acres of land on both sides of the Bug River. The size of the estate was reduced after the First World War, when the new Polish government under Marshal Pilsudski expropriated some of the land for the landless farmers who had worked for the count. After the expropriation, his estate still encompassed miles and miles of fields and forests, including many livestock farms and several satellite estates where different agricultural and forestry products were produced.

The Germans took over Adampol and two of its satellite estates, called Lesnichuvka and Natalin, to set up a labor camp. The camp was operated under the direction of a German SS officer, a storm trooper named Graf Zelinger. To obtain laborers, the Germans conducted selections from the trainloads of Jews taken to the Sobibor death camp, located nearby. They took only the healthiest and strongest-looking Jews.

Graf Zelinger organized different specialty shops, such as sewing factories, woodworking shops, metal works, and gold and jewelry engraving shops. There were rumors that they even had a top secret setup for making counterfeit American dollars and English pounds. They also took over the estate's farms and managed livestock production and the harvesting of grains.

All the slave laborers who were selected from the Sobibor transports had to be master craftsmen in their assigned fields. Graf Zelinger ran this vast enterprise as if it were his own, but all the products were shipped to Germany. Although he was an officer in the German SS, he wore civilian clothes and appeared to be less cruel than other SS soldiers were to the Jews. He kept telling his slaves that, if they worked hard, he would see to it that they would be spared from going to Sobibor.

At the end of each working day, the Adampol laborers went to their appointed barracks, men to one set of barracks and women to a separate set. There was a special section for the more attractive women and girls, picked from the trains that brought Jews from all over Europe to Sobibor. These females were kept for the pleasure of Zelinger's Ukrainian and Latvian guards, and sometimes for German soldiers.

Our group knew what was going on in Adampol because many of our people had relatives who had been sent there after the liquidation of the Wlodawa ghetto. Through the local villagers it was possible to communicate with the inmates of the camp. The inmates of Adampol wanted to believe that they would be spared, as Graf Zelinger had promised them, but we knew better. Our group decided to try to rescue as many of them as possible.

A Wlodawa teenager named Shenka was one of the Adampol Jews who had been picked to help the Germans in the animal hunt the previous winter. He had escaped during the great storm that stopped the hunt, and eventually he made his way to Chiel's group. Because of his familiarity with the layout of the camp, he was chosen to lead us into Adampol. Chiel assigned ten people to go with Shenka to see how we could get into the camp. The ten included myself, Symcha, Chanina, Velvale the Patzan ("Patzan" denotes a small person, as in "Little John") from Sosnowica, Chiel's brother Abram, Motel Barbanel, Moniek, Yankale from the Wlodawa ghetto, and another partisan from Sosnowica named Nisen.

We knew that the people in Adampol wanted to get out of there, but that they also feared conditions in the woods. They had heard about the raids the Germans had conducted during the winter, and about the large number of Jews that had been killed in those raids. I thought that if they could see us—live armed Jewish partisans—they would be more easily persuaded to try to escape.

Shenka knew a place at the back of the camp where the fence could be raised enough to let a person squeeze through. We sent him in first, and he went to the men's barracks where his father was. After a while, he came back with five Jews. What we learned from these five was that most of the people in the camp were afraid to leave and were resigned to their fate, hoping that Graf Zelinger would protect them. They were afraid of staying in the forest like us and thought our plan of a massive escape from the camp was an impossibility.

We went back to the woods with the five Adampol inmates. We had to rush because of the short summer nights. I suggested that we leave Shenka in the camp, to see whether the guards would notice the absence of the people who left with us. We told him we would come back the following night and that he should wait for us near the opening in the fence. We also told him to try to find other people who wanted to escape.

The next night we came back. Shenka took us through the fence and into the camp. He led us into an abandoned shack. We could see some flickers of light in certain barracks in the distance. It was close to midnight and pitch black outside. The shack was an old broken barn, and Shenka guided us to the steps leading into the cellar. There in the dark we met a group of Jews. We greeted them, but could not make out their faces in the dark. We were all armed, and Shenka went back outside to stand guard.

I told them we represented a large group of armed Jewish partisans who had come to rescue as many of them as we could. I said there were rumors that Adampol would be liquidated shortly. They wanted to know how they would exist in the woods. They were afraid the Germans would search for them in the woods and kill them. They said that, no matter how many partisans we had, we could not fight the German army. They felt the Germans were just too powerful.

We had to explain to them that the Germans had tried many times to kill us. It was true that they had superior forces to ours, but our bullets were just as deadly as theirs, and they were just as afraid of us as we were of them. I explained that the woods were our protection, and that it was easy to disappear into them. We had been in the woods for a long time, lived through many battles, and survived one of the coldest winters in memory. I showed them my gun and said: "Only this will save us. In the camp you are a prisoner. Don't think that the Nazis will spare you just because you are good craftsmen."

Some of the men we spoke with in the cellar left with us for the woods. A week later, we returned to Adampol with Shenka and got into the camp the same way. This time there was no need to persuade people to leave. There were about thirty men ready to go with us. We told them to wait while we went to the women's barracks, which were a distance away. The women knew from Shenka that we were coming, and they were ready. Ten women and thirty men left with us that night. As soon as we were outside the fence, a teenage girl named Rachel came over to me and kissed me, thanking me for helping to take them out. Some of the men that we took out had relatives among our group.

The people we took out of Adampol had no weapons, and we settled them in the Tabor. The women who came out included two sisters, Pesah and Temi, from Wlodawa, a girl from Hamburg, Germany, named Gretta, a girl from Warsaw named Rachel, Chasha from Wlodawa, and others whose names I cannot remember.

While escorting the Adampol contingent back to our base, we stopped in a village and asked the local farmers for wagons, horses, and food to take back with us. They gave it to us because we were armed. After we unloaded the food in our camp, we tied the reins to the wagons, pointed the horses in the direction from which we had come, and they found their way back to their owners.

A few days later another group of ours, consisting of about five partisans, went back to Adampol planning to take out an even larger group of people. This time I did not participate. Yurek from Zaliszcze, Yanche (Jacob) Barbanel (Motel Barbanel's brother), and three other veteran partisans went on this mission. They entered the camp and planned on staying there during the day to organize the escape. They hid their guns in one of the barracks.

One of the camp inmates apparently informed Graf Zelinger about the planned escape. In no time, a large detachment of SS men arrived from Wlodawa and surrounded the camp. It was obvious they had been informed about the planned escape. They immediately located and examined the spot in the fence through which the partisans had entered the camp. They told everyone in the camp—about eight hundred people—to assemble, and they marched them to a field outside the fence.

The partisans marched out together with the camp inmates. The SS men had ringed the field with machine guns, and the partisans realized what the Germans intended to do. Once in the field, they shouted to the others to run. Almost instantaneously, the Germans opened up with their machine guns, slaughtering the camp inmates who tried in vain to run to safety. Yurek was wounded in the hand, but he, Yanche, and one of the other partisans made it back to our base to relate this story. Very few of the camp inmates survived.

That was the end of the Adampol labor camp. In total, we had taken close to one hundred inmates out of the camp prior to the massacre in the field.

Shortly after the Adampol rescue, Moishe Lichtenstein began to realize he was losing many of his followers to our group. To retain intact what was left of his unit, he decided to leave us. One day, without notice, he and a group of about thirty people left the Ochoza forest, heading eastward toward the Bug River.

About a week later, a young woman named Chasha, who had gone with Moishe and his group, returned to the Ochoza forest and told us what had happened. While walking toward the Bug River, Moishe's group met some Russian partisans who joined with them. Aside from their rifles, Moishe's group also possessed a heavy machine gun, which Moishe entrusted to two of the Russian partisans to carry. Near the Bug River, they were spotted by a German patrol. A firefight ensued, and most of them swam across the river to the eastern bank. Some of them, along with the two Russians carrying the machine gun, escaped westward from the German patrol and began walking back to us. On the way back, they stopped in a village and asked a farmer to let them sleep in his barn for a few hours. They all fell asleep, leaving one of the Russians, named Volodka, with the machine gun to keep watch outside the barn. When they awoke, they found that Volodka, his Russian compatriot, and the machine gun were gone. They had been sleeping without a sentry. It could have been fatal if the Germans had discovered them during their slumber.

Moishe, with a few men, had also failed to cross the Bug River and had separately headed back to the Ochoza forest. When he joined up with the other contingent, which had returned to the forest, he asked the others what had happened to his machine gun. He was told that Volodka had stolen the gun and disappeared. He became enraged and vowed to get his gun back.

Moishe had heard a rumor that Volodka was in the village of Holeszow. Moishe took Shmuel Stul, Chaim Tencer, Motel Rosenberg, and Chasha with him. Upon arriving in Holeszow, they discovered a wedding in progress in one of the homes. They decided Volodka might be there, and they were right. He and the other Russian were at the wedding. Moishe entered the home and demanded that Volodka return the machine gun to him. An argument ensued. The groom asked them to step outside to settle their argument in order not to disturb his party. Moishe agreed and went outside with his four people. Volodka followed them. On the way out, he picked up the machine gun, which had been hidden near the door and covered with a cloth. As soon as he walked out, he opened fire, instantly killing Moishe, Chaim Tencer, and Motel Rosenberg. Shmuel Stul and Chasha escaped and came back to tell us the final part of this sad ending to Moishe Lichtenstein's leadership.

Months later, we heard about the partisans in Moishe's group who had managed to escape the German patrol by crossing the Bug River. After reaching the eastern bank, they met up with and joined different Russian partisan units operating in the area. Most of them survived the war.

Spies

Whenever a Jew in southeastern Poland escaped from a ghetto, a concentration camp, or a hiding place and could avoid being caught by hostile villagers, the Army Krajowa, the NSZ, or the Germans, they were directed by friendly villagers to our group in the Ochoza forest. Some came from great distances and walked for weeks trying to find us.

We kept a constant patrol around the perimeter of our base. It was very difficult for people who were unfamiliar with the area to find us. The patrol served to give us advance notice of the approach of unfriendly forces. It also served to pick up Jews who had been told that a large Jewish partisan unit operated in the area, and who were seeking safety within our ranks. We accepted everyone. Able-bodied adults joined the ranks of our fighters. The rest were put up in the Tabor.

Members of our unit often went to neighboring villages for food and information regarding the whereabouts of the Germans, and to meet with friendly villagers. Sometimes it was not easy to find our way back. We used an exceptionally tall tree as a reference point. It was an old oak tree that could be seen from miles away, and we often walked toward that landmark to locate our camp. Once we got closer to the tree, we could find our way to the base.

We were aware that the Germans knew about our unit, and that they were trying to infiltrate our area with spies in order to find the exact location of our camp. Anyone who was unknown to us and came close to our location was stopped and interrogated.

One day, Yanek from Wyryki was assigned to be one of our guards patrolling the perimeter of the base. He was one of the original members of Chiel's group, along with his brothers Yurek and Abram, and sister Tzesha. Yanek noticed an unfamiliar Polish man walking around in the woods not far from the base. He stopped the man and questioned him, but the fellow could not provide a satisfactory explanation as to why he was in the woods. Yanek brought him to Chiel at the base. We interrogated him and, after a little persuasion, he confessed he had been sent by the Germans to spy on us. We took him a distance away from the camp and shot him.

On another occasion a sizable force of our fighters was in the village of Maryanka, on the way back from a sabotage mission. Friendly villagers told us there was a group of Russian partisans in the nearby woods. The villagers were suspicious of this Russian group because they were all Asiatic and carried new German weapons. Also, they were dressed in decent clothes and did not look like Russian partisans. The villagers told us that these Russians were going around looking for other Russian partisan groups, claiming they had gotten lost after having had a battle with the Germans. We were told there were about twenty of them. We were aware that the Germans had been organizing fighting units from among the Russian prisoners of war whom they felt would be loyal to the Germans, and forming spy groups with them.

Our group passing through Maryanka consisted of about seventy armed fighters. Symcha and I volunteered to get closer to this suspicious group of Russians to investigate. Chiel told us to leave our rifles with our group in the nearby woods and to try to look like two villagers just passing through the area.

Unarmed, Symcha and I walked toward the area where we understood the Russians were camped. As we approached their camp, we heard a person, apparently their leader, speaking in German, and saw that he was not Asiatic. We did not walk directly toward them. We made a turn in the woods as if we were heading in a different direction. They stopped us and started to converse in Russian with us, asking if we had seen any partisans in the area. They wanted to know where we were from, so we told them that we had come from Maryanka. We said we were not aware of any partisans in the area but had heard that there were partisans in the Makoszka forest. While we answered their questions, our eyes took in their new German rifles and their new clothes, unlike anything Russian partisans would have available. They then released us, and we walked away. We were lucky they did not detain us and question us further. Apparently, they did not want to antagonize two local village farmers like us. We circled back to our group and reported to Chiel that they were German spies.

We decided to take care of this unit of spies. We surrounded their camp and called out in Russian that we were Jewish partisans, and that we wanted them to come out to us. They said that they were looking for Russian partisans, not Jewish partisans, and refused to come out. At that point, we opened fire on them. Ten of them were killed, including their German leader, and the rest scattered in the woods. We retrieved their good new German rifles. There were also many documents scattered about. From these documents, we discovered that they were a special intelligence detachment of the German army.

24

A Survivor of the Warsaw Ghetto Uprising

One day I was standing guard at one of the approaches to our encampment on the Zahajki village side, about a mile from our base. Through the underbrush, I noticed two people coming in my direction. I raised my rifle, and when they came closer I ordered them to stop and identify themselves. One man was a villager from Zahajki whom I knew. The other said he was Hershel Rubenstein, a survivor from the Warsaw ghetto uprising. I was both astonished and moved to see a Jew from the Warsaw ghetto uprising. In the woods we had heard many stories about the uprising, and about the heroic resistance the Jews had put up for four terrible weeks to hold off the German army. But actually seeing a man coming from that hell and finding his way to the Ochoza forest was hard for me to comprehend.

The villager left Hershel Rubenstein in my care and headed back toward Zahajki. When I was relieved at my guard post, I brought Hershel back to the group. News of his arrival spread like wildfire to all the separate groups at our base, and our people quickly gathered to see the man who had survived the legendary Warsaw ghetto uprising.

Prior to this, we used to sit around our camp fires and talk about the heroism of the Jews in Warsaw. We felt for them, being caught like rats in a trap, and it made us feel fortunate to be in the woods, free and armed with weapons with which to defend ourselves. The heroism of the Warsaw ghetto uprising had few parallels in the tragic history of the Jewish people. There, the starving remnants of the Warsaw ghetto rose up against the Germans in April 1943. With little outside help and no prospect of success, these courageous fighters kept the German army at bay for as long as Poland had resisted the German attack in 1939. Only after inflicting heavy losses upon the German forces sent to quell the uprising and the complete physical destruction of the ghetto by bombings and shellings were the defenders finally crushed.

Everybody gathered around Hershel, this legendary hero, to find out how he had saved himself, how he had escaped from the ghetto, and how he had come to us. Hershel was neither tall nor muscular. He looked to be about thirty-five years old, with dark hair, a wide nose, and very penetrating dark eyes. His left arm appeared paralyzed and hung at his side, twisted backward. He wore a black leather jacket and khaki pants which were stuffed into his boots, and a belt around his waist in which he had tucked a pistol. He was very friendly and tried to answer all our questions.

He told us that at the end of the uprising, some of the ghetto fighters had escaped from the smoldering ruins of the ghetto through the Warsaw sewers. They had emerged from the sewers beyond the ghetto wall. At that point, friendly Poles disguised as street cleaners had picked them up in a truck and driven them east into the woods outside the city. From there, he was directed from one village to the next by the Polish leftist partisans of the Army Ludowa, all the way to our base in the Ochoza forest.

In the Warsaw ghetto, Hershel Rubenstein had been a leader of the communist party. His group, together with other political groups like the Bund and the Zionist and religious groups, constituted the united front which had organized the uprising in the Warsaw ghetto. His left arm had been badly injured in the fighting. He had been running through burning buildings and had fallen from a second floor. His arm got caught on something as he fell, and it was pulled out of its socket. Without medical help, his arm had remained twisted backward and was useless to him.

We flocked around Hershel for many days and nights, hanging on his every word about his experiences. He told us about the hopelessness of the Jews' existence in the Warsaw ghetto. He described the starvation of men, women, and children; of bodies lying in the streets where they fell, either from starvation, disease, or arbitrary German shootings. He related tales of people being rounded up like cattle for transport for "resettlement" to the East. As the population of the ghetto became depleted by these roundups, people began to realize why no one ever came back alive from the "resettlements." He painted a picture of hundreds of thousands of Jews waiting for death. They were locked up behind the ghetto walls, which separated them from the hostile, anti-Semitic outside world. In that outside world, young thugs waited, ready to pounce on any Jews who attempted to sneak out and eager to turn them over to the Germans for a reward. The punishment for such attempted escapes was instant death. Finally, he described the desperation of people who decided that, rather than passively wait for transport to the death camps, they would make a statement by their gallant but hopeless uprising against over-whelming odds.

Like the others, I listened intently to Hershel's revelations. I kept thinking about my father, who had remained behind in Warsaw when I left the city in 1939. I knew I would never see him again.

Hershel joined our partisan unit and, despite his useless left arm, he proved to be a very brave and valuable fighter. He went out of his way to buck up our spirits whenever we were in a tight situation, during or after a skirmish with the Germans. He always compared our situation with that of the Jews trapped in the Warsaw ghetto. Such a reminder always made us appreciate the fact that, no matter what straits we might find ourselves in, we were still much better off than the people who had been in the ghetto. He was also an excellent speaker, and we all liked him. Many people in our unit had a nick-name, and Chiel named him Hershel the Commissar.

25

An Ambush and a Happy Reunion

Not long after Hershel Rubenstein's arrival, a friendly villager from Zahajki informed us that twenty German soldiers would be coming to the village the next day. The day following that, some were to continue on to other villages in the area, starting with the village of Holowna. The villager had learned this from the mayor of Zahajki, who was ordered to arrange transportation for the Germans. We learned that ten of the Germans would leave Zahajki, while the other ten would remain in the village.

We talked over this news with Chiel and decided to ambush the ten Germans who were to leave Zahajki. In order for them to travel from Zahajki to Holowna, they would have to pass by the edge of the Ochoza forest. At that point, there was a strip of road that curved into the woods.

About forty of us, including a few women, along with Chiel and Hershel Rubenstein (this was his first partisan action with us), started out for the point where the road curved into the woods. We had decided this would be the best place for the ambush. Vanka Kirpicznik of the Army Ludowa was aware of our plan and offered us a heavy Polish machine gun from his partisan force, along with two of his men to carry and operate it. They had gotten this weapon from a Polish army unit as it retreated from the Germans in 1939.

We reached the ambush point before dawn and camouflaged ourselves along the edge of the road. We waited there, lying on the ground, for several hours. Finally, at about eleven o'clock, we saw German soldiers approaching on three horse-drawn wagons, but there were closer to twenty of them instead of the ten we had expected.

The three Barbanel brothers and I, along with Chuna Kot from the village of Ninin, Hershel and his wife Hannah, Moniek and others, were lying at the bend of the road, and we saw the approaching Germans first. The machine gun had been set up by Vanka's two men, Yanek and Cesiek, a few feet from us on the back of a horse-drawn wagon. Further down the road were stationed Chiel, his brother Abram, Abram's girlfriend Dora, Yefim and his cousin Hershel from Kodeniec, Yurek and his brother Mortche from Zaliszcze, Lova from Parczew, Lonka from Parczew, Yanek and Yurek from Wyryki, the four brothers from Zahajki—Shloime, Dudke, Itzik, and Abram the Patzan—and many others.

We all waited for Chiel to give the signal to attack. We had not anticipated attacking that many Germans, but we were seasoned fighters with good weapons and a machine gun, so we felt confident.

We let the first two wagons pass, but as the third wagon came alongside us, Chiel gave the signal to attack. We opened fire in unison. The Germans jumped off the wagons and started running to the other side of the road, shooting back as they ran.

I noticed a Polish policeman jump off the back of the last wagon and recognized him immediately. His name was Zaremba, a participant in many local expeditions to round up Jews hiding in the woods. I had been told by Polashka that, when the Jews hiding in the Hola woods had been rounded up by the local villagers and marched to the Sosnowica police station, Zaremba had helped the Germans shoot the captive Jews. That was the roundup Manya, Moniek, and I had been lucky enough to miss because we had been at Stephan's house seeking food.

For the moment, I focused my attention on Zaremba. I shot at him from behind a tree and could tell that I wounded him. He shot back, missing me but killing my friend Chuna Kot, who was standing right next to me.

We kept up the shooting, and the Germans kept returning our fire. They had dropped to the ground to shoot at us, but they were exposed on the unprotected side of the open road while we were in the bushes with a good view of them. I tried to aim at Zaremba and, sensing that, he kept shooting back in my direction. One of his shots came so close it nicked off a small part of my left ear. Finally, I threw a grenade at the Germans, as did several of the other partisans.

One thing that failed to work was the heavy machine gun on which we had relied. It jammed almost immediately and was of no use to us. On top of that, we had not expected such a large group of Germans. Their horses became scared and ran away with the wagons. The fight lasted about twenty minutes. We then heard shots from the direction of Zahajki, and Chiel gave the order to pull out. I grabbed Chuna's rifle, and we all left.

We found out later from the local villagers that ten Germans were killed and many wounded in our attack. We could not discover whether Zaremba was among the casualties. We lost one man, Chuna Kot, a very brave young partisan. We learned that earlier the Germans had decided to double their force from twenty to forty and that about half of them had left the village that morning. When the twenty left behind heard our shooting, they started out toward the ambush to help their comrades. It was prudent for us to have pulled out when we did.

Shortly after returning to the Ochoza forest from the ambush, a group of Russian partisans arrived at our camp. Although there were eight of them, they called themselves "Shustka," which is Russian for "the six." Their group consisted of six Russians, along with two Jews from another part of the Makoszka forest. We had heard of the Shustka previously when we were in the Skorodnica forest. They were a splinter of Fioder's group (now departed for the Russian side of the Bug River), which had stayed behind. They were famous for their daring highway attacks on German transports. Also with them was little Itzik, whom we had adopted in the Parczew forest the year before and then had left with Vasil in Hola to recuperate. We were unaware of what had happened to him since the day the Germans had shot Vasil and we had been unable to find Itzik on Vasil's farm.

I was not at the base the day the Russians arrived. I was with a group on a mission to cut down telephone poles along a highway some distance away. Cutting down telephone poles was one of our most frequent missions. We would travel in small groups to a location tens of miles from our base. Then we would cut down a series of telephone poles in order to disrupt the Germans' lines of communication. The Germans frequently traveled in small groups to repair these telephone lines, so oftentimes we would stay in the area to wait for a German repair team, and then ambush them before returning to our base.

I returned from this particular mission two days after the Shustka arrived. On my arrival, Faiga ran over to tell me that Itzik was alive and had come to the base. I quickly went to find him, and we were overjoyed to see each other. We embraced and he even kissed me. Then he related what had happened to him.

He told me he had been very lucky because Vasil had taken good care of him, allowing his frozen toe to heal. Vasil had treated him like a son. The day he was in the barn and heard the Germans enter the yard, he thought he was finished. However, he kept repeating to himself that he was very lucky. He noticed a loose board in the back of the barn, pushed it out, and ran toward the woods. When he entered the woods, he heard the Germans following him, deeper and deeper into the forest. Finally, he climbed a tree to hide in its thick branches. The Germans headed in his direction, and at one point even stood under the tree in which he was hiding, but they never looked up. When darkness fell, the Germans left. Itzik climbed down from the tree and ran until he reached a field. At the edge of the field, he found a haystack. He made a hole in the haystack, climbed in, and immediately fell asleep. As he fell asleep, he kept repeating to himself that he was very lucky. In the morning, a villager and his wife came to get some hay and noticed him. Itzik started crying and told them the truth. He told them he was a Jewish boy whose parents had been killed, that he had been hiding in a barn and had run out when he heard the Germans coming. He told them that he had not eaten for two days and asked them to give him some food and to let him stay in the hole in the haystack. They talked it over and decided to take Itzik home with them. They kept him there for three weeks. During the daytime he was kept hidden in the barn. At night they took him into the house. One night the Shustka, along with two Jews, knocked on the house window. Itzik ran into the cellar to hide. When he heard they were partisans, he ran up to them and begged them to take him along. They agreed to take him with them.

Itzik was about eleven years old now and carried a pistol that the partisans had gotten for him. He had not had a haircut since we left him at Vasil's house, and his hair hung down to his shoulders. He looked to be half child and half adult.

The Shustka stayed with us for several days. They were on their way to the Russian side of the Bug River. They offered to continue to take Itzik with them, figuring that he would have a better chance to survive there since the partisans on the Russian side were better organized and more numerous. Itzik wanted to stay with us, but I explained to him that perhaps he would be better off on the other side of the river where he would be safer from the Germans. Moniek gave him a haircut, and Itzik said good-bye to us and left with the Shustka. I still had a warm spot in my heart for Itzik and was reluctant to see him go, but I knew he would be in a safer environment once he reached his destination.

26

Successful Raids After Joining the Army Ludowa

It was now the summer of 1943, and under Chiel's leadership our ranks had grown considerably. We now numbered about three hundred Jewish fighters, both men and women, and all armed. This was in addition to the approximately two hundred Jews we protected in the Tabor.

The Army Ludowa supplied us with military objectives and helped us in many ways. Their partisans accompanied us on some of our missions and provided us with weapons. They had a very good organizational base in the villages. Each village contained one person designated by the Army Ludowa to obtain information about German activities. That man would be our contact to supply us with information when we came into the village. He would also inform us of any villagers who cooperated with the Germans, and of other spies in the area. This information was very important to us. The other villagers were not aware of this person's activities.

After the surrender of the German army attacking Stalingrad and the lifting of the German siege of Leningrad in January and February of 1943, the tide of battle on the Russian front turned against the Germans. The local villagers were aware of the German reversals, and this caused them to cooperate more freely with the Army Ludowa and the Jewish partisans. There were no more instances of local villagers rounding up Jews and killing them or handing them over to the Germans. Because the Jewish partisans were armed and organized, and because we punished those villagers who collaborated with the Germans, the atmosphere toward us changed dramatically. We were respected and feared. Whenever we were in the Lubien area, I would stop at Stephan's farm. Now he was most friendly. He would put out food and drink for us. He respected our power and behaved as though he had forgotten that he had once threatened to kill me if I ever returned to his farm.

It was also easier now for the unarmed Jews from the Tabor—the elderly, women, and children—to seek food from the villagers. They knew they ran a lesser risk of being molested by the villagers, who feared retribution from Chiel's forces. On the other hand, the London-based Army Krajowa began to be more active. They also had partisan units in the area but did not have as much popular support as we did in the region of the Ochoza forest. They were stronger in the areas west of us, beyond the Wieprz River. Their leaders were officers of the prewar Polish army and civil administration.

When the Army Krajowa partisans were attacked by the Germans, they put up a stout resistance. They had very good weapons and leaders with good military training from before the war. When outnumbered by their attackers, they could scatter and return to their villages and their homes, melting into the local population. It was also easy for the Army Ludowa partisans to do the same. On the other hand, when faced with superior forces, the Jewish partisans could only fight or hide in the woods. We had no homes to go to.

The members of the Army Krajowa were very anti-Semitic, exhibiting the same attitudes they had held before the war. Now, however, they were armed and Jews were "fair game" for their attacks. Whenever they caught a Jew or a small group of Jews hiding in the woods or a village, they would kill them. Whether this was done on orders of their senior commanders or simply reflected their local leaders' inborn hatred of Jews, we never knew. Small groups of Jews, whether or not armed, were caught and shot.

I wanted very much to go to my hometown of Gorzkow, near Krasnystaw on the far side of the Wieprz River, to find out what had happened to my family—my grandfather, brothers, sister, uncles, aunts, and cousins. I was advised not to go there except as part of a large force. A twelve-man team of Army Ludowa partisans had gone to that area on a military mission. They were surrounded by men from the Army Krajowa and killed. Not one of them came back. Chiel's group was respected and feared because of our numbers, but as individuals our members were in danger, even in our own area, from the Army Krajowa.

Our group was an independent Jewish partisan unit, committed to fighting the Germans. In addition to our survival, our goal was two-fold—to avenge the murders the Germans had committed against our people; and to rescue as many Jews as possible and help them to survive.

In our area, we were a major fighting group upon which the Army Ludowa could rely to accomplish important military objectives. We cooperated with anyone who would fight the Germans. The Army Krajowa hated us because we were Jews, no matter how useful we could be to them in the battle against the Germans. They were deadly anti-Semitic and seemed just as intent upon killing Jews as they were in fighting Germans. We regarded them as just as great a threat to our survival as was the German army. It had nothing to do with political ideology. Few, if any, of our fighters were communists or leftists.

One morning, Vanka Kirpicznik visited us at our base in the Ochoza forest. When he arrived, I was sitting with Chiel and a few others under a tree, discussing the next move we were going to make against the Germans. Vanka told us about a very heavy cannon shell the Army Ludowa had located that we could use to blow up a train on our next mission. This heavy shell could be fitted with a fuse from a grenade and detonated from a distance. Blowing up a train was an exciting prospect to us. It was a major act of sabotage that we had not as yet attempted. Within our ranks were several men who had served in the Polish army before the war, where they had gained some familiarity with explosives. With this expertise and Vanka's cannon shell, we decided it was a worthwhile project and accepted Vanka's proposal.

Vanka brought the shell to our base and we figured out how to connect the fuse so that it could be detonated by wire from a distance. We decided to use it to blow up the train that crossed a bridge over a river near the village of Dubeczno, along the main rail line between Wlodawa and Chelm. The bridge was about thirty miles from our base in the Ochoza forest. We learned that a train passed there every midnight.

The group that went on the mission was seventy-five strong, including Chiel. The shell was over four feet long and very heavy. It took four people to lift it, and it could only be transported by horse and wagon. We rode to the Dubeczno area on wagons and reached the approach to the bridge well before midnight.

It was a pitch black night. To get to the bridge, we had to climb a very high embankment. Four people slowly carried the shell up the embankment to the rails on an improvised stretcher. Chanina and I, along with two other men, climbed up to the rail line and dug a pit under the rails in which to place the shell. The other four, who had hauled the shell up the embankment, kept watch and helped put the shell in place. At the bottom of the embankment, others in our group kept watch for German patrols. We attached a long wire to the fuse, which we ran all the way down to the riverbank below, about two hundred feet in length. We gave Chiel the honor of triggering the fuse.

It was almost midnight. Everyone was nervous and anxious to see this operation succeed. I climbed up a tree to watch for the oncoming train. Moniek put his ear to the rail to see if he could feel the vibration of the oncoming train.

I strained my eyes peering into the darkness for the train. Finally I saw a very small light, which quickly grew larger and larger. I rushed down the tree and Moniek jumped from the rail line, running to the riverbank below. The train was rushing toward us at a tremendous speed. We held our breath when the locomotive reached the bridge. Chiel triggered the fuse, and a tremendous explosion obliterated the bridge just ahead of the locomotive. The ground where we stood shook, and our ears hurt from the blast. The locomotive hurtled into the river forty feet below, pulling the rest of the train with it.

It was a military train full of hundreds of German soldiers. Some of them started jumping out of the train into the shallow water. They were running in all directions and appeared dazed and disorganized. We stood on the riverbank, firing our rifles at the mass of struggling men.

We heard one of the wounded Germans shouting "Muter, Muter!" I remember Velvale the Patzan from Sosnowica, standing next to me as we fired at the soldiers, murmuring: "They still have mothers. We don't have our mothers. They killed all of them."

After about fifteen minutes of rifle fire, we pulled out of the area, returning to our base on the wagons. The operation had been a great success. We heard later from the villagers that there were many German casualties in the train wreck, and that it took them several days to fix the bridge. This was the first of over twenty-five trains our group destroyed, either alone or in concert with units of the Army Ludowa. In later efforts, we used more sophisticated explosives.

One of our fighters, nicknamed Vuyo, was a native of the village of Dubeczno. He was about seventeen years old when we took him out of Adampol. His real name was Yankel Barbanel, a cousin of the Barbanel brothers.

Vuyo always liked to be close to Chiel. Wherever Chiel went, Vuyo followed, carrying his possessions, making him something to eat, getting an extra pair of boots for him on one of our *bombioshkas*, or getting him a bottle of schnaps, which Chiel liked. Wherever Chiel went, Vuyo was there too, like his shadow.

When the Germans ordered all Jews from the local villages to the ghetto of Wlodawa, Vuyo and his entire family had gone with the rest of the Jews to the Wlodawa ghetto. In one of the selections in the ghetto, his family was taken to the Sobibor concentration camp. Vuyo was sent to the Adampol labor camp. He worked there for Graf Zelinger until our partisan unit led him and other Adampol inmates to the woods in the spring of 1943.

Vuyo liked to tell us stories about his hometown of Dubeczno. He wanted to go there to show himself to the villagers. He wanted to prove he was still alive, and that he was a Jewish partisan, with a rifle and wearing a German military coat. The coat alone was a mark of distinction, as he had had to kill a German soldier to get it.

In addition to wanting to show off, there was another reason Vuyo wanted to return to his hometown. There was a big glass factory in Dubeczno, known throughout Poland, called the Dubeczno Huta. Before the war this factory had been owned by a Jewish family to which Vuyo was related. Now the owners were long dead, killed by the Germans along with the other Jews of Dubeczno. The Germans took over the factory and installed a Polish manager to operate it. The factory was operated day and night, making precision glass for the Germans. The Polish manager had a widespread reputation as a virulent anti-Semite. He had been instrumental in capturing a group of Jews, including Vuyo's uncle, hiding in the nearby woods. He then handed them over to the Germans to be shot.

We decided it would be worthwhile to destroy the Dubeczno Huta and thereby deprive the Germans of its output of precision glass. Thirty people from our group were assigned to this mission. We agreed that, if we caught the manager, we would let Vuyo take care of him. After dark, Vuyo led us to Dubeczno on several horse-drawn wagons. We took along several cans of gasoline, just in case we did not find the fuel tank Vuyo said was near the factory. We arrived in Dubeczno late at night. Vuyo led Symcha, Chanina, Chaim, and me directly to the manager's house, but he was not home. His wife was very scared when she saw us. She told us her husband had gone to Wlodawa that day and had not yet returned. The rest of our group went into the factory—a very large building—and told the workers who were there to get out. We located the tank of gasoline in a building next to the factory. We poured gasoline all over the factory and the manager's house, after chasing out his wife. We lit the gasoline and in no time the place was ablaze. We worked fast because a large detachment of Germans was stationed nearby in Wlodawa. We knew they would be able to see the flames against the dark sky and would come quickly.

Vuyo was very disappointed at not finding the manager, but he did manage to show off his German military coat to some of the Dubeczno factory workers. As soon as we were satisfied that we had destroyed the factory, we pulled out and headed back to the base on our wagons. Prior to setting the factory on fire, we removed the large leather belts from the factory's machinery to take with us. Leather was very scarce in wartime, and these belts could be used to make footwear. We later gave these belts to some of our friendly villagers as a reward for their loyalty.

A Sad Reunion

Among our military objectives were the destruction of food storage facilities used by the Germans, the burning of estates that supplied food for the Germans, and the destruction of small German outposts. During harvest time in the late summer of 1943, we focused our efforts on destroying all grain crops harvested and held for shipment to the Germans. For three weeks, we were busy burning estates and large farms which had their grains gathered for shipping.

In the village of Pachole, not far from the Ochoza forest, there was a large estate guarded by Germans and Polish police. The estate served as a storage place for grain and for large herds of cattle and pigs and other livestock which the Germans had requisitioned from area farmers for shipment to Germany. Our group decided to attack the estate, burn it, and kill as many guards as possible. Village informers told us the estate was lightly guarded.

We organized about one hundred men for this mission, which we conducted in broad daylight. Approaching Pachole, we passed many village farmers working their fields. Upon seeing such a large force of partisans emerging from the woods, they crossed themselves and ran home in fright. They realized something was brewing. We gathered all the wagons that had been abandoned in the fields and drove as fast as possible toward the estate in order to catch the Germans by surprise. Before we reached the estate, we jumped off the wagons and proceeded on foot. Chiel divided us into two groups. The first group was to burn down all the buildings and grain storage structures on the estate. I was in the second group, which was led by Chiel. The second group's objective was to rush the building where the guards lived.

Both groups attacked different parts of the estate simultaneously. Our group had one machine gun with us, carried by Dennis from Sosnowica, one of Chiel's relatives. As we rushed the guards' building, we opened fire with our weapons and with the machine gun, and the Germans began returning our fire. I got close to the building and threw in a grenade. There was a loud explosion, and then the Germans started jumping out the windows. We picked them off as they came out. They did not have a chance.

The entire estate was black from the smoke coming from the burning buildings. It was so thick that the dark smoke blocked out the sun and created the appearance of dusk. The cloud could be seen for miles. Our faces were black from the soot, and we looked like chimney cleaners. The animals from the barns were running loose in all directions.

About ten miles from this estate, in the town of Wisznice, there was a large German detachment. We knew that as soon as they saw the smoke they would head for the estate. We finished our job and left quickly for the woods. We were later told by the villagers that five German soldiers and five Polish police had been killed in the attack and that all of the estate buildings had burned to the ground. By the time the Germans arrived in trucks from Wisznice, we were deep into the woods.

During the late summer of 1943, we burned and destroyed dozens of large estates which supplied or served as food storage depots for the Germans. While proceeding on this campaign, I often thought of the nearby estate of David Turno, the wealthy Jewish farmer. His home had served as the area's synagogue for many years for the Jews in the villages surrounding Turno, such as Hola and Zamolodycze. When Manya and I had come to Hola in the fall of 1939, we often went together to David Turno's home. I remembered the Saturday services, the food he served after every service, and the pleasant times socializing with people. I also remembered my happy reunion there with my friend Yankel, with whom I spent long hours reminiscing about our days in the same Warsaw factory and living in the same Warsaw neighborhood. In the fall of 1942, the Jews of Hola and the surrounding villages had been ordered to move to the Wlodawa ghetto. David Turno and his family had to leave their home, and I never found out what happened to them. My friend Yankel also disappeared.

One evening, Chiel held a consultation with our group and we decided to go to Turno to burn down David's estate. It was far from our base in the Ochoza forest. Besides David's big estate with all of its mechanized harvesting machines, there were also two sizable farms in the village which had two big harvesting combines. These two farms were storage or supply sources for the Germans, so these were included in our plans to be destroyed. David's estate was located at the top of a hill at one end of Turno. The entire village was about two miles long, and at the opposite end were the other two farms.

About seventy people from our group took part in this night-time mission to Turno, including a number of our female fighters. Among them were Faiga, Dora, Hannah, and Rostka. Chiel divided our force in half. He led one half to David's estate on the hill. The other half, including myself and the Maryanka partisans, went to the other two farms at the opposite end of the village.

Everything went according to plan. We went straight to the barns on the two farms, and with big hammers we smashed the combines and then set fire to the barns loaded with grain. We worked quickly, and in about half an hour our job was completed.

At the other end of the village, Chiel with his group did the same thing. In no time, the entire village was lit up from the towering flames shooting into the sky from the blazing barns at opposite ends of the village. The glow was visible from miles away. Our group started pulling out toward David's estate, where Chiel and his men were supposed to wait for us. Halfway there, we heard shots and machine gun fire from the end of the village we had just left. In no time we saw a large force of Germans coming toward us. We fired back and kept running toward David's estate on top of the hill. The glow of the flames silhouetted my group, exposing us very clearly to the Germans. Chiel saw the seriousness of our situation, and he and his men started shooting over our heads at the oncoming Germans. This slowed them down somewhat and gave us a chance to join the others at the top of the hill. Together we answered their gunfire, slowly pulling out of the estate.

While running from the burning estate, I noticed a bulky form crawling on all fours, like an animal, and making very strange noises. It tried to stand upright but could not, and fell back down. I pointed it out to Symcha, running next to me, and we both decided it might be a human being, perhaps a Jew. We each took hold of one arm and dragged him along with us. The fight continued around us. We ran several miles from the estate, and then stopped to rest and look at this heap of a man. He was covered with hair down to his waist. His clothes were in shreds, and he could not stand on his feet. He looked like a skeleton and had no teeth. From his mumblings I discovered that this being was my friend Yankel, David Turno's nephew from Warsaw. He was half delirious and did not recognize me. I understood from his mumblings that he had dug a hiding place under the feeding troughs for the cows. No one knew he was there, and he had been able to survive on the food in the troughs and the milk from the cows. He had been in this hiding place for almost a year, but the heat from the burning buildings had driven him out of his hiding place.

We continued on to the village of Mosciska, where we put him on a wagon to take him to our base. Moniek cut his long hair, and we tried to feed him, but he could not hold down any food. He was extremely weak, and a few days later he died from his malnourished state. We buried him in the woods. Afterward we grieved for what had happened to a good human being, my friend Yankel.

28

A Second Encounter with Zaremba

Part of our sabotage work was aimed at wiping out all German/Polish outposts. We wanted to destroy their administrative records to diminish their ability to collect food quotas from the farmers, and in general to disrupt their control of the area.

We lacked enough manpower to attack larger German garrisons in the cities, but we liquidated the smaller outposts. By this time we felt free, more or less, in the area in which we operated. More often than not we stayed in village houses instead of the woods. Every villager was assigned several men to be housed and fed, and every few days we changed to another village, so as not to be a burden for too long. The only time we stayed in the woods now was when a large concentration of Germans arrived in the area and an attack was anticipated, but this did not happen often.

We tried to avoid confrontations with the Germans inside the villages in order to spare them from being destroyed. The villagers respected us and provided us with intelligence about German troop movements. Toward the end of 1943, the Germans seldom ventured into the villages. They were fully occupied on the Russian front and could not spare many troops to clean out the partisans from the countryside.

The village of Krzywowierzby was a county seat from which the neighboring villages were governed. All administrative offices from the area were there, and all taxes and deliveries of livestock and produce to the German administration went there. There was also a Polish police station there that was frequently visited by the Germans.

At one of our conferences with Chiel, we decided to attack the county seat of Krzywowierzby and to liquidate this outpost, destroying records and killing as many Germans as possible. We had heard that one of the Polish policemen stationed there was Zaremba, a very vicious man. We had many reasons to remember him, all of them bad ones. He had guided the Germans on many expeditions when they had gone into the woods to kill Jews.

We had previously encountered Zaremba in the spring of 1943 in the Ochoza forest when we ambushed the two wagonloads of German soldiers outside Zahajki. He was their guide at the time, and his bullet had killed a very brave partisan, Chuna Kot. At that time I had shot Zaremba in the face, but he had survived.

We hoped to find him this time in Krzywowierzby. With Chiel in the lead, about seventy-five of us attacked the outpost late one afternoon. The attack was swift and well coordinated. Armed with two machine guns, grenades, and our rifles, we surrounded our two main objectives, the police station and the administrative building. Dennis from Sosnowica handled one machine gun, and Lonka from Parczew handled the other one. Participating in the attack were two Patzans, or "little ones." One was Velvale the Patzan from Sosnowica, who, although the older, was very short in stature. The other one was Abram the Patzan from Zahajki, who had grown up in the woods with his three brothers and was now about twelve years old. Both Patzans were very good at hitting targets with grenades and so were very valuable to us on this mission.

As usual, I was together with the Maryanka group, including the three Barbanel brothers (Symcha, Chanina, and Chaim), Yefim, Yurek from Zaliszcze, Hershel and his wife Hannah, and Abram Grynszpan. We were all hardened fighters who had fought the Germans in numerous actions, and we were fearless and full of passion. Having lost our families, taking revenge on the Germans was almost considered a holy act for us.

We attacked and easily gained entrance to the administrative building. The employees ran out, and we quickly burned the building down. The occupants in the police station were all killed. Some died from our grenades, and the rest were killed by our gunfire when they escaped from the police station and attempted to put up some resistance outside the building. I spotted the hated Zaremba running from the police station, but he did not get far. I fired at him and saw him fall.

It quieted down, and we proceeded to burn the police station. From behind the police station came a single shot and then several. A wounded policeman had been hiding there and started firing at us. Yefim was hit and went down, seriously wounded. His cousin Hershel noticed where the shots had come from and tossed a grenade which finished off the policeman. The buildings were all on fire as we pulled out of the town.

We learned later that fifteen Germans and Polish police had been killed in the raid, including Zaremba. Yefim had taken a bullet in his chest, but we nursed him back to health. He was able to go on many other actions with us after he recovered. The bullet, however, is still in his body to this day.

29

Donachy Gets Her Revenge

Whenever we were at our base in the Ochoza forest, the people who lived in the Tabor would come to visit their returning sons or daughters or to visit friends. We visited them in the Tabor also. I liked to listen to them because they talked about their lives before the war. Not being a native of that area, I found these stories very interesting.

The older members of the Tabor were the leaders of their camp. They organized the distribution of food and counseled people on problems that arose. These elderly Jews were considered very wise, and we consulted with them often. The three leading elders of the Tabor were Abram from Zaliszcze, Yankel from Holowna, and Nuchem from Krasnowka. Abram had two sons who were partisans, Yurek and Mortche. Yankel had two daughters and a son, Shmuel (nicknamed "Soltis"), who was a partisan. Nuchem had a family in the Tabor also.

When we visited the Tabor, we often encountered one woman who always told stories about her village of Zahajki. We called her "Donachy." Her husband's name probably was Don, and that is why we called her that. She had two young daughters with her and also took care of a four-year-old boy whose family had been massacred by the Germans. His name was Aaron, but because of his young age she called him Aaraly.

When Donachy had escaped to the woods, she entrusted her house and possessions with a neighboring villager. Many others had also done this. The village of Zahajki was close to the Ochoza forest, and Donachy would often go to the village to get food from her old neighbors and to check on her house.

She always talked to us about her house, her barn, and her cow, from which she had previously gotten milk and butter. She told us she hoped and dreamed for the day when the war would end and the Germans would be chased out of Poland. Then she would be able to go back to her home in Zahajki and start to live again like a human being. Whenever she saw Chiel she would pester him to attack Zahajki. She would either tell him that Germans were there or that, even if there were no Germans, in Zahajki he could catch the many collaborators who had led the Germans to the Jews hiding in the woods. We explained that we were in fact taking revenge on the collaborators, but that did not seem to appease her. Her main concern was inducing us to attack Zahajki.

One evening Donachy came running from Zahajki to Chiel with news that there was a wedding in the village. "So what if there is?" Chiel chided her. She explained that one of the collaborators was making the wedding for his daughter. She told us there were eight German soldiers attending the wedding, and that it would be easy for us to kill them. When the four Zahajki brothers heard this news, they pressed Chiel for permission to take a force of partisans to Zahajki.

The four brothers were seasoned partisans. They had gone into the woods after the rest of their family had been killed by the Germans. This was even before the order was issued for all the village Jews to go to the Wlodawa ghetto. In the woods they found a small group of five escaped Russian prisoners, and together they roamed the forest as an armed band. They ambushed Germans on the roads and developed a reputation as fierce fighters. The four brothers joined Chiel when he organized his Jewish partisan unit, after he had arrived from the Makoszka forest in the winter of 1942. They had been well schooled by the Russians in fighting tactics.

The oldest of the four brothers, Shloime, was about twenty-five years old. He was tall and broad-shouldered, with a dark complexion, curly thick black hair, and a fierce look in his eyes. He carried a German rifle and wore a pistol at his side.

The second brother, Dudke, was also tall, dark, and fierce-looking, but not as broad-shouldered as his brother. He looked a little less menacing than Shloime. He also carried a German rifle and wore a German hat at a rakish angle on his head.

Itzik, the third brother, was tall and very skinny. The youngest brother, Abram the Patzan, was about twelve years old. He had dark eyes, a round face, and high cheek bones. Abram was a very fast runner and an excellent shot with the short cavalry rifle he carried. He disliked being called Patzan ("little one"). He wanted to be treated as an equal. He smoked cigarettes and even drank a little with the older partisans. He could ride a horse and had proven himself many times as a fearless fighter against the Germans. In battle, he would curse them aloud and cry with the anger he kept inside him.

A group of about twenty of us, including the four Zahajki brothers and Donachy, started out for Zahajki, only a few miles away. We heard the music from the wedding party as we approached the village. When we got closer we spread out and surrounded the house. Inside the house, we could see people dancing and could make out the German soldiers among those dancing. The four brothers rushed in first and shouted the order: "Hands up!" Panic broke out. All the guests started to run, including the collaborator who had hosted the wedding. He jumped through a window, but Donachy, who was outside, spotted him. We brought him back and shot him.

We did not want to fire in the house, as we did not want to hurt the guests. We let them all run out. The Germans were left standing with their hands up. We shot them all and left their bodies in the collaborator's house.

Moniek and Abram quickly busied themselves with gathering the remaining food and drink from the party to take back to our base. Donachy made a point of showing herself to the guests who were running from the house. She told them that this was in revenge for the Jewish families they had previously turned over to the Germans to kill.

30
The Sobibor Death Camp

By the end of the summer of 1943, all the ghettos in the cities and towns had been liquidated and their Jews sent to different concentration camps. Those from our area were taken by train to Sobibor, near Wlodawa and about twenty miles from where we were operating. Sobibor's crematoriums worked at full speed, twenty-four hours a day. Trains brought Jews from all over Europe to be gassed there and then tossed in its giant ovens.

In the meantime, the news from the Russian front was encouraging. The Germans were retreating. When we periodically met with Vanka and other leaders from the Army Ludowa, we took the opportunity to listen to Vanka's radio. We heard the war news broadcast from Moscow, which revealed how bad a beating the Germans were getting. They were losing more and more Russian cities to the Russians. This news made us hopeful that someday the Germans would lose the war, and we would be free people again. We were proud that we could contribute to their defeat, if only in a small way.

However, it was very disturbing to know that, only twenty miles from us, in this dreaded place called Sobibor, our fellow Jews were being killed by the thousands every day, and there was nothing we could do to stop it. In several group discussions, I pressed Chiel to move our group closer to Sobibor. Then we could investigate in the villages around the concentration camp how tightly the camp security was maintained. Perhaps with a large force consisting of all our partisans and with help we might get from the Army Ludowa, we could work out a plan to attack the camp and free the prisoners.

We broached our idea with Vanka, and on one occasion with Mietek Mocha when he came to the area. Mocha was the leader of the Army Ludowa in southeastern Poland. I was hopeful that with their help we could carry out an attack. They agreed that something should be done, but nothing ever materialized.

Chiel was a very good organizer and strategist. Before we went into a fight, he would investigate all available sources of information to ensure that it would not be a losing battle. I and many others helped to persuade him to move closer to Sobibor to investigate.

A large group of us went with Chiel toward Sobibor. Our Maryanka group knew the area very well, including the villages around the concentration camp. We passed several villages along the way. In each of them, there were many Army Ludowa sympathizers who were eager to give us information. They told us that the area around the camp was mined. We asked if they knew of any Jews who had escaped. The answer was no. We were told that the camp was guarded by a combination of German SS men and Ukrainian and Latvian guards, totaling at least three to four hundred soldiers. We were also told there were three lines of electrified wire fences around the camp, and three lines of mines outside the fences around the perimeter of the camp. From time to time a wild animal from the surrounding woods would wander into the vicinity of the camp and would explode a mine. Then the entire camp perimeter would be illuminated by searchlights.

This news was very discouraging. We could not attack a force that outnumbered us and was protected by such defenses. After dark, we got as close to the camp as we thought we could without being detected by the camp guards. The camp was surrounded by a large forest, but powerful lights from the camp swept the edge of the woods. From a distance, we could see the fires belching from the tall smokestacks of the crematoriums. We saw that it was impossible for us to storm this camp. The security was too strong and the risks too great.

Before we started to pull back, we decided to fire our weapons in unison to let the Jews inside know that they had friends thinking of them on the outside. We fired three salvos and then pulled back. Immediately after we fired our weapons, sirens sounded and what seemed like a million guns and machine guns began firing from the camp. The entire area lit up with searchlights. Even after we had walked several miles from the camp, we could still hear the shooting.

We stayed in that general vicinity for about two weeks. During this time, we took the opportunity to blow up a German freight train that was going to the front with weapons and supplies.

Several weeks later, we moved on to the nearby village of Wyryki. We found out from our contact there that inmates of the Sobibor death camp had just revolted. They had killed many of their guards and broken out of the camp. Most of the inmates had been killed in rushing the fences and braving the mine fields, but many of them had survived. Some of the survivors were still in the surrounding forests.

We stayed in this area longer than we had planned, crisscrossing the woods and talking to villagers in the hope that we might find some of the Sobibor inmates who had escaped. One night, while passing through a village, I and a few others went into a farmer's house to ask for food. Inside the house, we heard a noise coming from the next room. I asked the farmer what it was. He became visibly nervous and told us there were two men there, one with a gun, and that they too had come for food. When they heard our knock on the door, they had hidden in the next room. Chanina, who was with us, approached the closed door and asked in Russian for the people inside to open it. Then I went to the door and announced in Yiddish that we were Jewish partisans and asked them to open the door. The door swung open to reveal two men who were very happy to see fellow Jews. One was Boris from Slonim, a city in White Russia. The other was Wladek, who came from Warsaw. They told us there were three of them, and that the third one, whose name was Atleta, had gone to another house for food. With Boris and Wladek, we left the farmer's house and went looking for Atleta. We found him after visiting a few nearby houses. He carried a pistol that he had taken from a German guard. He was a seventeen-year-old boy from Warsaw, of average height but extremely strong, and therefore the Germans had nicknamed him Atleta (which means "the athlete"). According to the other two, his real name was Leon, and he had killed two Germans with his bare hands at the time of the uprising. The other two looked like walking skeletons. We took all three of them with us into the woods. They told us the story of how the revolt was organized and how they had killed many of the German and Ukrainian guards. They said that many Jews had escaped and that there might be more of them in the woods. We searched for another few days but could not find anyone else.

They also said the inmates had heard our three salvos the night we were outside the camp a few weeks previously. When that happened, the Germans had sounded the alarm and chased everyone out of the barracks. They ordered the camp inmates to lay face down on the ground, with the guards pointing their guns at them. The Germans were afraid there would be an attack on the camp, and in that case they had planned to shoot all the inmates. They did not want anyone to get out alive to tell the story of what had happened in Sobibor. We learned later that soon after the revolt the Germans destroyed the entire camp, taking pains not to leave any sign of the gas chambers and crematoriums.

We took the three escapees with us, and after a period of recuperation they made excellent partisan fighters. All three survived the war and settled in Israel. When we had returned to the base, they related in detail how the Sobibor revolt had been organized. The camp was divided into separate sections. One was the crematorium section. Separately, there were different working shop sections occupied by tailors, shoemakers, carpenters, goldsmiths, and other craftsmen. There were also warehouse sections where the inmates sorted, for shipment to Germany, clothes, jewelry, toys, human hair, and gold teeth taken from the gassed bodies before they were thrown into the ovens. Trainloads of people, mostly Jews, were brought to the camp daily from all over Europe. Most of the Polish Jews came in cattle cars, packed like sardines. They were in transit for many days without food or water. They were half starved coming from the ghettos even before they were packed into the cattle cars. When the trains arrived in Sobibor, many were already dead. The dead bodies were taken from the trains by wagons, pulled by camp inmates, directly to the crematoriums. The work of unloading the transports had to be done very quickly. The SS men and Ukrainian guards would beat and chase people coming off the trains so they could not orient themselves as to where they were and where they had to go. Within twenty minutes an entire trainload of several thousand Jews had to be emptied.

Sometimes the trains brought Jews from Western European countries like Holland, Belgium, and France. These trainloads came in regular passenger cars, which seemed very comfortable. The Jews from the Western European countries did not come from ghettos, as had the Polish Jews. They were dressed nicely and came with their luggage. Their children even brought their toys with them. On the way, they had been served food in the dining cars. They were told that they were being taken east to provide labor in support of the German war effort. When they arrived on the platform they were greeted by the same SS guards who, just hours earlier with the previous transport of cattle cars, had been beating, shooting, and unleashing dogs on the Jews. With smiles on their faces, they greeted these Western European Jews. They told them to leave their luggage on the platform and that the porters would bring it to the waiting room. The Jews were very satisfied, and some of them even tried to tip the porters who helped them down from the train cars. The porters consisted of camp inmates, referred to as the platform brigade. The platform brigade was forbidden to talk to the new arrivals, under threat of punishment by death from the SS. Nonetheless, some of them nodded their heads in the direction of the crematoriums, with their smokestacks constantly belching the blackened ashes of burned bodies, trying to show the new arrivals what was going on. The platform brigade knew that, within an hour, these people would be turned into ashes by the efficient German operation.

In the waiting room, the new arrivals were told to get undressed, men separate from the women and children, and to put their clothes into packages. Camp inmates then cut the women's and children's hair. Afterward, the Jews were told to go into the shower rooms. They were told that when they came out they would get back their bundle of clothes. Up to this point the SS had been polite. Once the people were led naked to the passageway bearing a sign on top marked "Shower Rooms," the SS started yelling, "Faster, Faster!" pushing and clubbing them. Some of the Jews started resisting, and their terror was very great. Some were shot right in front of the shower rooms, which were really gas chambers. Once inside the "Shower Rooms," the doors were closed and poison gas was dropped into the chambers. After several minutes of agony and screams the occupants were dead. Their bodies were then carted by camp inmates to the crematoriums to be burned in large ovens.

The October 14, 1943, revolt in Sobibor was organized by two men. The first was Sasha Pechersky, a Russian Jew and Russian officer, who led the few Russian prisoners of war in the camp. The second organizer was a Polish Jew named Leon Feldhendler. Both men survived the revolt. No one knew, shortly after the uprising, how many Jews had been killed in the revolt. Approximately six hundred had rushed the fences, many to be mowed down by machine gun fire from the guards or to be caught on the electrified fence or blown up in the surrounding mine fields. Weeks later, small groups of three or four survivors made their way to our base after wandering in the woods. Many told us stories about the escape and about those who were attacked or murdered in the woods by members of the Army Krajowa.

I remember three female Sobibor survivors who came to us about a month after the revolt, having been directed to us by a friendly villager. One was Edek, the second was Ulla, and the third was a Dutch Jew named Cathy. When Moniek from our Maryanka group saw Cathy, a tall girl with red hair, he was immediately attracted to her. He convinced us that we should include her in our group. She eventually was given a rifle and went on many missions with us, proving to be a very capable partisan fighter.

Altogether about fifteen survivors of the Sobibor revolt managed to make their way to our base. Most made very good partisans, were in many battles with us against the Germans, and survived the war.

31

On the Offensive in the Fall of 1943

During the fall of 1943, we did not stay very long in one place, not even at our base in the Ochoza forest. In the past, we would go on a mission and then return to the base. Now a group of us would leave the base for a week or two, completing several sabotage missions before coming back. We destroyed food storage facilities, cut down telephone poles to disrupt German communications, sought out collaborators, and attacked and destroyed small German and Polish outposts.

The Germans did not show themselves very much in the villages now. They stayed mostly in the cities, and so we were able to sleep in the village homes. We stayed in the ones closest to the woods, just in case of trouble.

Back at the base, we would march and sing Polish, Yiddish, and Russian partisan songs. Moniek always carried a harmonica, and when we marched and sang he would accompany us on his harmonica. We had good rifles and grenades, and because most of our activities were conducted at night we had equipped ourselves with flashlights. Some of us had pistols. Most of this equipment had come from our skirmishes with the Germans. Some of our fighters were dressed partially or entirely in German uniforms. Many, including myself, refused to wear them (except perhaps a good pair of German boots) because we hated what they symbolized to us. Additionally, I felt that, depending on the circumstances, it could be dangerous if we were mistaken for Germans by friendly forces.

Whenever we returned to our base in the Ochoza forest, the people from the Tabor were very happy to see us. Some of them had sons and daughters among us. After a few days of rest at the base, we would start out again on a series of new missions.

At one point we received orders from Army Ludowa headquarters to destroy four road bridges in the area. One was near Lubartow. Another one, near Parczew, was the largest of the four bridges. Chiel assigned four different groups to destroy the bridges. I led a group of about fifty fighters assigned to the Parczew bridge.

It was close to midnight when we reached the Parczew bridge. At a nearby village, we ordered some of the villagers to supply us with wagons and to load them with straw. Several wagons were loaded in no time. We also appropriated several cans of gasoline from the village and instructed the villagers to break up the bridge with their axes, saws, and crowbars. After the bridge structure had been severely damaged, we emptied the straw onto the bridge, poured petrol on it, and set fire to it.

The wooden frame of the bridge burned brightly, and the flames were visible for miles. I was sure that the Germans stationed in Parczew would see the glow and send a force to investigate. We had to work fast and get out of there. The night was almost over, and we had several miles to walk before reaching the forest.

While marching on the road back to the forest, in the distance we saw a convoy of trucks coming in our direction. We could not tell what they carried or how many of them there were. We quickly moved off the road and hid behind some low bushes. Many trucks passed by at high speed. We decided to wait until the end of the convoy and then attack the last few trucks.

Suddenly one of the trucks pulled to the side of the road not far from us and stopped. The others continued to pass it. About ten Germans emerged from the stalled truck and milled around the vehicle, pointing flashlights at the motor under the upraised hood. We held our fire since the other trucks were still passing by. We figured that we should wait until the end of the convoy before we attacked. When the last truck passed by the stalled one, we opened fire on both of them. The moving truck immediately lurched to the side of the road near us and stopped dead. For about five minutes we kept shooting furiously at the two trucks without letting up. For a while, the Germans answered our fire. Chanina and I each threw a grenade at them. After a few intense minutes of firing, there was no further resistance or movement from the trucks, which had been turned into blackened, charred shells.

We started to pull out fast, because several of the trucks which had previously passed by had stopped, turned around, and opened fire on us. We were not anxious to start a fight with a large German force. We did not know how many Germans had been killed, but we saw many lying on the road around the trucks. Later we were told by people in the area that the two charred trucks had remained on the side of the road for many days. They also reported that the convoy we attacked had been heading toward the bridge we had destroyed. The Germans had had to reroute the convoy, and it took several days for them to repair the bridge. When we reported to Chiel that we had not only destroyed the bridge but had also ambushed part of a German convoy, he congratulated us.

Another time, we received orders to liquidate the spies and collaborators who worked for the Germans in the nearby villages. These people were reporting to the Germans on our movements and the movements of units of the Army Ludowa. For this task, we received help from local villagers who had been working secretly with us. In the villages of Kszyvy Bor and Chmielow, we shot soltys (village elders) for their open collaboration with the Germans. In the villages of Krasnowka and Zinki, we did the same thing.

On another occasion, we found ourselves in the area of Zamolodycze. We had a force of about one hundred fighters. Our Maryanka group, including Faiga, presented a proposal to the others. We suggested that, since we had such a large group at that time, we go to Zamolodycze and take revenge on certain local villagers. They were the ones who had gone to the woods to round up the Jews who had escaped from the village in 1942 in order to avoid being forced into the Wlodawa ghetto. The villagers had marched the Jews back to Zamolodycze, locked them in Faiga's house, brought the Germans from nearby Sosnowica, and then watched as the Germans took the Jews out one by one and shot them. Only Faiga, Manya, Moniek, Yosel, David, and myself had survived that massacre by running away when the villagers sought to march us out of the woods.

Faiga, who had shed many tears for her murdered family members, was the person who most wanted us to take revenge on these villagers. She knew each person in the village, having been born and raised there. All the villagers knew her family as well as all the other Jews from the neighboring villages who had been rounded up. Her father had been a shoemaker and had done work for these people. Her brother Mendel had been a carpenter and also had done work for the villagers. The only one from her entire family left alive was

Faiga, and she carried within her a tremendous desire to avenge their deaths.

Faiga recalled each person who had been in the group that had rounded up the Jews in the woods. She also had kept a mental list of those who had shown a special satisfaction in catching the Jews, and those who had hung back and just been part of the mob. There were not many in the latter group.

We went from house to house in the village, taking out only those who had most actively participated in taking the captured Jews to Faiga's house to be killed by the Germans. The ones who had been merciful, and who had let Faiga escape, were spared. We killed about fifteen villagers. That was the largest act of revenge we ever took against collaborators.

Shortly after our detour in Zamolodycze, we received orders to go to the village of Kaplonosy. A large estate there, guarded by German SS men and Polish police, was being used as a storage depot for livestock and produce for the Germans. Our objective was to destroy this large estate, kill the Germans that guarded it, and burn the foodstuffs stored there.

Chiel took about sixty partisans on this mission. We were divided into two units. One unit of about thirty, including the Maryanka fighters and myself, was given the task of attacking and destroying the warehouses. They were a short distance from the main administrative buildings where the SS guards were housed. Our second unit was to hide as close as possible to the administrative buildings. Our hope was that when the Germans heard the first unit's attack and saw the warehouses burning, they would rush out from their quarters to the scene of the attack. Then our second unit would be able to slip into the vacated administrative buildings to burn them.

Everything went according to plan. My unit broke into the warehouses without meeting any armed resistance and set fire to them. The fire spread very rapidly, as there was a lot of dry straw around. The Germans rushed out of their quarters toward us, shooting everywhere, and we fired back. In the meantime, the second unit broke into the administrative buildings, set them on fire, and started shooting at the SS guards. At that point the Germans, realizing they faced partisans both in front of them and behind them, started running in different directions, seeking to avoid encirclement. We killed about six of them and about ten Polish police. The rest escaped. The estate was destroyed, both of our units met at the appointed area, and we left the vicinity. We suffered no casualties but were all very black from the soot.

We marveled at the constant movements of the officials of the

Army Ludowa. The Army Ludowa's high officials and military commanders would come, stay with us for a while, and then leave, all without advance notice. We never knew where they came from or where they were going when they left. These activities continued despite the presence of the local Gestapo, with all its informers watching the movements of virtually everyone. In spite of the constant Gestapo surveillance and the general terror created by the Germans, each village had its secret members who worked for the Army Ludowa and made it possible for the secret functioning of that organization.

Chiel's force was respected by the leadership of the Army Ludowa. As a result, they trusted us with important missions. They knew they could depend on us because as Jews we had no homes to return to and no families to go back to. We had no choice but to fight. Our mission was to fight, take revenge, and destroy the enemy.

We were often given special missions to escort leaders of the Army Ludowa or deliver important papers to the Russian (eastern) side of the Bug River. The partisan movement on that side of the river was much stronger and better equipped than in our area. They cleared out the Germans from large areas and built small airstrips where Russian planes could land with supplies. They were in constant touch with the Army Ludowa headquarters in Moscow.

On one of these special missions we lost a very good man, Hershel Rubenstein. He had been one of the leaders of the Warsaw ghetto uprising and, after escaping the ghetto ruins, had been directed to us by the Army Ludowa underground. On this particular mission we had to escort several high-ranking members of the Army Ludowa to the eastern side of the river. About twenty of Chiel's partisans, including myself and Hershel Rubenstein, accompanied them across the river. We had a local villager as a guide who knew the shallow spots in the river, and it was relatively easy for us to cross.

At first, everything went smoothly. Once we were on the other side we were met by a Russian partisan patrol, which took us by wagon to the partisan base about twenty miles away. The mission was done, but we stayed a few days in the woods with them before starting back to our side of the Bug. While crossing the river, we were spotted by a German patrol on the western bank. They started shooting at us. We were almost to their side of the river and could not go back. We answered their gunfire as we struggled to wade through the waist-high water. When we reached the western bank, we drove off the German patrol. Then we realized that Hershel was missing. No one had seen what had happened to him. It is likely he had been hit by a bullet, fallen in the water, and drowned. He was unable to swim because of his paralyzed arm. We never found his body. Hershel Rubenstein's death was a big loss to us.

In the course of traveling through the woods on our missions, we sometimes came upon small groups of two or three Jews. Some had escaped from a concentration camp, or had left a hiding place where they could no longer stay, or had been discovered and chased away by unfriendly farmers. If they managed to avoid being captured and killed by the Army Krajowa and we spotted them first, we would bring them back to our base. If they were fit to fight, we gave them weapons and accepted them into our partisan ranks. Most concentration camp escapees were too weak and emaciated to be fighters. Those unable to fight, as well as children and the elderly whom we found in the woods, were brought to the Tabor. Once there, we helped them with food and anything else we could get for them.

On one occasion as we were walking in the woods, we came upon a little six-year-old boy sitting by the side of a road at the edge of the forest. He was sobbing and did not run when he saw us from a distance. It was late afternoon, and we stopped to get a closer look at him. We thought he was a Jewish child and so started to talk to him in Yiddish. He responded immediately to a familiar tongue. He told us that a friendly farmer in Kodeniec had kept him hidden for a long time. Finally, the farmer could no longer keep him. The farmer brought the boy to this spot in the woods and told him to sit there because Jewish partisans were known to pass this way and might find him. The child's name was Zishky. We took him with us to the Tabor in the Ochoza forest, where the people in the Tabor took good care of him.

Another time a group of our partisans returned to the base with a boy about ten years old, whom they had found near the village of Skorodnica. He was tall for his age and very thin, with rags for clothes. His name was Moishe. A friendly villager had told the partisan group that a Jewish boy came to him every few days begging for food. The villager told us he thought the boy must be hiding somewhere in the nearby woods. Our partisans stayed around the vicinity of Skorodnica for a few days, hoping the boy would return again to the farmer for food. That is exactly what happened. When they tried to approach him, the boy started running. They hollered in Yiddish that he need not be afraid because they were Jewish partisans, and he returned. He told them that for several months he had been hiding in the woods. He came from the village of Kolacze. His father, mother, and two little sisters had been hiding from the Germans in

Kolacze. His parents had given him to a farmer to work as a shepherd, hoping that he would be able to save himself. Several months before we found him, he learned from the other shepherds that his entire family had been caught by the Germans and killed. He got scared and ran away, leaving the farmer's cows in the field. He had heard that there were Jewish partisans in the area, whom he hoped to find. In the meantime, he begged the local farmers for food and slept in a haystack in a farmer's field. The partisans brought him to our base, and we kept him in the Tabor. We took him with us on *bombioshkis* in the area of Kolacze because he knew all the farmers there. He would tell us which farmers had been kind to him, so that we would not bother them. He also pointed out those farmers who had been inhospitable toward him. We made it a point to seek out those farmers for food.

I distinctly remember Yom Kippur in the fall of 1943. We did not have a calendar to tell us that it was time for this holy Jewish holiday. However, the three leading elders of the Tabor—Abram from Zaliszcze, Yankel from Holowna, and Nuchem from Krasnowka—were all pious Jews and kept track of when the holidays arrived.

It happened that our entire group was together at the base during this holiday. On Yom Kippur eve all the partisans and the people from the Tabor came together for the Kol Nidre service, which is the solemn opening to this very solemn holiday. Abram from Zaliszcze had a very thick prayer book which he had somehow saved. The prayer book contained the Hebrew prayers for all the Jewish holidays. We made a big fire (at night the Germans did not come into the woods). There were about five hundred people around the fire, and Abram started chanting the sad melody of the Kol Nidre. For all of us, it brought to the surface memories of being home with our families and going to synagogue on this sacred night. Everyone was simultaneously crying and praying, while Abram chanted the Kol Nidre. We had lost our families, and none of us could be sure of our future.

As we sat around the fire, we could hear the noises of the night owls and other animals. It was cold and the autumn sky was clear and full of stars. We sat and watched the shooting stars, and from the depth of the Ochoza forest we sang the prayer of Kol Nidre. The next day was Yom Kippur and we stayed together. Most of the people observed religious practice by fasting, and Abram recited prayers throughout the day.

Destruction of Our Base
in the Ochoza Forest

Usually the Germans followed a pattern when they intended to attack us. They would travel to a nearby village the night before. The following morning, they would carry out their attack on a certain part of the woods, often shelling us with artillery from a distance as a prelude to the attack. We usually had friendly villagers tell us that the Germans had come or were coming to the area, and this gave us a chance to withdraw in the face of a large German force.

In the fall of 1943, shortly after Yom Kippur, the Germans surprised us with a change in tactics. They came in the morning in large numbers, straight from faraway Lublin, with their trucks and heavy weapons. It happened that all the partisans were away from the base on missions at the time. On our return, as we were passing through nearby villages, we heard from the farmers that there had been a large massacre at our base. When we got there we learned that about seventy-five women, children, and elderly people in the Tabor had been killed in the attack. At this time of the year the swamps in the Ochoza forest were practically dry, which had made the area more accessible than usual to the Germans.

From local villagers and from survivors of the attack we later came across, we pieced together what had transpired. We were told that the people who were keeping guard around each island of the Tabor had sounded the alarm when the approaching Germans were sighted. For defense when the partisans were away, the people in the Tabor had about forty rifles. They were mostly old weapons from the First World War—some were French, Russian, and Austrian.

The leaders of the Tabor had sent out scouts to the adjacent islands. The scouts warned the people that the Germans were trying to set up a trap in a nearby treeless field. They advised that it was better to stay put in the forest and swamps until night, when they would try to leave in the direction of the Zahajki woods.

Late in the morning, the Germans attacked from three sides, leaving an apparent escape route toward the open field. Panic broke out among some of the people. They started running in all directions, mostly to the open field. The Germans had hidden soldiers behind several haystacks and a barn that ringed the field. When people ran into the field, they were mowed down by machine gun fire.

Many people who were running escaped the fire. While running and holding her three-year-old daughter, Chanche Barbanel was grazed by a bullet that passed through her hair and set it on fire. Her little girl kept pleading with her mother, "Please don't drop me," when she saw her mother's hair on fire. Chanche held on to her daughter, and the two of them, along with her husband Motel, survived the attack and ultimately the war.

The forty people with weapons spread out, forming a defense on the main island. In unison they fired a volley at the Germans and then kept up a constant rifle fire at the attackers. The Germans continued their shooting, but because of the large number of guns fired by the defenders in their initial volley, the Germans did not immediately move in closer. This gave the unarmed people time to scatter in the woods. The Germans did not know that the defenders holding them at bay consisted of a small number of boys and elderly men, some of them in their sixties and seventies.

Many people who did not panic and run into the open field saved themselves by hiding in the underbrush and in the swamp, as instructed. The shooting went on the entire day. The forty armed Jews defending the main island slowly retreated from the base, to cover the escape of the others. They stayed together, keeping up their fire to prevent the Germans from freely hunting down the Tabor people. Given their age, inexperience as fighters, limited weaponry, and the overwhelming number of their attackers, the forty defenders gave a good account of themselves, both in terms of tactics and accuracy of fire. Their rearguard action undoubtedly saved many of the Tabor people by slowing down the attackers and by drawing the Germans' attention to their small group. Their constant rifle fire inflicted many casualties on the Germans. For almost all of them, this was their first opportunity to avenge the cruelties that had been committed against their families. Unfortunately for many of them, this opportunity was also their last. By the end of the day, most of the forty defenders had been killed. By evening, the Germans pulled out, taking with them their dead and wounded. The surviving Jews buried their dead. Then they went into the swamp and forest to gather the survivors who were hiding, and together they left for the Zahajki woods.

When we arrived at our base, there was no one there. All we found were broken pots, scattered clothing, and turned-over shelters. We searched the swamps and found more dead Jews, whom we buried. We also collected a number of survivors of the raid in the nearby woods.

We stayed in the Ochoza forest for a short time longer, in order to allow other units of Chiel's force to join up with us upon returning from their missions. During this time, we found out from the villagers that a Polish forester who lived in the village of Kaplonosy had led the Germans to our base. We also learned that the German garrison from the town of Wyryki near the Bug River had taken part in that raid. We found the forester in his home in Kaplonosy and shot him. Much later we had the opportunity to attack the garrison in Wyryki and killed many of the Germans there. After all of Chiel's units had rejoined us, we left for the Makoszka forest, about twenty miles away, together with the survivors of the raid we had found. Later, we joined up with the other Tabor survivors of the raid who had left our base before we arrived there.

33

Destruction of the Ostrow Lubelski Garrison

The Makoszka forest covered a vast area. The local German garrisons would not venture into the forest unless joined by large forces brought in from other areas. If we were informed by the local villagers of the movement of such large forces in our direction, we pulled out if we had time. If we were surprised by such a force, we fought back, but this was not always advantageous for us.

The town of Ostrow Lubelski was located near the Makoszka forest, south of Parczew. There was a sizable German and Polish garrison of over a hundred men stationed there, which harassed the partisans. They did not openly attack the partisans in full force. This was left to the larger German forces. However, soldiers from the Ostrow Lubelski garrison would ambush partisans on the roads bordering the forest, then return to their well-fortified positions in the town.

At this time our ranks consisted of about 300 armed fighters, many equipped with submachine guns. We received orders to attack and destroy the Ostrow Lubelski garrison and city hall. A force of just under one hundred Army Ludowa fighters joined us for this attack. We started out through the forest toward Ostrow Lubelski late one afternoon. Each man carried plenty of ammunition and two hand grenades. Before we left the woods, Chiel divided the group into two units. The first unit was assigned to storm the quarters where the German and Polish garrison was housed, destroying the garrison and demolishing the building. The second unit was assigned to destroy the records in the city hall by burning it down and to seek out German collaborators.

Dennis, the young partisan from Sosnowica and a relative of Chiel's, carried and operated a heavy machine gun. His helper, who carried the heavy ammunition, was a fifteen-year-old fighter named Sam. We nicknamed him Polimiot because that was the name of the weapon whose ammunition he carried.

When we left the woods we still had a distance to walk toward the town. Some wagons carrying wood passed us, and when they saw us, the drivers whipped their horses to go more quickly. When we noticed a large number of empty wagons coming down the road, we stopped them and rode them the rest of the way to town. From a distance, we could see the top of the Ostrow Lubelski church. Soon we reached the town and divided into our previously assigned units. I was in the unit assigned to attack the garrison.

We commenced the attack just after sunset. Firing our guns, we rushed the German command building. I remember Chiel yelling: "Get the murderers," as we ran. The Germans barricaded themselves inside the building and fired back at us through the windows. We dropped to the ground to avoid their fire, crawling to get close enough to throw in grenades. As I tossed a grenade through a window, I noticed the German fire on my right concentrating in the direction of Moniek and Chanina, who were behind me. Moniek fell and dropped his rifle. He appeared dead. The Germans stopped firing in his direction. Chanina kept up his fire. I jumped up and threw my second grenade into the window on my right. The grenade exploded, followed by several secondary explosions, and pieces of masonry began falling from the building.

Dennis kept up a steady fire from his heavy machine gun as the Germans started running out of the building. Chanina yelled to me that Moniek was killed, but I had a feeling that he was faking. I knew Moniek was a good actor and yelled back for Chanina to keep firing. I was right about Moniek. He was okay.

The Germans never had a chance. There were too many of us, and we overwhelmed their defensive positions. We burned down the city hall and German command center and wiped out the garrison in less than an hour. In that space of time, we rounded up and shot some of the civilian collaborators too. We quickly gathered together our forces and pulled out of Ostrow Lubelski. We had killed the bulk of the German garrison (which included some Polish police), and the remaining defenders fled to the countryside.

34

Escape from Encirclement

From our informers in the Parczew area, we learned that the Germans were preparing a major attack in the Makoszka forest. A large concentration of Germans, together with artillery and armored vehicles, were massing in the villages around Parczew—a sure sign they were about to launch an attack in the forest. We received an order one evening from the Army Ludowa high command to pull out of the forest as soon as possible. In our area, in addition to our force, there were also an Army Ludowa group and a Russian partisan unit, each consisting of about eighty fighters. The order applied to these two groups as well.

That same evening, we gathered together the people of the Tabor, who were camped in the nearby woods. We told them that we and the other two partisan units were moving out of the area, and that we expected a major German offensive imminently. We advised them to move immediately to the Ochoza forest to avoid this attack.

Most of them heeded our advice and started getting ready to go, but some hesitated, especially those who came from Parczew and the surrounding villages. They figured they could find safety in the vastness of the forest, and that the Germans would not find them. However, the great majority of the Tabor group, under the leadership of their elders, left in a hurry that night for the Ochoza forest. We made sure that those who were capable carried guns.

At dawn, we were attacked. The Germans brought in many troops from the Russian front (which was not far from the forest by this time) for the attack. The Russian army was pressing the Germans back now. The Germans realized that the partisans might hinder their retreat and so decided to try to eliminate this threat.

They cordoned off our area of the woods with troops and artillery and subsequently opened up a tremendous artillery fire on the forest in our vicinity. We tried to cut through the surrounding ring. The machine gun and rifle fire was very heavy, and we had to retreat back into the woods to a different area, hoping to be able to find another route of escape.

The Germans did not advance very far into the forest. They thought we were a very large force from the heavy fire we returned. But they kept the woods sealed. They started out with artillery shelling and then brought in several planes, which circled low over the trees, dropping bombs. The trees caught fire. The planes could not see us under the thick forest foliage, but they dropped their bombs anyway. The shelling and bombing continued for the entire day. We knew the woods very well and tried to cut through the German ring several times, but we were blocked at every turn.

We were a combined force of almost five hundred partisans. By this time, our group consisted of about three hundred fighters. The Russian contingent of about eighty men was part of the Voroshilov battalion, the rest of which was stationed on the eastern side of the Bug River. They had very good heavy machine guns. The Polish Army Ludowa group, also about eighty men, were mostly new recruits, but very brave men.

We tried to disengage ourselves from the German cordon, moving to a different part of the woods. We hoped that toward evening the Germans would pull out, because they had never before fought with us at night. Toward evening we moved in the direction of the village of Uhnin, hoping to break out there. Uhnin was at an edge of the Makoszka forest, from which we could follow small patches of woods that would lead us all the way south to the Ochoza forest.

We probed the ring in the Uhnin area, and the encircling forces started shooting at us. We answered them with our fire. Then we heard them ordering us, in Russian, to surrender. This order was transmitted over a loud speaker. The speaker said: "We are Russians. Our leader is General Vlasov. We have it good with the Germans. Surrender and come with us and be part of us. We don't want the Jews, but you Russians are our brothers."

This part of the enemy ring was manned by soldiers referred as the "Vlasovis." They were former Russian prisoners of war, willing to fight on the Germans' side, who were organized under the command of a former Russian officer named General Vlasov. They did not have a reputation for being good fighting men. Our group became enraged at confronting these turncoats, especially our Russian partisans, who immediately fixed bayonets on their rifles. We threw ourselves at the Vlasovis, tossing grenades and spraying submachine gunfire. It was getting dark, and we knew this was our chance to break through. With shouts of "Traitors of the Motherland" coming from our Russians, we rushed straight at them. In a few short emotional minutes we overran their position in fierce hand-to-hand combat. The Vlasovis were massacred, many on the points of the bayonets used by our Russians, who seemed more concerned with pursuing and killing every one of the hated Vlasovis than with leaving the encircled area. It was dark by the time we mopped up the Vlasovis and, having suffered few casualties, we were in a hurry to get as far away as possible. The few Tabor people who had not escaped the previous night followed us. We walked the entire night, finally reaching the Ochoza forest where we rejoined the bulk of the Tabor people.

The next several weeks in the Ochoza forest were very difficult for us. We were frequently attacked by German units and were forced to be constantly on the move while protecting the Tabor people. Finally, we received information from our informers that a very large force of German troops was concentrating in the villages around the Ochoza forest. We did not know if this was happening because the Germans were following us, terrorizing the villagers for more food supplies, or simply killing people for supporting the "bandits" (as the Germans referred to the partisans). In the meantime, German soldiers were going around to the villagers with bags and baskets, taking whatever items of value they could find, without any official orders. We were advised by our friendly informers to pull out of the area to avoid another clash with a large contingent of the regular German army.

At that time, a section of the headquarters of the Army Ludowa was stationed in the Ochoza forest. Chiel, along with several of our group, went to visit the Army Ludowa command to get new instructions and to find out what the situation was. Bolek Alef and Mietek Mocha, two major figures in the Army Ludowa, were there at the time. In consultation with the Army Ludowa, the decision was made to "lay low" and watch the German movements for the next few days. We knew that an attack by the Germans could happen at any time, since they were concentrated in great force. We felt it would not be wise for us to confront the Germans in a frontal fight.

We decided to go east, and perhaps cross the Bug River to the Russian side. We were exhausted from all the fighting and felt there was no place to go except across the river. We knew that on the Russian side there were large areas controlled by Russian partisans. It would give us a chance to rest for a while, free from another German attack. We relayed this request to the Army Ludowa leadership, but they disapproved of our plan. In the meantime, more and more German troops poured into the surrounding villages. We decided to act on our own plan and told the Tabor people they could come with us if they chose. We took most of the Tabor people eastward with us, and the remainder scattered throughout the forest.

In a small village not far from the Bug River, we went at night to the house of a friendly local priest and asked him to take us to the shallowest point of the river. He led us to a spot where the water was waist deep, and with our weapons over our heads we crossed, with the priest leading the way. When we got to the other side, we directed him to go back.

We did not want to stay close to the river in case we were spotted by a German patrol, so we proceeded on foot several miles deeper into the woods. As the sun came up, we were still very wet and the weather was very cold. It was late autumn, 1943. We sat down in the woods to dry ourselves. At that point, we had no idea where to go, so we simply sat there in the woods.

A few hours later, a Russian partisan on a small horse spotted us and trotted over to our resting place to investigate. We told him who we were, and he went back on his little horse to report. About a half hour later, a group of ten men came and asked for our commander. A group of about seven or eight of us, including Chiel, Lonka from Parczew (who had been with Chiel from the very beginning of his partisan unit), Yurek from Zaliszcze, Symcha, and myself, went with the group to the Russian partisan commander, who was not very far from where our group had camped. We explained who we were and why we had come. We told him that we were a group of Jewish partisans working with the Army Ludowa. We explained that we had been in a battle with a large force of Germans in the Makoszka forest a few weeks ago. We had fought our way out, killing many Germans and Russians from the Vlasov army, which was fighting on the Germans' side. Lately, we explained, we were in the Ochoza forest when a new concentration of Germans was brought into the area. We felt we were not in a position to confront a force of that size, and since we were close to the Bug River, we decided to cross over and stay on the Russian side for a while.

They took us deeper into the woods and told us to wait there.

Several hours later, the battalion commander arrived on a horse. He was a young man, and very friendly. He told us he had heard of the good work the Army Ludowa was doing, and he was glad we had saved ourselves from the Germans. He welcomed us.

Our immediate problem was food. The Russian partisans were not in a position to feed all of us. They brought us some bread and potatoes but told us not to go for food to the farmers there, as they were very poor. After we were there a few days, the Russian battalion commander visited our encampment to make the following announcement: Since we were Polish citizens we would have to go back across the river to Poland. However, since we were there and were exhausted from our battles with the Germans, they would let us stay with them for two weeks. We had no desire to stay there much longer anyway, because there was no food to be had. The Russians appreciated our problem, and they solved it in a unique way. There was a pond nearby where carp were commercially raised. The fish were already grown to full size. The Russians let some of the water out of the pond to make it easy for us to catch the carp and told us that we could have as many as we wanted. For two weeks we ate carp—boiled carp, fried carp, grilled carp. We remembered these fish for years to come, and appreciated the Russians' willingness to share with us whatever they had.

When we returned to the Polish side of the river, we were glad to be back in our own territory. We learned that during the two weeks we had stayed with the Russians, the Germans had conducted raids in the woods and villages in the area. When we returned, however, they were gone. They could not afford to deploy large forces in the countryside for very long when they were taking such a beating at the Russian front.

We had not wanted to stay with the Russian partisans indefinitely, as we would have lost our identity as a Jewish partisan unit. We would have been purposefully absorbed and scattered among the different Russian partisan groups. That is what happened to other smaller Jewish fighting units, like the remnants of Moishe Lichtenstein's group who had managed to cross the Bug River to the Russian side. There was no such thing as a separate Jewish partisan group in Russia. Another reason we decided to come back was because we knew the territory on the Polish side. We knew the local people and were an important and respected part of the Army Ludowa. Additionally, we felt a big responsibility for those of the Tabor people who had chosen not to follow us to the Russian side.

Once back in the Ochoza forest, we reestablished contact with the

Army Ludowa command and also rejoined our Tabor people who had stayed behind. The Army Ludowa command told us that the Germans had been very active in the area for the two weeks we were away. We felt we had been wise in going over to the other side of the Bug River when we did.

35

Murder at the Hands
of the Army Krajowa

We were told that a Russian plane
had dropped weapons for the Army Ludowa, some of which were to
be given to us, in the vicinity of Siedlce. This must have been by
error, because Siedlce was far north and west of us. The Army
Ludowa people in the Siedlce area hid these weapons for us, and we
were instructed to go there to pick them up. About fifteen people
were selected for this mission, five from our group and ten from the
Army Ludowa. Our men consisted of Abram from Zmiarka, Dennis
from Sosnowica, Eli from Parczew, and two fighters whose names I
cannot recall. The leader of the mission was Yanek of the Army
Ludowa.

Yanek and some of our men were familiar with the territory that
had to be traveled. About fifteen miles from Siedlce, they entered a
villager's home to rest. They ordered the occupants not to leave the
house in case they were German collaborators or Army Krajowa
members. But a little boy about eight years old slipped out through
the attic and let the neighbors know that a group of heavily armed
partisans had come into their home. Soon afterward the house was
surrounded by about a hundred armed members of the Army Krajowa. They asked for someone from the house to step outside and
talk things over. They warned that, if no one came out, they would
storm the house. Yanek, the mission's leader, went out to them and

told them that he was with a unit of the Army Ludowa from the Makoszka forest. The leader of the Army Krajowa force responded by saying that the Army Ludowa was working together with Jews and communists and therefore was an enemy of the Army Krajowa. Yanek explained that they were all Polish patriots and that their only enemy was the Germans.

At that point, the Army Krajowa leader demanded that those in the house give up their weapons and leave the territory quickly. He gave them five minutes to come out and surrender their weapons. The Jewish fighters were definitely against giving up their weapons. Abram said that the Army Krajowa was no better than the Nazis, and once they had given up their weapons they would surely be killed. He felt it would be better to open fire on them and run. Yanek and the rest of the Army Ludowa men hesitated, saying that the Army Krajowa would never do a thing like killing them.

Dennis challenged that belief by asking why the Army Krajowa wanted their weapons, since they had enough of their own. Meanwhile, time was going by and five minutes had just about passed. Yanek was the first to throw out his rifle, and another of his men followed. At that point, the five Jewish partisans opened fire and stormed out running. The surrounding force immediately attacked those in the house and those running from it.

It was a massacre. Of the fifteen men on the mission, only two of the Jewish partisans returned—Abram, who was wounded in the hand, and Eli, who was wounded in the foot. Army Ludowa people in the vicinity later told us that the thirteen dead partisans had been buried in a mass grave.

News of these terrible murders stunned us all. We found out that the owner of the house in which the fifteen partisans had been surrounded was the commander of the Army Krajowa in that area. Many of our fighters and those from the Army Ludowa were ready to go back to that village to take revenge for this heinous crime. The Army Ludowa leadership was against taking revenge. They pointed out that the Germans would love to see the partisans fighting each other.

In the village of Grabowka, our group of three hundred Jewish partisans, together with a large number of Army Ludowa men, organized a meeting to protest the murders committed by the Army Krajowa. Several regional leaders of the Army Ludowa, including Vanka Kirpicznik, came to the meeting. A large crowd of neighboring villagers, who were sympathizers of the Army Ludowa, were also invited to the meeting. All the Army Ludowa leaders condemned the brutal murders committed by the Army Krajowa, but warned us not to be provoked into answering murder with murder. In spite of what had happened near Siedlce, we were told that we should encourage collaboration with the Army Krajowa in fighting the Germans until we were rid of them. After the war, we were told, we would settle with the murderers. I later learned that after the war the Polish government did indeed make the local Army Krajowa leader pay for this crime. He was put on trial, convicted of the murder of thirteen partisan fighters, and sentenced to a long prison term.

This incident was not our only fatal run-in with the Army Krajowa partisans. Four or five months later, in the spring of 1944, a small group of Chiel's men went into the village of Maryanka to get some food. Among them was Chaim Barbanel (the oldest of the three remaining Barbanel brothers), his brother Chanina, Geniek (a relative of the Barbanels), Yankel (Vuyo), and Velvale the Patzan from Sosnowica. On their way back to the woods, they were ambushed by an Army Krajowa unit. In the fight that ensued, Chaim was killed. The others escaped and upon their return told us what had happened. We lost a very courageous partisan in Chaim. The irony is that, after so many battles with the Germans, he was killed by the Army Krajowa and not by the Germans. Even though we fought the same common enemy, the Army Krajowa took every opportunity to kill Jews. It even sometimes seemed that they were more interested in killing Jews than in fighting the Germans.

We later obtained from an informer the name of the individual who had masterminded the ambush in which Chaim was killed. He paid for his crime with his life.

36

Our First Parachute Drop

In late 1943, we were stationed in the village of Old Grichovy, not far from the village of Rudka where the local Army Ludowa command was located. I often accompanied Chiel to Rudka to hear the latest news from the Russian front and to talk about our future military activities. On one such occasion we were told about an upcoming Russian parachute drop of weapons for both us and the other local Army Ludowa partisans. There had been previous drops of weapons, but not in our area. This was to be the first drop for our group. Chiel and I were to keep it a secret from our force until the time came to receive it. We were the group that was given the job of arranging the pick up.

Several days later, after dark, Chiel gave the order to ready two wagonloads of dry wood and three wagonloads of straw. A large group of us traveled with the wagons about five miles into the woods to a spot where there was a large clearing. The group was wondering what we were about to do. Finally, Chiel told them that, when the order was given, we were to scatter the wood in several bundles encircling the clearing, and then we were to wait for an airdrop. We had to wait several hours, during which Abram Bochian, the clown, kept us amused with his jokes and imitations.

At about ten o'clock that night, we lit the bundles of wood and waited. We kept scanning the sky. It was a cold night and the sky was very clear. By about midnight, everyone was getting impatient and beginning to doubt that anything would happen. The lighted bundles of wood, around which we huddled for warmth, were burning low. Then we heard the faraway sound of airplane engines. The men were ordered to throw more straw and wood on the fires, and the flames immediately shot up. The aircraft started to circle the clearing, flying lower and lower. Chiel fired a flare gun in the air, lighting up the clearing even more.

All of a sudden we saw a parachute coming down. A few of us ran toward it. It landed several hundred feet from the fires. After that, several more bundles, six in all, came floating down toward us. We kept looking for more because we knew that a man and woman were also supposed to be dropped.

Finally, a man landed right in the center of the clearing. We waited for the woman, but we did not see anyone else. When he landed, the man held a revolver in one hand and a knife in the other, with which he cut himself loose from the parachute. For a few moments, he kept us at a distance with his revolver. He uttered a password, and Chiel answered. After that he put the revolver into his pocket, and we approached him. He told us that the woman, named Tania, had jumped right after him.

A few of us unharnessed the horses from the wagons and rode on horseback in several directions. We scoured the woods, calling out her name. Others went on foot and searched for several hours over many miles. While searching through the woods, I heard a faint rustling noise in the distance. I called Chanina, and together we reached the source of the rustling, where we found the woman trapped. Her parachute had become entangled in the top of a tall tree. We helped her down and found she was uninjured. She was dressed in a Russian military uniform with a round fur cossack hat. After exchanging the password, we brought her back to the group in the clearing.

We returned to the base and eagerly unpacked the bags. In the first one we found fifteen brand new submachine guns, called PPSZs, with seventy-five bullet magazines in each, and plenty of ammunition. Another bag contained six heavier caliber submachine guns called Dichterovy, with fifty-five bullet magazines and additional ammunition. The Dichterovy had a longer range than the PPSZs, and their bullets could do more damage. One bag contained boxes of German ammunition, since we used many German rifles and pistols that we had acquired in ambushes and fights with the Germans. Another bag contained various mines and explosives for blowing up bridges, buildings, and trains. These included English plastic mines, which were equipped with a timer. When thrown at a locomotive, they would seal onto the metal and could not be removed without exploding. They could be set for specific times to explode. Another heavier bag contained five PTR antitank guns, which were each almost ten feet long and weighed about forty pounds apiece. Included in the bag were very large shells for these guns, designed to pierce the heavy plating of a tank. Later, on several occasions, we used these guns to shoot down German planes. The last bag was full of propaganda literature in Polish and Ukrainian to be distributed to the villagers. We shared the contents of all these bags with the Army Ludowa. We also brought the two Russian parachutists to Army Ludowa headquarters.

Receipt of this airdrop was a tremendous lift to our morale. After all the casualties we had suffered and cruelties that had been inflicted on our families, for the first time we felt there was a friendly power that had stretched out a helping hand to encourage us to go on fighting. Although we later received more airdrops and other Russians parachuted into our area during the war, these later events could not compare with the excitement and feeling of hope that this initial drop brought to our group. It made us feel we were an important part of the Allied armed struggle against the Germans.

We immediately put the new weapons and mines to good use. Chiel gave orders to blow up a train that traveled east on the Lukow-Lublin line, quite a distance from our base. This train passed over a bridge near a wooded area. Some of our fighters were familiar with this area. We were ordered to blow up the train and destroy the bridge. Five of us, including myself, were given the new submachine guns. We were instructed in how to handle the mines. They were much lighter to carry and much simpler to detonate than the cannon shell we had previously used, which took four men to carry up an embankment. The new mines could be carried by one man and had much more destructive force. We did not need a wire to set them off. They were detonated by remote control, by a timer, or simply by contact. We could be some distance away and still watch the results.

We met no resistance at the bridge, as it was unguarded. We planted the mines to explode from the weight of the train cars. The mines went off with a tremendous explosion, while we were safely at a distance. We were told later by the local Army Ludowa sympathizers that the bridge collapsed, with the locomotive and several cars falling into the water. The rest of the cars derailed and plunged down the railroad embankment.

At the same time, Chiel had sent another group equipped with the new mines to the Chelm-Wlodawa railroad line. Upon their return, that group told us they had blown up a German troop train. The explosion had derailed several cars and killed many German soldiers.

37
The Winter of 1943—44

During Christmastime 1943, we were stationed in the woods near Kodeniec. Some of the villagers invited us for a Christmas meal. Ever since the Russian army had gone on the offensive following the Battle of Stalingrad, the local villagers had started to feel that the Germans were not invincible and that it was possible they might even eventually lose the war. In such an event, some villagers were concerned they might be accused of collaborating with the Germans and that those who had caught Jews and Russian ex-prisoners and turned them over to the Germans might have to pay for their crimes. Given those fears, the entire population of the village was now friendly to us and asked us to share the meal with them.

There were few Germans in the countryside now, as they were needed on the Russian front. We felt safe about quartering ourselves in the villages unless we heard that large German forces were coming into the area, in which case we pulled out into the woods. We always avoided an open fight with large German units. In a pitched battle, they could always get reinforcements, but we could not. Our strategy was to attack, inflict maximum damage, and disappear. Of course, our biggest asset was the dense forest in the area, some of which was virtually impenetrable in parts.

About ten or twelve of us were assigned to each house for the holiday meal. The people in each home prepared a very nice dinner, with food and homemade bimber (which had a very high alcohol content). As often happened, when bimber was available some of our men had too much of it and got drunk. In the middle of the festivities, a messenger arrived to tell us that a large force of Germans was coming into the area. Chiel gave the order to pull out to the woods, but we had a problem with the men who were drunk. We had to use wagons to take them with us.

We learned later that this large force of Germans went from village to village—through Lubien, Wyryki, Zahajki, Hola, Zamolodycze, and others—looking for what they called "bandits." However, they did not look for us in the woods. In our condition, we were lucky they did not.

Besides our sabotage work, we were also asked to distribute the literature the Russians periodically dropped to us along with the weapons. Groups of our partisans, together with Vanka Kirpicznik and others from the Army Ludowa, went among the villagers handing out this literature. It urged the destruction of livestock and produce held for the Germans and tried to recruit new members into the ranks of the Army Ludowa. The literature stated that the war would not last much longer, that the Russian army was chasing the Germans closer and closer to the Polish border, and that if the local people would help in the struggle they would be rid of the Germans that much faster.

We tried to build up a good relationship with the villagers and took from them only our barest necessities. We knew all of them and tried not to go to the poorer farmers. To the poorest ones, we never went. Mostly we would go to the larger estates.

On one occasion, a villager from Zahajki came to us and complained that some Jewish people had come to his house and had taken not only food but clothing and household possessions that they could not even use. Chiel assured the villager that he would put a stop to this. We went to the Tabor in the Ochoza forest, and we found out that the people who had done this were mostly youngsters. They had spent several parentless years growing up in the woods and just did not know any better. We told them they would be punished if they did it again, and we urged the Tabor elders to supervise the youngsters' actions more closely. We assured them that we would try to supply them with their needs.

During the winter, the farmers did not work in the fields and the evenings were long. The women of the villages would meet in someone's house to do certain types of work and socialize at the same time.

The teenage girls would get together, about a dozen to a house, bringing their spinning wheels to spin the flax that grew in the summertime. The flax had been dried in the sun and then broken up and combed to make small packages. During the long winter nights, the women took out these packages and spun them into a type of fine yarn. The yarn would then be used to make a rough linen, from which they made linen shirts and pants. Some of them even embroidered the shirts.

These gatherings in a farmer's house were called *pratky*, a Ukrainian term. While they worked they sang, told stories, and attracted the local teenage boys, who also came over to socialize during the evenings. The girls tried to show off with the speed of their spinning.

In other farmers' homes, groups of girls got together to pick the hard stem parts from goose feathers, so that the feathers could be used for making pillows and feather beds. This was a tedious and long job. After the girls finished one household's feather needs, which took several evenings, they would go to another household to reciprocate with the help they had received, until all of them had completed their work. Our partisans were welcome to come into the farmers' homes in the evenings and talk and spend time there.

On Sundays the village youths arranged dances called *zabavy*. Several of our fellows sometimes dropped in on these dances, and we would have to watch them to make sure they did not "get lost" with some of the village girls, or get drunk. We felt responsible for each other and had to remember that we were still forest people, with a deadly enemy around us.

In late December 1943, we received orders to destroy a very large estate near the village of Jedlanka. It served as a storage depot for grain and livestock from the surrounding farms prior to their shipment to Germany.

We were stationed at the time in the Makoszka forest. Chiel assigned about fifty partisans to destroy this estate. Included in this mission were our Maryanka group, Yurek from Zaliszcze, Abram Bochian, Sucha Korn, Yurek from Wyryki, Lonka from Parczew, Vuyo, myself, and others.

After we had burned and destroyed the entire estate and were in the process of pulling back, we saw a truck coming toward us on the highway. We quickly hid in the woods bordering the highway, and prepared to ambush the truck. As the truck reached us, we opened fire. After a few shots from our automatic weapons, the truck stopped on the side of the highway. Inside were four German soldiers and a young woman. One of the Germans was wounded in our ambush. We interrogated them and found out that one of the soldiers was not German. His name was Yanek, and the woman was his girlfriend. He was armed with a German machine gun and wore a German uniform. He started begging us not to kill him. In a very excited tone, he told us that he was fed up with the German army and that he had wanted to desert many times but had not found an opportunity to do so. He pleaded with us to give him a chance to prove how much he hated the Germans. He swore in Czech that he would be a good partisan and fight the Germans. We understood his language as it was similar to Polish and Russian. He was crying as he begged for his life. We usually did not trust a German in such a situation, but in this instance I felt that we could take a chance with Yanek. We talked it over with the others and decided to take him and his girlfriend with us, but to watch him closely. We emptied the truck of its contents, which consisted of boxes containing perfumes, soaps, and other toiletries. Then we took the three Germans into the woods and shot them, taking their rifles, pistols, and the machine gun. We returned to our base in the Makoszka forest and later distributed the toiletries among local village women.

Yanek turned out to be a very trustworthy partisan and a good fighter. When we ambushed a German convoy or derailed a railroad transport, he in his SS uniform with his German machine gun proved very useful. While the Germans were running in confusion, Yanek would be blasting away with his machine gun, killing many of them before the Germans could figure out that he was not one of them. Yanek fought in many battles with our group and survived the war.

In the winter of 1943–44, Chiel's partisans were camping in the village of Koniuchy, about ten miles from the Ochoza forest. We had to stay there for several days. Six of us, including me, were assigned to go on a *bombioshka* to another village. We had been told that this other village held a large estate and several affluent farmers. One man in our group, Shmuel, knew the village. He was the son of Yankel of Holowna, who lived in the Tabor.

It took us about half the night to walk there. We expropriated a horse and wagon when we got to the village. We loaded it up with items such as meat, bread, and other foods from the estate and smaller farms. On the way back the snow, which had been falling steadily, turned into a raging storm, and we were unable to see the road. The snow was whipped so fiercely by the wind that it stung our eyes, forcing us to cover our faces.

As we approached Koniuchy, it started to dawn. The snow let up a little, and we noticed a man running toward us from the village. He stopped and told us that a very large force of Germans had come into the village during the night, and that our group had pulled out because it was too large a force to confront. He said Chiel had told him to be on the lookout for us and to warn us about the Germans.

We left the wagon with the food on the road and started running toward the woods. A half mile ahead of us was a sparsely wooded area, and much farther were the denser woods. As it got lighter, some of the Germans from the village noticed us and started shooting in our direction and chasing us. It was hard to run because of the deep snow. We shot back and that slowed down our pursuers a little. As we ran toward the trees, I realized that the weight of my warm jacket was slowing me down. I took it off, dropped it, and continued running.

Finally, we made it into the heavy woods unharmed. Only one of us, Shmuel of Holowna, knew the area, but none of us knew where Chiel and the group had gone. Our guess was that they would return to the Ochoza forest, so Shmuel led us there. It took a good twenty-four hours for us to reach the Ochoza forest, but we had guessed correctly and Chiel was there with our group. They had been very concerned about us and were very happy to see that we had made it back. Chiel apologized for leaving without us, but he explained that he could not risk a battle with such a large German force.

In early January 1944, a new group of Jewish partisans arrived in our area. They came from the Janowski forest on the western side of the Wieprz River, west of Lublin. They were directed to us by Mietek Mocha, the leader of the Army Ludowa in the Lublin area. There were about forty people in this group, and most of them were Jewish ex-prisoners of war. They had been in the Polish army when the Germans overran Poland in 1939 and had been taken prisoner. Initially, they were held in different POW camps together with the other Polish soldiers. Later, when the wholesale slaughter of Jews began, they were taken to a labor camp near Lublin and treated like all the other Jews at that time, experiencing hard work, starvation, torture, and death.

Later, in 1941, when Germany attacked Russia and captured Russian prisoners by the hundreds of thousands, these Jewish POWs were assigned to build barracks for the Russian prisoners in the Lublin area. While working on these buildings, they somehow contacted the Polish underground. In return for a lot of money, they were promised weapons, which were never received. However, the underground helped them to escape into the woods. Once in the woods, they suffered many casualties, both from the Germans and the right-wing Army Krajowa. They finally obtained some weapons and organized themselves into a partisan group in the Janowski forest.

They were joined later by other Jewish escapees from area ghettos, and in 1943 they joined the Army Ludowa as a Jewish partisan unit. Since most of them had military training, they were able to do a substantial amount of sabotage work against the Germans. However, the population in the area was all Polish (as opposed to our area which was mostly Ukrainian) and very anti-Semitic, constantly informing the Germans of the whereabouts of the Jewish partisans. Additionally, the Army Krajowa and NSZ were predominant in that area. The Army Krajowa and NSZ would attack any Jews they could find, whether unarmed refugees or armed Jewish partisans.

Mietek Mocha and the other Army Ludowa leadership felt that this group of Jewish partisans could accomplish more in our area of the Makoszka forest, where there was a larger concentration of Jewish and Army Ludowa partisans. They ordered them to move eastward to our area and join Chiel's group. During their journey to us they had to cross the Wieprz River, at which point they were attacked by Germans and lost several people. In early January, they finally reached us.

They were a good bunch of hardened partisans, disciplined and friendly. Their leaders were Mietek Gruber, Franek Blaichman, and a partisan named Dvoretski. We were glad to welcome them to our group and their noncombatants to our Tabor. They were amazed at how large a group we were and how freely we could maneuver in the area. This was because we were a large force and had liquidated most of the small German outposts near us. The larger German forces did not often come into our area because they were busy at the front. Having come from an area where the Army Krajowa and NSZ were predominant, they were also surprised that the local population behaved in a friendly manner toward us.

We called this group of partisans the Lubartow group, named after the town of Lubartow where they had come from, west of the Wieprz River. We took them with us on our missions. Together with them, we blew up trains and ambushed German convoys on the highways. Soon they were fully integrated into our force. We appreciated their expertise in explosives, as they had been trained in their use in the military before the war. Dvoretski was especially expert when it came to explosives.

Spring 1944

By the spring of 1944, our group of Jewish partisans had grown to about four hundred fighters. This was in addition to approximately an equal number of Jewish noncombatants we protected and supplied in the Tabor. Our fighting force had increased in number, not only with the arrival of the forty partisans of the Lubartow group but also with the trickle of Jews whom we constantly picked up during our maneuvers in the woods.

In the spring of 1944, the military activity intensified in our area of the Ochoza woods. Russian partisan units arrived from the other side of the Bug River. They were known by the names of the founding fathers of the 1917 Russian Revolution. Some were called the Voroshilovcy, the Budiennys, the Chapayoveys, and the Charneys. They rested a while in our area, then proceeded farther west, always staying ahead of the retreating Germans, who were being pushed back by the Red Army.

One such Russian partisan unit, under the command of General Kolpak, was of exceptionally large size. More like an army than a unit,the ten thousand men that came through our area did not even comprise the entire force under Kolpak's command. Some were still on the eastern side of the Bug River. Very heavily armed, with artillery, flamethrowers, and antitank guns, they were heading southwest toward the Carpathian Mountains, leaving in their path the destruction of any German forces they encountered. They were so large a group that when they stopped to rest they had to spread out through dozens of villages and towns.

Our partisan unit was stationed in the village of Rudka when the forward patrol of General Kolpak's force arrived. Chiel and several of our men on horseback rode to General Kolpak's headquarters in a nearby village. They met with the General, who told Chiel that the Russian army was advancing rapidly, but that the retreating Germans could still do a lot of damage. He advised Chiel to be careful, especially since we were a small partisan unit compared to his. General Kolpak offered us several new heavy machine guns and some medical supplies (all of which Chiel accepted), and wished us luck. After a day's rest they moved out, passing through the village of Rudka on horses, wagons, and on foot. Their horses pulled light artillery pieces and wagons full of ammunition and supplies. As we watched them, we wondered how they could travel in such a large force so openly with the Germans all around. We also fought the Germans and inflicted many casualties on them, but our tactics were never to expose ourselves like they did. We would attack and then disappear into the woods.

As Kolpak's soldiers passed through the village, we saw that the force was composed of many nationalities. There were dark faces, light faces, and Asian faces, but the most noticeable thing was that they were all young faces, often in their mid- to late teens. The soldiers were dressed in all kinds of clothing, some wearing half German uniforms and half civilian garb.

Rumor had it that there were many Jewish partisans in Kolpak's army. We kept staring at the soldiers as they marched by, trying to recognize Jewish faces. It was not that hard to tell. When we saw a Jewish face we called out "Amchu?" and they answered with the same word. Then they called out the names of the cities they had come from, many of which were Polish.

Among their cavalry force, I noticed a young boy on a small horse. He looked to be about thirteen years old, with a short cavalry rifle slung over his back and a pistol at his side. He wore a leather jacket with a fur collar and was riding with a group of tall strong-looking teenagers and smoking a cigarette. When I noticed this little partisan my heart started beating fast. He looked just like little Itzik. I ran closer to him and called him by name. He saw me and called out, "Uncle Hershel!" He rode over and, leaping from his horse, jumped on top of me and kissed me, and I hugged him back. He could not stay with us very long because his column was moving out. But in a few short moments, he told me that General Kolpak was like a father to him and had made him a cavalry soldier. He boasted that they were beating the Germans and insisted he was still a very lucky person. Then he jumped back on his horse and rode off to rejoin his departing unit, waving a farewell from a distance.

A little later in the spring of 1944, part of our unit was stationed in the village of Bojki. The local Army Ludowa leaders were there with a force of men, along with some Russian partisans. A few people were playing their harmonicas, and some partisans and local village teenage girls were dancing outdoors.

The music stopped abruptly when a courier rode into the village in great haste. I was standing next to Chiel, Symcha, and Bolek Alef, one of the Army Ludowa leaders. The courier told us he was from a unit of about one hundred Army Krajowa partisans, which was surrounded by a larger force of Germans on the estate of Wielka Zawiepszowka near the village of Wolka, about eight miles from us. The courier said his partisan unit was under heavy attack and badly needed our help.

Bolek Alef suggested that our group of Jewish partisans go to their aid. He said that this would show the Army Krajowa how well we could fight and our willingness to cooperate with them. Our fighters were reluctant to help the Army Krajowa because of their strong anti-Semitic attitude and their murder of any Jews they encountered. We had not forgotten our thirteen partisans they had murdered near Siedlce. However, at Bolek Alef's insistence, we agreed to go.

In a few moments, we grabbed our weapons and headed to the estate on wagons. Bolek Alef joined our force, consisting of about two hundred heavily armed men, many carrying PPSZs and Dichterovy automatic weapons. As we approached the village of Wolka, we could hear shooting. We divided our force into three groups and positioned ourselves at three points outside the German unit encircling the estate. In unison, we launched our attack on the Germans' rear, taking them completely by surprise. The encircling Germans were about equal in number to our attacking force of two hundred partisans but now found themselves pinned down between the defenders' fire and our automatic weapons fire. In short order, many of the Germans were killed and the rest fled into the countryside.

It was a big victory for the partisans, and the Army Krajowa commander thanked us for our help. He told us that the Germans would have overrun them soon had we not arrived on the scene, as his men were almost out of ammunition. His force had also suffered heavy casualties. We made sure he knew that it was Chiel's Jewish partisan group that had come to his rescue. Even this, however, did not stop the Army Krajowa from their continued attacks on unarmed Jews and small units of our partisans.

We later learned that the Army Krajowa had been holding a party on the estate when the Germans launched their attack. It was a puzzle to us that the Germans had done this. From our experience, the Germans and the Army Krajowa partisans in our area generally avoided each other and chose to attack the Army Ludowa and Jewish partisans instead.

At the beginning of May 1944, we received word from Army Ludowa headquarters to expect a visit from the commander-in-chief of the Army Ludowa, General Rola Zimiersky. The order directed us to inform not only our men of his visit but also the other Army Ludowa units and friendly villagers in our area. We were to arrange a large gathering to meet the General. For several days we practiced marching and singing in unison to our march step. Michael from the Lubartow group was especially knowledgeable on this subject, and he conducted our practices. We hoped to make a good appearance for the General, who was going to inspect a parade of all the local partisan units.

We were anxious to hear what the General had to say to us. At the designated time, we congregated in a large clearing in the woods. General Zimiersky arrived together with several high-ranking officers of the Army Ludowa and two photographers. They brought with them a bulletin from headquarters which was distributed to all of us. The bulletin gave us the latest war news and informed us about the atrocities inflicted on the civilian population by the retreating German forces. We focused especially on the news of the most recent successful offensive of the Red Army as it approached the Bug River, and the news of the heroic fighting of the Army Ludowa all over Poland.

The partisans marched in front of the dignitaries very smartly, although they were dressed in many different nonmilitary outfits. Two civilians entertained us with jokes and anecdotes. After the speeches, the General shook hands with all the partisans. He made it a point to talk with Chiel's Jewish partisans, asking if any of us had heard from relatives. He was aware of the genocide the Germans had conducted against Jews.

General Zimiersky (and later Army Ludowa headquarters) advised

all the partisans to leave the area and head westward toward the
Vistula River. They warned that the main German army would be
retreating through the area and that we might be caught and destroyed by them. The Polish Army Ludowa in our area agreed to
follow this strategy. The westward movement of the Army Ludowa
partisans was a strategy devised by the Army Ludowa in concert with
the Russian high command. This strategy ensured that strong Polish
partisan forces would always be ahead of the front as it moved west,
continuing to harass the retreating German army.

We talked it over with Chiel. We knew that we would not be
welcome in the Vistula River area west of us, where the Army Krajowa and the NSZ were the dominant partisan forces. We were well
aware of how anti-Semitic the local populace was there. Also, we were
aware that the Vistula River area was sparsely wooded and therefore
not conducive to our type of guerrilla warfare. Finally, we were
unwilling to abandon the people of the Tabor, toward whom we felt
a great responsibility.

Chiel presented these arguments to the local Army Ludowa leadership, consisting of Mietek Mocha, Captain Zemsta, and Bolek Alef.
They understood our unique situation and agreed with us. They
knew we were familiar with this area and that its population was
friendly to us, which would not be the case in the more anti-Semitic
areas to the west. They recognized that the woods, being so dense
and impenetrable, were a great asset to us, and they knew that unlike
other partisan units, we protected a large number of noncombatants
in our Tabor.

Mietek Mocha, Captain Zemsta, and Bolek Alef prepared to leave
for the west with close to a thousand Polish and Russian partisans,
transporting many new weapons which had recently been airdropped
by the Russians. They asked Chiel to provide them with a group of
our fighters as guides who were more familiar with the terrain to
accompany them westward. Chiel assigned a group of close to thirty
people to go. Among them were Yurek from Zaliszcze and his girlfriend Rostka, Franek Blaichman, Nicoli Berezin, and Hanka.

About two weeks later, Yurek, Nicoli, and the women returned.
The others trickled back in small groups later on. They reported that
the Army Ludowa force had been attacked by a larger German unit,
which had been informed of their location by the Army Krajowa and
the NSZ. These two groups would rather openly collaborate with the
German army than help the Army Ludowa or us, even though we
were all supposed to be fighting together with the Russians to free
Poland from the Germans.

The entire Army Ludowa group had crossed the Wieprz River and proceeded to the village of Dombrowa. It was early in the morning and the group was camping in a small and not very dense woods when their forward scouts brought the news that a large force of Germans with trucks and artillery was coming toward them from the direction of Lublin. The Germans headed straight to the spot where the Army Ludowa group was camped, having been tipped off by the Army Krajowa.

When the group was alerted to the approaching Germans, they took defensive positions to counter the impending attack. The Germans began the attack by trying to storm the wooded area and overrun the partisan force. A lengthy battle ensued, and the Germans were finally repelled from the woods. After a while, several German light aircraft appeared in the sky and began bombing the woods. The partisans had antitank guns with them and aimed them at the planes, downing two of them. The air attacks stopped only once darkness fell. Then the partisans tried to move out as fast as they could, using the darkness as cover. They buried their dead in the woods and headed toward the village of Romblow. Before dawn the next day, they divided into two groups and took up defensive positions in some wooded areas around Romblow. The Army Ludowa group was led by Mietek Mocha, Captain Zemsta, Bolek Alef, and Captain Kolka. The Russian group had its own leaders. Each took up a different area to defend against the attack they were sure was coming. When the Germans launched a frontal attack, the Army Ludowa partisans were in the area of heaviest fighting against the regular German army and SS troops. Such a frontal attack was a mistake for the Germans, as the partisans were heavily armed. The Germans were again repelled with heavy losses and called in more air strikes and artillery fire. Many of the partisans' wagons with supplies, weapons, and ammunition were hit in the bombing and shelling. Hundreds of Germans were killed and about thirty partisans died in that day's battle.

When evening came, the partisan leadership decided on a new strategy, in order to avoid more losses. They divided into yet smaller groups, seeking separately to break through the German encirclement in the dark. Mietek Mocha and Bolek Alef went separate ways with their men and got through to the Janowski forest. The Russian group broke out also, but Captain Zemsta's group decided to come back east to us. They escaped from the Romblow area without casualties and, after walking for hours, they stopped to rest at a village. Apparently they were betrayed again by Army Krajowa members in the village. The Germans surrounded them there. Captain Zemsta was hit by a bullet in the face as he ran out of one house. Yurek and Rostka, who were nearby, saw him fall. Nicoli Berezin was wounded in the hand. Most of the rest of Captain Zemsta's force fought their way out and managed to make it back to us in small numbers to tell the story. Hearing of their experiences, we were glad we had chosen not to move west to the Vistula River region.

With the departure westward of most of the Army Ludowa units and Russian partisans, the Army Krajowa became more and more aggressive in our area, not toward the Germans but toward the Jewish partisans. They sent out feelers asking us to join them, but we knew they could not be trusted.

In June of 1944, the Army Krajowa invited Vanka Kirpicznik (who had not moved westward with the rest of the Army Ludowa) to a meeting near Ostrow Lubelski. The purpose of the meeting was to talk about uniting the two partisan movements in activities against the Germans. Vanka came to us and asked Chiel for several of our men to accompany him to this meeting. Chiel asked me to be one of the group to go. I refused and pleaded with Vanka not to go because I did not trust the Army Krajowa. I felt this could be a trap. I argued that the Army Krajowa was planning to destroy us. They ambushed and killed our people wherever they could. They had ambushed and killed Chaim Barbanel in the village of Maryanka just a week prior to this invitation. They had also earlier killed a group of thirteen Jewish and Army Ludowa partisans near Siedlce when they had gone to retrieve weapons from a Russian airdrop. They had ambushed and killed a group of ten of our partisans on a mission west of Krasnystaw, and had killed many others on different occasions. But Vanka argued that, since we Jewish partisans had rescued an Army Krajowa group at the estate of Wielka Zawiepszowka near the village of Wolka, they might be more cooperative now. Besides, he wanted to hear what their plan was for cooperative activities. Vanka was a stubborn and fanatic idealist and patriot. He wanted to explore any chance of cooperation with the Army Krajowa to fight the Germans.

Vanka left for the meeting with about twenty partisans, some from our group, including Velvale the Patzan from Sosnowica, who upon his return told us what had happened. The group was ambushed near Ostrow Lubelski by Germans. There were rumors that the Army Krajowa had informed the Germans of the group's position. They fought their way out with few losses, but the biggest loss was that of Vanka, who was killed in the ambush.

Vanka was a native of the Wlodawa area and had been a communist before the war, like Mietek Mocha. He was the first to organize partisans in the Wlodawa area. The first time I met him, I was working for Stephan in Lubien in 1941 after the Germans had attacked Russia. He was in the woods looking for escaped Russian ex-prisoners of war to try to organize them into a fighting unit. Later, I learned that he was the one who had organized Fioder's group of Russian ex-POWs in the Makoszka forest. When we met in the Skorodnica forest, he directed us to Chiel's group in the Ochoza forest. We had both recognized each other at that time. In the course of my contacts with the Army Ludowa leadership, Vanka and I had developed a warm friendship.

The First Battalion of the Army Ludowa, which he had commanded, and of which Chiel's force was a part, was renamed the Jan Holod Battalion after he was killed. Jan Holod was Vanka's real name. His death was a great loss to the Army Ludowa and to me personally.

A Pitched Battle

In mid-June of 1944, the news was good. The Red Army was moving closer to the Bug River. Over the radio we heard that the Allied forces had opened a second front in Europe by crossing the English Channel and were fighting the Germans in France.

We were in the Makoszka forest when we learned that a force of about two hundred Russian partisans had arrived from the other side of the Bug River and were stationed in Wola Wereszczynska, a very large village. Most of the Army Ludowa and the Russian partisan units had left our area to go further west to the Janowski forest. We moved toward Wola Wereszczynska to be closer to this Russian force, whose leader's name was General Baranovski. We were about four hundred strong, both men and women fighters. For safety's sake, we left the Tabor people back at our base in the Ochoza woods.

After consulting with our group, Chiel decided to go into Wola Wereszczynska to meet the Russians. It would be advantageous for us to be near another large friendly force until we heard from Army Ludowa headquarters as to further operations. Chiel and a group of us went to the Russian camp in the village to meet the General. He was a short, stocky man dressed in farmer's trousers, and he received us cordially. After we introduced ourselves, he told us he had heard of our partisan unit. He introduced us to his wife, who traveled with him, and poured us a drink. He came out of the village to meet the rest of our force and was impressed with the weapons we had and the discipline we showed.

We set up base not far from the Russians at the opposite (eastern) end of the village. We found out that there was another Russian partisan force of about two hundred men nearby, called the Charney unit, named after its commander. The Charney unit was based in a neighboring village about five miles from Wola Wereszczynska.

General Baranovski was a strict disciplinarian. He ruled his men with an iron fist and frequently punished them for insubordination, just as in a regular army. One day a woman from a neighboring village came to his headquarters with a complaint that one of his men had raped her while on a food expedition. He had all his men line up and asked the woman to identify the man, which she did. Baranovski conducted a trial, after which the man was sentenced to death and shot.

He administered his unit in an organized military fashion. He ordered groups of men to mend clothing and uniforms and to repair shoes. He built a steam bath so that the men could wash themselves and disinfect their clothes.

His men had been safer on the eastern side of the Bug River because of the larger numbers of partisans operating there. They had gained control of wide areas of the countryside, so their bases were safe. The Germans did not operate in those areas where the partisans were very strong. The partisans treated those "liberated" areas as their own territory and treated the people in the villages as their own. They did not go to the villages for clothing, and food was obtained in an organized fashion.

On our side of the Bug, it was quite different. The partisan forces were not as organized or as numerous as in the Russian territory. We were pursued by the Germans and could not remain in one place very long. We also had the Army Krajowa and civilian spies to watch out for.

At one of our meetings with Chiel, I suggested that we might persuade the General to move to a different area. His unit had been in Wola Wereszczynska for a few weeks before we had arrived there, and by this time we had been there for about two weeks. I felt that by this point the Germans knew of our whereabouts, and we would soon probably have to confront them. Our group's strategy had always been to avoid a frontal attack. We could not match the German military strength nor could we call in reinforcements like the Germans did. Our tactics were to commit acts of sabotage and move on, but when we were attacked we fought courageously.

Chiel agreed with my suggestion and broached the possibility of relocation with General Baranovski. The General, however, had his own ideas, and perhaps his orders. "When they come, we'll fight them," he said. We were uncomfortable staying in one place for so long, but did not want to appear to the Russians to be any less brave than they were. This was especially so in light of General Baranovski's "let them come and get us" attitude. Also, the General succeeded in persuading Chiel that our joint force of about six hundred fighters could stand up to a German attack.

A few days later, we received word from local informers that a large force of Germans from the Wlodawa area was headed in the direction of our village. We were told that they were very heavily armed, transporting artillery and heavy machine guns. The next morning a German airplane circled over the village. Symcha Barbanel and Boris (who had joined us after escaping from the Sobibor concentration camp) were on horseback patrolling the outskirts of the village. The plane strafed them with machine gun fire. They were not hit, but Symcha's horse became frightened and threw him. Boris jumped from his horse, and they both ran for cover.

Once the Germans had spotted our force, we knew we would be attacked shortly. General Baranovski's two hundred Russians took up defensive positions on the west side of the village, near a cemetery. The General gave orders to dig trenches in the cemetery, and we did the same on our side of the village. We could not tell which side of the village the Germans would attack.

Before dawn the next morning, Chiel told me to climb up a tall fireman's tower about a hundred feet beyond our trenches to look for the German force. I had a good view of the area. The village was surrounded on three sides by a forest, about a half mile from the village outskirts. The fourth side of the village was open to fields. From my observation post, I soon saw a group of Germans emerge from the woods, approach the end of the village occupied by Chiel's force, and then stop. After a while, they melted back into the woods, as if they had finished reconnoitering the approach to the village. I hollered down to Chanina, who was standing next to the tower, and told him what I had seen. He ran back to the group to relay the news. We all knew that an attack was expected any minute. Chiel sent a message to the Russians to let them know that the Germans were about to attack our end of the village. In response, General Baranovski moved some of his Russians over to where we expected to engage the enemy.

In a short time, I saw a very large force of close to a thousand German troops emerge from the woods. As they advanced, they let loose a tremendous concentration of artillery and heavy machine gun fire toward the village. By this time, I had climbed down from the tower and rejoined my group. Some of us were in trenches that we had dug, some were positioned in and behind houses and barns, and others were hidden behind trees.

We held our fire as the Germans approached the village. At the point when several hundred of them were at the outskirts of the village and approaching our hidden positions, we opened fire. The fighting was intense and lasted a long time. Our machine guns became red-hot from constant firing. We threw grenades and even used our PTR antitank guns against the attackers. We were more or less cornered, but the Germans were exposed in the open in front of us. After fierce fighting, they finally pulled back toward the forest, leaving their dead and wounded in and around the village. We had suffered few casualties in the battle because we had been firing from sheltered defensive positions.

We knew this was only the beginning. Soon another wave of Germans approached the village from the woods. Simultaneously, five German planes flew in and started bombing and strafing our end of the village, blowing up many of the houses in which we were positioned. This caught us by surprise, and we started pulling back to the western end of the village where the Russians were located. The village was on fire, and it was difficult for us to retreat. We darted from house to house and from tree to tree, seeking cover from the oncoming Germans and the aerial attacks.

As I ran toward the Russian positions, a bomb fell right in front of me and made a big crater in the ground. Luckily, it did not explode. The tremendous impact, however, threw me to the ground. I must have been unconscious for a few seconds, but then I picked myself up and ran further toward the other end of the village.

When we reached the cemetery where the Russians were dug in, we formed a defensive line with them. We shot at the planes with our rifles and machine guns but to no effect. Our combined force had several antitank guns designed to destroy tanks by shooting horizontally. Nicoli, a tall Russian and former navy man who was the only survivor of a battleship that had been sunk near Sevastopol, was crouched near us with one of these antitank guns. We suggested to the Russian that he aim his gun vertically and shoot at the planes. It took several men to hold the gun upright. He hit one plane, which caught fire and crashed. Then he hit another. It crashed in the woods farther away.

At this point, the second wave of advancing Germans entered the eastern portion of the village. They quickly reached the cemetery and launched a frontal assault on our combined partisan force. General Baranovski ran through the Russian trenches without his hat, which he had lost somewhere, giving orders to keep shooting and withdraw further to the extreme western end of the village and then into the woods beyond. Chiel kept shouting encouraging words to us, telling everyone to keep firing and not to panic as we retreated to the woods. A wheat field ran from the western end of the village to the woods, and we had to cross this field. That was the most dangerous spot because we were in the open, exposed to the strafing of the planes. In that wheat field we lost about eighteen partisans, mostly Russians, crossing to the woods.

We gathered at the edge of the woods and formed a defensive line, camouflaged behind the thick underbrush. The Germans kept advancing in our direction from the village. In the meantime, we had sent a messenger to Charney's Russian partisan unit stationed about five miles from us. About one hundred of his men arrived at this point and reinforced our line at the edge of the woods, waiting for the Germans to come closer. We were now a combined force of almost seven hundred fighters. The Germans were less than three hundred feet from us and not yet able to see us when we opened fire.

It was a massacre. The massed firepower from our light and heavy automatic weapons mowed down the advancing Germans, who were completely exposed in the open wheat field. They withdrew back to the outskirts of the village. For the second time that day, they suffered heavy casualties and were forced to retreat. By this second time, they seemed disoriented and demoralized, as if they had not expected to meet fierce resistance from partisans. Their planes continued to circle over the woods, dropping their bombs. This did no damage to us because the planes could not pinpoint our location under the protection of the foliage.

Well over a hundred Germans had been killed or wounded. The battle had lasted the entire day. The Germans landed small planes to take away their dead and wounded. Despite the intense fighting, our combined partisan force had suffered relatively light casualties, mostly while crossing the open field from the village to the forest. At the end of the day the Germans pulled out. That night we left toward the Makoszka forest, stopping in a village for some food.

In the Makoszka forest we met small groups of Jewish, Russian, and Polish partisans. Many were remnants of the thousand-man Army Ludowa and Russian partisan force that had moved westward from our area in May. They had fought and lost a pitched battle against a larger German force near Romblow. Afterward, they had scattered in small groups to head eastward back to our area.

The Russians, under General Baranovski, traveled to the Bor forest, not far from the Makoszka forest. General Baranovski, we later learned, was a Hungarian Jew who had been a general in the Russian army.

40
Liberation

In the beginning of July 1944, we received another Russian airdrop. This time, however, the Russian planes did not drop weapons. Instead, eighty men parachuted down to us. They were members of the Polish Kosciuszko Battalion, which had been organized in Russia and had fought alongside the Red Army. They were regular army men, dressed in full Polish army uniforms and wearing the traditional Polish military four-pointed hats with an eagle on the front. Their outfits were identical to prewar Polish army uniforms, except the eagle on their hats did not wear a crown. These soldiers were very well equipped and even carried a two-way radio. Some of them were Jewish, as was their leader, Captain Trucker. The Polish villagers were overjoyed to see soldiers in Polish uniforms. They crossed themselves and hugged and kissed the newly arrived soldiers. These eighty Polish paratroopers stayed in our area and fought under the Army Ludowa command.

Since most of the Army Ludowa partisans had left previously to go further west, new units of the Army Ludowa were being formed in our area. These new units were organized under the leadership of Captain Korchinsky, a veteran Army Ludowa partisan who had fought in the Spanish Civil War. There were also new Russian partisan groups in the nearby woods. They had traveled from the eastern side of the Bug River to harass the retreating Germans. In total, our forces now numbered about eight hundred fighters, consisting of Chiel's Jewish partisans, the eighty Polish paratroopers, Captain Korchinsky's Army Ludowa men, and Russian partisans under the command of General Baranovski. All of these fighting units operated together at this point to maximize the impact of our forces. Our Tabor people remained safely hidden at our base in the Ochoza woods.

Long columns of German trucks and tanks kept moving westward from the approaching front. The Germans were now retreating en masse. They were not only using the highways but also the side roads, fields, and wooded trails. For a two- or three-week period, we were constantly ambushing their columns, especially on the wooded trails. Our PTRs came in very handy. Many of the German tanks went up in flames from their armor-piercing shells. The German tank crews would then jump out of their burning tanks, only to be met by our fire.

Our group of Jewish partisans stayed together and fought with a vengeance. We attacked the Germans in the woods at close range. Our ambushes took them completely by surprise, and they seemed disoriented as they retreated in defeat.

Sam (nicknamed "the Polimiot") carried a PTR. Whenever he hit a German tank and it caught fire, he would let out a loud "Hurrah." Yakubovich, who had lost the khaki army hat he always wore, also carried a PTR, which he used with devastating accuracy. Velvale the Patzan, from Sosnowica, effectively performed his special talent—tossing grenades. I remember many of our fighters who furiously attacked the retreating Germans—Chiel, Yefim, Yurek from Zaliszcze and his girlfriend Rostka, the brothers Yanek, Yurek, and Abram from Wyryki, Abram (Chiel's brother) and his girlfriend Dora, Adam from Parczew, Sucha Korn, Abram from Zmiarka (who had previously suffered a wounded hand in an attack by the Army Krajowa), Buchali and Lonka Fefercorn from Parczew, Abram Bochian, Zalman from Parczew, and of course our Maryanka group including Symcha, Chanina, Moniek, Hershel and his wife Hannah, Chaim Weisman, Motel Barbanel and his wife Chanche, Faiga from Zamolodycze, Chanche from Kodeniec (Yurek from Zaliszcze's aunt), the four Zahajki brothers and Boris. The Lubartow group, led by Mietek Gruber and Franek Blaichman, fought bravely alongside us. Our female partisans were equally active fighters—sisters Pesah and Temi from the Adampol labor camp, Tzesha (Yanek from Wyryki's sister), and Cipora and her sister from Holowna. Besides using their weapons, the women also carried first aid kits and nursed the wounded when necessary. There were many more fighters whose names I cannot recall.

We hit the Germans hard as they attempted to retreat. Many of our fighters were cursing as they fired, rejoicing that the tables were now turned on the Germans. Our combined partisan force destroyed many enemy columns. Our aim was to block the Germans' retreat, so that they would be captured by the advancing Red Army.

The Germans understood our objective and appreciated the threat we represented to their avenue of retreat. One morning in July, large units from several divisions of the retreating German army attacked us from all sides. They surrounded the entire Makoszka forest like an iron ring, trying to block our escape from the woods. They probably figured that by their sheer numbers they would annihilate us. They kept launching attacks into the woods. We would fight back and then retreat deeper into the forest. This went on for hours. The Germans did not penetrate deep into the woods, so we could retreat after each attack. Toward evening, we decided to split into smaller groups and to fight our way out of the encirclement by cover of night.

General Baranovski's Russian partisans left us and went back toward the Bor forest. Our unit and the other Army Ludowa group waited for orders from Army Ludowa headquarters. Captain Korchinsky and Captain Mara were the two commanders at Army Ludowa headquarters, several miles deeper into the woods from us. They were supposed to have joined us to make plans as to which way to break out of the encirclement. We waited through the evening, but no one showed up. Finally, Chiel and several others rode on horseback to Army Ludowa headquarters. They discovered the headquarters was deserted, except for one man who had remained behind with a message for us. He directed us to head toward the Ostrow Lubelski area and try to break through the German ring there. If we were successful, we were to link up with the Russian partisans in the Bor forest.

We abandoned all our supplies so that we could move quickly in case of another engagement with the Germans. The men carrying the PTR guns were unwilling to part with them, even though they knew it was difficult to maneuver with them in the dense woods. After several hours of walking, we approached the edge of the woods near the Ostrow Lubelski area. The Germans somehow spotted us and directed a tremendous artillery barrage in our direction. The barrage came from the vicinity of Ostrow Lubelski, which was where we had intended to slip through the German encirclement. By this time, it was pitch dark and the Germans could not see us very well. They kept shelling the area without causing us any damage. However, we realized we could not pass through the enemy ring in the Ostrow Lubelski area once the Germans had been alerted to our presence.

We moved away to a different area. As we approached the edge of the woods a few of us, including Symcha and myself, were sent out into the open as a forward patrol. We were immediately spotted by German troops who started shooting in our direction. We withdrew back into the woods to our group, which moved deeper into the forest. We tested a few other spots in the enemy cordon, and each time we were detected and fired upon. We were surrounded no matter where we went, and we were beginning to feel we had little chance of slipping through the German lines.

We moved deeper into the woods and decided to split up into smaller groups, each one heading in a different direction. I was left leading a group of about thirty partisans. They consisted mostly of the Maryanka group, including some women, along with a few men from Parczew and from Wlodawa. The men had to abandon their PTRs. We walked in the woods in the dark in the direction of Ninin, not knowing what had happened to the other groups.

Approaching Ninin, we ran into more German fire and were forced to retreat back into the woods. With the onset of daylight, we decided to lay low, hidden in the dense forest. We realized that the entire Makoszka forest was surrounded on all sides. We did not know what had happened to the rest of our unit, and we were tired, thirsty, and hungry.

Fortunately, we were in an area of the forest where we had buried slonina for just such an emergency. I and a few others in Chiel's force had been assigned to keep track of all the places where we had hidden caches of this salted pork. We located the buried slonina and were glad to find it well preserved. We helped ourselves to the pork, which made us very thirsty, but that could not be helped.

We knew the Germans were in a general retreat and would eventually have to start moving out of the area, but we did not know when. We thought the best move for us would be to head north to the Parczew end of the woods. A major highway passed through there, and the German front seemed to be moving westward through that area. At this point, we were a small unit, no longer seeking to attack retreating German columns. Instead, we were caught between the German reserve forces and their frontline troops. Now we were seeking simply to survive in an ocean of enemy soldiers.

Abram Bochian and the other Parczew men knew this area very well. They suggested that we leave the woods and cross the highway at night. They knew of several individual farmhouses on the outskirts of Parczew where we might hide out.

It was a fantastic and dangerous plan, but it was the only way we could escape the German encirclement. From three days and nights of constant running and fighting, we were exhausted, hungry, and thirsty, and we felt we had to take a chance. We hoped the Germans would not think that we would dare venture to the open outskirts of Parczew. Our plan was to cross the highway at night and enter a nearby house. We could hide there during the day and the next night slip into another village bordering Parczew, without actually entering Parczew. We would then continue, following patches of woods, away from the Parczew area and in the direction of the Bor forest.

We moved to the edge of the woods near Parczew and observed long, unending lines of heavy German military transports filling the highway. On the other side of the highway we visually measured a half mile of fields before one could reach the nearest farmhouse. The Germans did not bother to guard this side of the forest, probably assuming that partisans would not emerge into this open area so close to their main forces. We lay down along the highway in a ditch behind some shrubs and waited for a lull in the traffic. Although it was pitch black, the transports drove without lights. It was raining hard, and we were drenched and hungry. The transports continued moving without a letup. We realized we were in a bad position now that we were out of the woods. We had to make a move before daylight, as we were exposed and would be visible to the Germans by dawn.

While we were lying there we heard a plane drone overhead. It dropped a cluster of flares, like a chandelier with many bulbs. The flares hung in the air for about fifteen minutes and lit up the entire strip of highway. We crouched deeper in our hiding place behind the shrubs to avoid detection. As soon as the flares died out, there was a short lull in the traffic. We immediately darted across the highway. We ran across the open field and entered the first house we encountered.

It was a farmhouse and the people inside were visibly scared when we stormed into their home. We told them we were partisans and meant them no harm. We ordered that no one leave the house. In a short time it started to dawn. We watched the inhabitants of the house closely. I posted a man at each window, so no one would slip out. We were afraid of being betrayed.

The livestock in the barn nearby started making noises, wanting to be let out to pasture, but we did not let anyone leave to take care of them. After a while, a neighbor knocked on the door to find out why the animals were not being let out. We let him in, then kept him imprisoned in the house also. Soon his wife came looking for him, and we kept her in the house too. Then the children came looking for their parents. By noontime, there were about forty people in the house—our thirty partisans and the ten people under our guard.

We peeked out the windows and saw German soldiers running, not only on the highway but through side roads and fields. Then it got quiet. Later in the afternoon, another neighbor came into the house and told us that the Germans had left Parczew and that Russian soldiers were at the other end of town. We did not believe him. We could not imagine that this was the end of German occupation.

We continued to look through the windows and soon saw a Russian tank coming toward us on the highway. It was followed by foot soldiers and a field kitchen. Well behind that was a long column of tanks, each bearing the star of the Red Army.

We ran out toward the highway, a half mile from the house, waving our hands in the air. The lead tank pulled over to the side and a Russian came out of the tank toward us, followed by a few foot soldiers. Seeing a band of people with weapons, they kept their distance while asking who we were. We told them we were Jewish partisans who had been fighting the Germans. They saw that our weapons were Russian just like theirs. They came closer, and we hugged and kissed them and cried for joy. They took us to a jeep at the back of the column, where their commander greeted us very warmly. The Russian commander said that for us the war was over, but they still had to chase the Germans back to Germany.

It was a moment of great joy for us, and at the same time one of great sorrow. We could not help but think of the multitudes of our people who had perished and of our loved ones who had not survived to see this moment.

Chaim Weisman could not stop crying. He had lost his entire family in the woods in German raids, with the exception of his little girl Bebale. She had survived so many German raids and had taken care of him like a mother. But in these last few furious days, while trying to break out of the woods, we lost her during a German attack and never saw her again. Now Chaim was all alone, having lost his wife and all five children.

The Russians fed us from their field kitchen, for which we were very grateful. Then we climbed on top of their tanks and rolled into Parczew with our Russian liberators. They let us off in Parczew and continued westward toward the retreating Germans. After disembarking from the tanks, we walked through the streets of Parczew. Some of the natives recognized our Parczew partisans and expressed amazement that there were still Jews left alive. Bochian took us over to the house he used to live in. It was currently occupied by a Polish family that was plainly not happy to see him. The other Parczew partisans—Lonka, Buchali, Edek, Adam and Sucha Korn—also went to look for their homes.

In Parczew we learned that the only resistance group that had suffered losses during the final few frantic days of fighting was a unit of Army Ludowa partisans under Captain Mara's command. We were supposed to link up with them and go together to the Ostrow Lubelski area. They had left the Makoszka forest ahead of us. The unit was spotted in an open area while trying to cross a railroad line and was attacked by a large force of Germans. They retreated into the woods but lost more than a dozen men, including Captain Mara. Captain Korchinsky's group survived unscathed.

The next day was July 22. We left Parczew and headed for Kodeniec. There we found Chiel with the rest of the group, including the people from the Tabor. Luckily our group had suffered few losses those last few days. Altogether, Chiel's partisans numbered about four hundred fighters, and the Tabor people consisted of approximately the same number.

From Kodeniec, we all headed to Lublin on Russian army trucks. All along the highway to Lublin, we saw signs of the fierce fighting that had occurred. The highway was strewn with burned-out German tanks, trucks, and cars, many lying upside down, and the bodies of dead German soldiers were everywhere.

Lublin became the temporary Polish capital and the temporary headquarters of the Russian and Polish armies. Warsaw and the western half of Poland was still in German hands and would not be completely liberated until 1945. Lublin was not badly damaged, but the signs of war were everywhere. The city was filled with damaged buildings and abandoned German military equipment. The Lublin city government allocated several buildings, which had been abandoned by the Germans, for temporary living quarters for the partisans and provided us with food rations.

Soon afterward, Jewish survivors started arriving in Lublin from the liberated areas—from death camps, from the forests, from bunkers and other hiding places. Many Jewish children, hidden by friendly Polish villagers during the German occupation, were pouring into the city of Lublin every day. We did our best to help these survivors. We appropriated two additional large buildings on Lubartowski Street. One was the I. L. Peretz Building, the prewar Jewish writers building. It housed the adult survivors, and another building nearby housed the children. The city gave us beds and food for the survivors. We also organized the first Jewish committees to represent these survivors. Our group of Jewish partisans participated actively in these committees, especially with regard to coordinating the efforts of the various relief organizations. The survivors kept coming daily to our buildings to inquire about their families, hoping some had survived. The committees organized a registry of the first survivors to arrive, so all the later arrivals could search the registry for their relatives and also register themselves.

Soon after the liberation, help started to arrive from abroad. The American Jewish Joint Distribution Committee, the Red Cross, and the Hebrew Immigrant Aid Society (HIAS) sent food, medicine, and other necessities which were distributed among the survivors. The survivors committees we had organized worked with these organizations in support of their relief efforts.

Most of the survivors from the concentration camps were young people. The few older survivors were from the woods and various hiding places. The survivors, especially those from concentration camps, were from various European countries that the Germans had at one time occupied: France, Belgium, Holland, Hungary, and of course Poland—as well as from Germany itself.

Most of the survivors were individuals whose families had been wiped out. They clung to each other like family. Young men and women, being without families, tried to pair up. They wanted to belong to someone, to start a semblance of a family, and not to be alone. Although many had different languages and cultures, somehow they got together and found mates.

In Lublin, I met my cousin from Gorzkow, Zindel Honigman, along with his wife Betty and their six-year-old daughter Fella. In 1942, Betty and Fella were taken by train from the Izbica ghetto to Sobibor. Betty found a small crack in a corner of the train car and pushed her then four-year-old child out of the moving car. Then she slid through the crack and fell from the moving train. After she found her daughter, who miraculously had survived the fall, she walked back to Gorzkow. There she was hidden for short periods each by several friendly farmers until the end of the war. Her husband Zindel had, however, ended up in Sobibor. He was a big husky man, so he was put on a work detail cutting down trees in the surrounding woods. One day he and two friends, Shlomo Podchleb- nik and Moishe Merenshtein, a native of Gorzkow, were taken by the guards to carry buckets of water for the rest of the men working in the woods. The three of them overpowered and killed their two Ukrainian guards and escaped into the woods. This occurred before the Sobibor uprising. The three men found their way back to Gorz- kow and survived by hiding in the nearby swamps and woods. After the liberation, Zindel joined his family and came to Lublin, where I met them.

I wanted to go home to Gorzkow to find out what had happened to my family. I met a farmer who had been a neighbor of ours in Gorzkow and who came to Lublin on business. I knew him well and trusted him. He told me not to go home because it was dangerous for a Jew to show up in Gorzkow. His name was Fidetzky, and his home was three houses down from our home. He knew my family very well and told me the story of what had happened to the Jews in Gorzkow.

In the summer of 1942, the Germans had forced thousands of Jews (from other areas of Poland) into the small village of Gorzkow. They packed them into the Jewish homes like sardines, and the ones who could not fit into a house stayed outdoors. When even more Jews arrived in Gorzkow, the Germans decided to move all of them to Izbica where they established a ghetto. The people were marched the five or six miles on foot to Izbica. When the Izbica ghetto became too overcrowded, the Germans began to move the Jews by train to the Sobibor death camp to be killed.

Farmer Fidetzky also told me what had happened to two of my brothers, seventeen-year-old Moishe and thirteen-year-old Motel. They were rounded up with all the other Jews in Gorzkow and marched to Izbica. They escaped from the Izbica ghetto and walked back to Gorzkow. They hid there in the woods and in the limestone pits, which abounded in the area. One night they went to the home of a former neighbor asking for food. He told them to wait in his barn while he brought food out to them. They waited in the barn and after a while the neighbor brought a gang of anti-Semites to the barn. The gang brought clubs into the barn and clubbed Moishe and Motel to death. Fidetzky told me that many Jews from the Gorzkow vicinity who went to local farmers for food were murdered in the same way by local gangs of anti-Semitic Poles.

When I think about my father or the rest of my family—my sister, my grandfather, his wife and two children, my aunts, uncles, and their families—I do not know how they died. I only know they all perished, probably in the gas chambers at Sobibor. However, having been told how Moishe and Motel met their deaths, I cannot erase that scene from my mind. I continue to see that scene in my dreams. The pain I feel from that memory is still strong after all these years, and always will be.

Disillusionment and Departure

Our Jewish partisan unit had spent years in the woods fighting the Germans, not only to survive but also with the ultimate goal of ridding the Germans from Poland. In our many missions and battles, we had fought alongside the Polish partisans of the Army Ludowa, who shared this common goal. Additionally, we had received the cooperation of most of the villagers in our area of operations, who also shared this common goal. With the liberation of our area, we expected to be greeted as heroes for having successfully fought the common enemy to help free Poland. Instead, our Jewish partisans were confronted with just the opposite reaction and were saddened to realize that Polish attitudes toward Jews remained the same after the war as they had been before the war.

The newly created Polish government offered the Jewish partisans jobs in the government administration in Lublin. We were also given positions in local police forces. However, in these jobs, we quickly experienced resentment and hatred directed at us by our anti-Semitic Polish coworkers. In some cases, we were attacked in public by gangs of former Army Krajowa units.

At first, some Jewish people tried to fit into life under the new government. However, I was gradually persuaded that there was no longer any place for Jews in Poland. In the first year after liberation, hundreds of Jews who had come back from concentration camps, the woods, and various hiding places were killed, both individually and in mass pogroms, by the Polish population. One of the most dramatic pogroms occurred in July 1946 in the town of Kielce, where a large number of Jews were killed or wounded in a single day of mob violence. Pogroms against Jewish survivors broke out in many Polish cities and towns, such as Krakow, Chelm, and Rzeszow.

We were clearly made to feel that our coming back was a disappointment to the Polish people. They had hoped and assumed that the Germans had successfully wiped out all the Polish Jews. They resented the surviving Jews because they feared that the survivors would seek to reclaim their homes and businesses. Polish anti-Semitism did not abate with the liberation from German occupation. The survivors who went back to their hometowns and villages were met by a very hostile local population.

Abram Bochian, together with some other Parczew Jews, decided to return to their hometown to live. They felt secure because they were familiar with members of the newly appointed left-wing government there and the local police chief. They felt that, as ex-partisans, they would be shown consideration and be allowed to get back some of their possessions. After a few days there, they were attacked by Polish anti-Semites. In the attack, Abram Bochian was shot and killed. Abram Bochian, the heroic partisan, who had fought so bravely against the Germans, who had lost his entire family in the woods, and who had made us laugh in the tightest situations, was not killed by a German bullet but by the Polish people in his own hometown.

Similar tragedies occurred in other cities and towns across Poland, when Jewish survivors went back to their hometowns to see what was left of their families, homes, and possessions. In Lublin, mobs of anti-Semitic Poles killed a number of Jewish survivors. Among those killed in Lublin was Leon Feldhendler, one of the two leaders and organizers of the revolt in the Sobibor death camp. He was originally from Zolkiewka, a small town near my hometown of Gorzkow. Another survivor who was killed was a young man, named Blank, from the town of Izbica, also near Gorzkow. He had moved back into his prewar home. Anti-Semitic Poles broke into his house at night and shot him.

Even Chiel Grynszpan was the target of this type of violence. He had taken a job as a policeman in Hrubieszow, a city southeast of Lublin near the Bug River. An Army Krajowa group sent him a package of flowers containing a bomb. When he opened the package, the bomb was triggered and exploded in his hands. He suffered injuries from the blast but luckily survived.

The combination of having no family members left alive, together with the hostile and often deadly reception given by the Poles in their hometowns, led to a migration of many of the remaining Polish Jews. As soon as the rest of Poland was liberated, the Jewish survivors began moving into the cities closer to the German-Polish border, like Lodz, Wroclaw, and Szczecin. The goal was to get into Germany and then into the American-occupied sector of Berlin, where the American government through the United Nations Relief and Rehabilitation Agency (UNRRA) had established refugee camps, referred to as displaced persons camps, or simply "DP camps." We hoped to be able to emigrate from there either to Palestine or to other Western countries. We could not see ourselves starting a new life in Poland, after the Poles had helped kill all our families.

I and many of my partisan friends joined in this westward migration. We crossed the German border without incident. Then we reached the American Zone in Berlin and registered ourselves in the local UNRRA DP camp. In a short period, the camp had filled up with survivors, and we and many others were moved farther west into Germany. I and many of my partisan friends tried to keep together. We were sent to a DP camp named Garbazai outside the town of Wassenberg, about thirty miles west of Düsseldorf.

I found out through the camp grapevine that my two brothers Meyer and Irving had survived, and two months later they joined me at the camp. Our meeting was very emotional. I had not seen them since before the war. In September 1939, Meyer had accepted the offer the Russians had extended to Polish Jews in the Russian-occupied area west of the Bug River. Those Jews were allowed to pull back with the Russians withdrawing from that portion of Polish territory which they had occupied in the just-ended German-Polish-Russian war and which, by the terms of the 1939 German-Russian pact, belonged to Germany. Shortly afterward, Stalin decided to transport those Polish Jews who had accepted this offer away from the militarily sensitive German-Russian border. They first were sent to an area of Siberia, east of Novosibirsk, and later to Tashkent in Soviet Central Asia. There they were safe from the war zone and, once hostilities had ended, they returned to Poland to find that their families had been killed. Irving had survived the war by hiding in caves in the Lublin area, obtaining food from local friendly farmers.

Some people in our DP camp who left for Palestine were intercepted by the British navy and interned in camps behind barbed wire in Cyprus. Many, with the help of HIAS, tried to immigrate to the United States and other Western countries. In February 1947, my two brothers, the Honigmans, and I took a small troopship leaving Hamburg for the United States. It was a very rough, stormy crossing, and it took us ten days to reach the United States.

Living in a free country like the United States may be taken for granted by many, but not by the survivors of the Holocaust. We were met here with friendship and given opportunities to start a new life that we could not have previously imagined. Many of my partisan friends came here too, and now live in cities all over the United States. Many also settled in Israel, Canada, Brazil, Argentina, Australia, and France, but none remained in Poland. We keep in touch, attend one another's family celebrations, and always reminisce when we are together about our miraculous survival during the war. Although it causes us pain, we do it every time we meet. For me personally, my wartime experience is permanently stamped in my memory. I know I will carry that experience in my mind as long as I live.

EPILOGUE

Harold Werner died on December 4, 1989, after battling a long illness for several years. He spent much of his last two years of life in a hospital bed, from which he focused his energies on dictating this book to his wife Dorothy. In November 1989, he finished his work on the book and turned it over to his wife and children for publication. He died two weeks later.

GLOSSARY OF NAMES

NICKNAMES AND FIRST NAMES	FULL NAMES
Adam from Parczew	Adam Winder
Chanina Barbanel	Henry Barbanel
Chasha	Ann Lederman
David ("the tall one") from Sosnowica	David Friedman
Dora	Dora Grynszpan
Faiga	Faiga Rosenblum
Franek Blaichman	Frank Blaichman
Hershel and wife Hannah from Skorodnica	Hershel and Hannah Berkowitz
Mietek Gruber	Samuel Gruber
Moniek	Moishe Rotstein
Mortche and Yurek from Zaliszcze	Morris and Joe Holm
Polimiot	Sam Goldwasser
Rostka	Rostka Holm
Symcha Barbanel	Sam Abarbanel
Tzesha from Wyryki	Tzesha Blaichman
Velvale the Patzan	Velval Litwak
Yanek, Yurek, and Abram from Wyryki	Jack, Yurek and Abram Pomeranc
Yankale from Wlodawa	Jack Lederman
Yefim	Joe Rolnick

INDEX

Aaron "Aaraly" (orphan boy), 167

Abarbanel, Sam. *See,* Barbanel, Symcha

Abram from Wyryki, 144, 223

Abram from Zaliszcze, 167, 182

Abram from Zmiarka, 194–95, 223

Abram the Patzan from Zahajki, 150, 165, 169, 223

Adam from Parczew, 223, 228

Adampol labor camp, 158; prisoners from, 94; rescue of Jews from, xviii, 137–42

Administrative records, destruction of, 164–65

Agricultural training camps, 8

Airdrops, 197–200, 222

Alef, Bolek, 190, 210, 212, 213

Alter, Viktor, 18

Ambush of Germans, 123–24, 129; Ochoza forest, 165; Zahajki, 149–51

American Jewish Joint Distribution Committee, 52, 229

Anti-Semitism, xx, xxiii–xxiv, xxv, 6–10, 206, 230; of Army Krajowa, 155–56; of German

occupation forces, 14–15; in Gorzkow, 230; post-war, xx–xxi, 232–34; in Warsaw, 53

Army Krajowa ("Land Army"), xx, 134, 155–56; and Army Ludowa, 212–14; Jewish partisan aid to, 210–11; and Jews, 194–96, 206, 214–15, 232, 233; and Sobibor death camp survivors, 174

Army Ludowa ("People's Army"), xx, 134, 147, 170, 180, 210, 220–21; Army Krajowa and, 155; and German attack on partisans, 188–93; and German retreat, 224, 228; and Jewish partisans, 135, 154–59, 177, 193–95, 206, 211–12, 232; and Ostrow Lubelski garrison destruction, 186–87; Polish paratroopers and, 222; weapons for, 199; westward move, 212–14, 216

Arranged marriages, 54–55

Atleta (Sobibor death camp survivor), 172

Austria, German Anschluss, 4

Balackov (General), 33

Baranovski (Russian partisan General), 216–18, 220–21, 224

Barbanel, Chaim, 87, 96, 116–18, 196, 214; Dubeczno Huta raid, 158–59; Krzywowierzby raid, 165; foraging expedition, 127; rescue of Jews from Wlodawa ghetto, 122–23; and Zahajki ambush, 149

Barbanel, Chanche, 91, 123, 184; and retreating Germans, 223

Barbanel, Chanina, 87, 89, 97, 99, 102–3, 107–8, 115–18, 172, 177, 196, 218; Adampol raid, 138; and blowing up of train, 157; Dubeczno Huta raid, 158–59; foraging expedition, 127; Krzywowierzby raid, 165; Ostrow Lubelski garrison raid, 187; and parachute drop, 198; and retreating Germans, 223; and Wlodawa Jews, 119; and Zahajki ambush, 149

Barbanel, Esther, 96, 116, 117

Barbanel, Henry. See Barbanel, Chanina

Barbanel, Motel, 91, 123, 184; Adampol raid, 138; and retreating Germans, 223

Barbanel, Rachmiel, 87, 90, 91

Barbanel, Symcha, 87, 89, 97, 107, 116, 118, 191, 218; Adampol raid, 138; and attack on Germans, 109; Dubeczno Huta raid, 158–59; foraging expedition, 127; and German spies, 144–45; Krzywowierzby raid, 165; and retreating Germans, 223; Turno estate raid,

162–63; and Zahajki ambush, 149

Barbanel, Yanche, 140

Barbanel, Yankel. See Vuyo from Dubeczno

Barbanel, Yosel, 80, 81, 85–86, 87–90, 97, 117–18; frozen feet, 102, 105

Bar Mitzvah, 46

Bashis, Sarah, 40

Batalione Chlopsky ("Farmers' Battalion"), 134–35

Bathhouse, Gorzkow, 41

Beatings of Jews, 7–8

Berezin, Nicoli, 212, 214

Berkowitz, Hershel and Hannah. See Hannah, Hershel from Skorodnica

Bet Din (Jewish court), 37

Blaichman, Franek (Frank), 206, 212, 223

Blaichman, Tzesha. See Tzesha from Wyryki

Blank from Izbica, 233

Bochian, Abram, xxi, 103–4, 132–33, 136, 197, 203, 223, 226, 228, 233

Bojky (village), 210

Bombardment of Warsaw, 11–14

Bombioshkas (food-foraging expeditions), 101, 132–34, 204–5

Bor forest, 221

Borgenstein, Sucher, 49–50

Boris from Slonim, 172, 218, 223

Boy babies, birth of, 35

Bridges destroyed by partisans, 177–78, 199–200

Buchali from Parczew, 223, 228

Bug River, 16, 17, 20–22; crossings, 180–81, 191–93

Endecia (National Democratic party), 6–7, 135
Endek party, 6–7
Equipment of Jewish partisans, 176
Erlich, Henryk, 18
Escaped prisoners, Jewish, 205–6
Estates, destruction of, 160–63, 179, 203–4
Explosives, Lubartow group and, 207

Faiga from Zamolodycze, 80, 85–86, 88, 97, 107, 113, 118–19, 152; and attack on Germans, 110; cooking by, 114, 120; and retreating Germans, 223; revenge, 98–99, 178–79; in Skorodnica forest, 89; Turno estate raid, 162; weapon for, 103
Falk (knitting factory boss), 50–51
Farmers: Germans and, 60–65; Jewish, in Poland, 16–17
Farmer's Battalion (Batalione Chlopsky), 134–35
Farm life, 28–31, 57–67, 72–73; winter, 68–70, 202–3
Fascists, Polish, 135
Fefercorn, Lonka. See Lonka from Parczew
Feldhendler, Leon, 174, 233
Fidetzky from Gorzkow, 230
Financial market, Warsaw, 3
Finkelstein, Sarah, 40
Fioder (Russian partisan leader), 91–92, 102, 104, 128
Flax, spinning of, 203
Flight into the forest, 75–78

Food: destruction of German supplies, 160–63; of farm family, 58; foraging expeditions, 101, 108, 114, 127, 204–5; Gorzkow village, 38, 40; for Ochoza forest people, 132–34; for partisans, 120; Warsaw bombardment, 12–14
Foraging expeditions, 101, 114, 132–34, 204–5; Karolin settlements, 127; Skorodnika forest, 108
Forced labor, 25, 26–28; Adampol, 137–38
Forest: flight into, 75–78; Zamolodycze raid, 81–86. See also Makoszka forest; Ochoza forest; Skorodnica forest
Freedman, Aaron, 1–2, 17, 55–56, 66, 71
Freedman, Chaia, 1–2, 16, 65–66, 67, 75, 78, 81
Freedman, Lazar, 16, 17,
Freedman, Manya, 1–2, 16, 25–26, 53, 63, 71, 75–76, 88, 161; change of farms, 67; departure from Warsaw, 17–20; farm work, 28, 29, 58; fate of, 92, 128; flight into the forest, 74–78; Hola visit, 65–66; in Skorodnica forest, 89, 91–92; in Zamolodycze woods, 79–86
Freedman, Rachmiel, 1–2, 16, 25–26, 53, 66, 71
Freedman, Shifra (aunt of Manya), 16–17, 75
Freedman, Shimon, 17, 26, 66
Freedman, Shmuel, 1–2, 16, 71, 75, 78; departure from Warsaw, 17–20; in Warsaw bombardment, 12–13